CHRIST WILL COME AGAIN

Christ Will Come Again

Hope for the Second Coming of Jesus

Stephen Travis

Hodder & Stoughton
LONDON SYDNEY AUCKLAND

Copyright © 1982, 1997 by Stephen Travis

First published in Great Britain under the title
I Believe in the Second Coming of Jesus 1982.
First published under the present title 1997.
This edition first published 1997.

1 3 5 7 9 10 8 6 4 2

British Library Cataloguing in Publication Data
A record for this book is available from the British Library

ISBN 0 340 66512 2

Typeset by Hewer Text Composition Services, Edinburgh
Printed and bound in Great Britain by
Cox & Wyman, Reading, Berkshire

Hodder and Stoughton Ltd
A Division of Hodder Headline PLC
338 Euston Road
London NW1 3BH

Contents

Introduction

We live at a time of ends and beginnings. Announcing that the End is Nigh used to be a part-time job for stern-faced men pacing city-centre streets with sandwich boards. Now it is a major industry providing work for authors and TV documentary-makers. At the turn of the millennium 'The End' is big business. Walk round a bookshop and you will find titles like *The End of Work, The End of Economic Man, The End of History and the Last Man, The End of the World, The End of the Future*. And that's only the tip of the iceberg. There are over 150 books in print with 'End of . . .' in the title! There is a sense that the old world is crumbling, and anxiety about what may take its place.

But there is another group of people working overtime to offer visions of a new future. Management consultants, futurologists and gurus of every kind compete to tell us how the world will be in twenty or fifty years' time—and how we can keep ahead of the game. And politicians talk confidently of the new millennium into which they are leading us.

Most people are a long way from this heady talk. Despite what they see on their TV screens of ethnic conflict and ecological ruin, they sense that predictions of cosmic catastrophe are a little over the top. Yet they could hardly be described as optimists. Experience has taught them that it is unwise to hope for too much. As the old certainties fade and we move into a period of increasing change and uncertainty, there is no agreed vision of the future we expect or desire. Surrounded by a collection of competing visions, hope wavers.

And we have learnt to be suspicious of people whose visions of the future are pressed too eagerly upon us. When the politician, the salesman and the business consultant set out their stalls we ask, 'What's in it for them?' 'Why are they trying to manipulate us?' 'What kind of power game are they playing?' And so the selling of hopes becomes the source of cynicism.

Yet human beings cannot live without hope. When we have no goal to set our heart on, when we can see no pattern or purpose to our life, when we realise that our life's achievements fall short of the ideals we may once have had, when we can see no ultimate value to our life, we fall prey to despair. 'Life isn't worth living any more,' we are tempted to say.

The issue is thrown into sharp relief by the prospect of our own death. World heavyweight boxing champion Muhammad Ali once said, 'I'm scared of no one. I'm only scared of death.'

Consider two great men of the twentieth century. Sigmund Freud (1856–1939), who has shaped modern thought more than most people, was obsessed with death. He was certain that he would die at forty-one. Then at fifty-one, at sixty-one and sixty-two. When he was seventy, he wrote that he would die in his eighty-second year. His colleague and biographer, Ernest Jones, recorded that Freud would frequently part from him with the words 'Goodbye. You may never see me again.'

Freud concluded one of his essays with these words: 'If you want to endure life, prepare yourself for death.' When he was sixty-four, he was broken by the death of his daughter. He wrote in a letter that he wondered when his own time would come and that he wished it might be soon. 'I do not know what more there is to say,' he continued. 'It is such a paralysing event, which can stir no afterthoughts when one is not a believer.' And in his seventies he wrote: 'What good to us is a long life if it is difficult and barren of joys, and if it is so full of misery that we can only welcome death as a deliverer?'

C. S. Lewis (1898–1963) also was overwhelmed by grief at the death of his wife, as he recorded in *A Grief Observed* – the basis of the film *Shadowlands*. As a Christian believer he found his faith shaken to the foundations. But gradually his sense of God returned. He found himself led back into trust, hope and what he described as 'unspeakable joy'.

In the summer of 1963, he suffered a heart attack and lapsed into a coma. He recovered, however, and lived quietly and happily for a few more months. He wrote to a friend: 'Though I am by no means unhappy I can't help feeling it was rather a pity I did revive in July. I mean, having glided so painlessly up to the Gate it seems hard to have it shut in one's face and know that the whole process must some day be gone through again . . . Poor Lazarus!' And to another friend he wrote: 'When you die . . . look me up . . . It is all rather fun—solemn fun—isn't it?'

The God of hope

In a world where so many people dare not hope for much, the story of God's purpose for the world comes as good news which generates hope. In preparing this book for its new lease of life I have become more convinced than ever of the centrality of this hope for Christian belief. Three convictions in particular have made their mark on me.

First, the mainstream churches are paying a heavy price for the widespread abandonment of a full-blown biblical hope. On the one hand, we have left the field open to enthusiasts for a particular kind of interpretation of the book of Revelation. They seem to offer a vivid hope of security under God's sovereignty amid the upheavals of the end of the world, but in fact are peddling a kind of fatalism which masquerades as hope. On the other hand, our hesitation and frequent silence about two articles of the church's creeds—the final coming of Christ and the resurrection of the dead—leaves us with a diluted message to meet the needs of today's world. Unless we can speak of a creator and saviour God whose intention is always to bring about something *new* in the world and in the lives of individuals, we have little to offer.

Second, the focus of our hope is Jesus Christ himself.

7

The themes dealt with in this book are often thought of as a rag-bag of unrelated ideas, among which Christians can choose the items they fancy. I have tried to show that they hang together because they all are related to Christ, and to remove any of them has an effect similar to removing a wing or tail-fin of an aeroplane. The coming of Christ was the goal of the expectations described in the Hebrew Scriptures. Christ's final coming marks the completion of God's work, which was begun with his first coming. Resurrection is the destiny of those who are united with Christ and share in his destiny. Our relationship to Christ is the standard by which the destinies of human beings are ultimately determined. The purpose of Christ embraces not only the human race but the whole of creation. Christ himself is the distinctive and unifying feature of Christian hope.

Third, to argue whether hope for individuals is more important than hope for the rest of creation, or whether hope for a life beyond death matters more than hope for the transformation of this world, is to set up false distinctions. The purpose of God described in Scripture is to bring the kingdom of God in its perfection. And that means there is hope for the coming of Christ in glory, hope for our resurrection to eternal life, and hope too for God's transforming presence within history.

Old and new

I have been able to make only limited revisions to the text of the book—altering some of the illustrative material and bringing factual information up to date. In two areas the original date of publication will remain obvious. In chapter four, where I discuss the 'dispensationalist' interpretation of Christ's second coming and related events, the authors with whom I debate are not so prominent now. The popular writers and televangelists who have taken their place are presenting very much the same message. Yet Hal Lindsey, whose *Late Great Planet Earth* sold by the million in the

1970s, remains the most influential of them all. His book was reissued in 1992, and in 1994 a sequel appeared, *Planet Earth—2000 A.D.: Will Mankind Survive?* (Palos Verdes, Calif.: Western Front).

The discussion of Marxism in chapter seven was written before the extraordinary collapse of communism in Eastern Europe and the break-up of the Soviet Union. I think my analysis of Marxism was not too wide of the mark. But, like everyone else, I was taken by surprise by the speed of the collapse. Since 1989 we have observed the confusion and the enormous human suffering now that powerful forces, which were for so long repressed, have unleashed their destructive energy. Yet in the long run, like the Hebrew prophets, we may discern in the collapse of ruthless dictatorships the hand of God who overthrows the oppressor and works towards justice and harmony.

But that is to anticipate the rest of the book, whose theme is as vital as ever. May it help its readers to 'be ready at all times to answer anyone who asks you to explain the hope you have in you' (1 Peter 3:15).

Chapter 1   The Beginning of Hope

'Hope is the enemy,' wrote the American novelist Henry Miller in *Tropic of Cancer*. He was denouncing the brand of hope which copes with present distress merely by looking for something better to turn up round the next corner. It refuses to look present realities in the face and to set about changing them. It leads, not to defiant action against the prevailing evils, but to life in a fantasy-world, hermetically sealed to keep out the cold of reality. It is escapist, defeatist, trivial. Hope is the enemy.

And there are many who think that Christian hope is that kind of hope. To believe in life after death, they say, saves you the trouble of making the best of this world. And anyone who expects the second coming of Christ is a certified drop-out from social responsibility. That, I believe, is a profound misunderstanding. This book will try to show why biblical hope is no enemy, but a friend without which the human race is indeed lonely.

Hope—in the sense of an expectation that God is working out his purpose through history, and will lead the events of history and the lives of men and women towards a goal—was born in Israel nearly four thousand years ago. Such hope is by no means a commonplace notion accepted by most human beings until 'modern man' came along to question it. This was illustrated when the World Council of Churches Faith and Order Commission met in Ghana some years ago. A Methodist minister from Sri Lanka told how he had invited some Hindu friends to give an account of the hope which motivated them. It turned out not only that they had great difficulty in understanding what he was driving at, but also that the Tamil language has no word for what Christians mean by hope.[1] There simply is nothing comparable to the biblical concept of hope in the great religions of the East.

Belief in a God who has a purpose in history and a goal for human lives was *given* to Israel by God.[2] In this chapter we look at four parts of the Hebrew Scriptures to see how this hope was expressed.

The God of promise

From their very beginning the Israelites were a people on a journey—a journey towards the destiny which God had set before them. That is what made them distinctive. The journey began when God called Abraham to leave his home in ancient Iraq. We cannot say what religious experience prompted Abraham to set out with his family, his servants, his cattle and his considerable wealth. But we *can* say that with Abraham there began God's grand design to bring blessing to the whole world. And what began as the journey of a nomadic group became the pilgrimage through history of a people loaded with hope.

Hope was based on a threefold promise given to Abraham at his call, according to Genesis 12:1–3:

> The Lord said to Abram, 'Leave your native land, your relatives, and your father's home, and go to a country that I am going to show you. I will give you many descendants, and they will become a great nation. I will bless you and make your name famous, so that you will be a blessing. I will bless those who bless you, but I will curse those who curse you. And through you I will bless all the nations.'

There was, first, the promise of *a land*. It was at the time a land full of Canaanites, and fertile only in parts. Yet it was a country, a homeland, given to Abraham and his descendants by divine guarantee. It would stretch from the border of Egypt in the south-west to the River Euphrates in the north-east (Genesis 15:18), and would belong to Abraham's descendants 'for ever' (Genesis 13:14f.; 17:8).

Secondly, there was the promise that Abraham's descendants would become *a great nation*—their number as countless as the specks of dust on the earth or the stars in the sky (Genesis 13:16; 15:5).

The third, climactic part of the promise is the promise of *blessing*. The blessing is for Abraham, his descendants, and through them for all nations. Does the Hebrew of Genesis 12:3 mean that God will bless the nations *through* Abraham and his descendants (GNB text)? Or that the nations will see Abraham so richly blessed by God that they will conceive no greater blessing for themselves than to be blessed like him (GNB margin)? It matters little, for in either case the message is that God's blessing of Abraham is but the beginning of something that will overflow to all mankind.

Later (Genesis 17), the promise was repeated in a different form. God made a covenant with Abraham—a pact whereby God undertook to fulfil the promises already made, and demanded in return that Abraham and his descendants express their obedience to God's will, especially by circumcising their male children. Circumcision was to be the sign that the Israelites were God's covenant people, enjoying a special place in his plans for the world. But the 'covenant' was not just a business contract. It was a relationship: 'I will be your God and the God of your descendants' (Genesis 17:7). This is the first example in the Bible of the often-repeated covenant promise—'I will be their God and they shall be my people.'

Those eleven words sum up the whole purpose of God for the human race. We are made for relationship with our Creator. And the descendants of Abraham constantly looked back to him as the man in whom God had begun the task of leading people from a dark and chaotic world towards their true destiny. To him God had given promises, and these promises became the source of Israel's life and expectations. The promise of the land was not forgotten when a famine took Abraham's great-grandchildren into Egypt. For it was to occupy the land that Moses led the Israelites out of Egypt, and Joshua led them in conquest of Canaan. The same promise brought confidence to David and Solomon at a time of expansion. It brought comfort and hope to Jews exiled to Babylon in the sixth century.

The remarkable thing is that Abraham's descendants clung to those promises through thick and thin. When times were bad, as they were during the exile (587–539 B.C.), the promises enabled Jews to preserve their national identity and to go on believing that God had a plan for them in their homeland. Just as God had called Abraham and given him the promises before Abraham did anything to earn God's favour, so again, despite their failures and their experience of disaster, God would restore them in sheer grace and faithfulness to his word. And in the good times, such as the period of David and Solomon's powerful empire, they did not abandon their forward look. They might have said, 'Now the promises are fulfilled—we are a great nation, we possess the land, we are full of God's blessing. Therefore we have no need of hope.' The temptation to think like that was certainly present. Yet hopes for the future continued to flourish. The God who had acted repeatedly in their history would continue to act, writing his plans into the pages of history.

God is the God of promise.[3] That belief was etched deep in the mind of Israel. It preserved them from understanding their history as comparable to the endlessly repetitive cycle of nature, which formed the basis of the religion of their Canaanite neighbours. The God of Israel made promises announcing the coming of realities which as yet were hardly dreamt of—his word 'brings into being what did not exist' (Romans 4:17). Thus he taught his people never to think of the present situation as God's final act, but always to fix their gaze and their hopes on the future, the time of fulfilment. He set them on a journey. As long as the promises to Abraham lacked total fulfilment, the journey must go on. And certainly in one respect—the blessing for Gentiles—the fulfilment seemed a long time coming.

14

The hope of the prophets

The prophets' business was, amongst other things, to declare the intentions of God about the future. They did it in many ways, with a rich variety of emphases. In these few pages, therefore, we shall not attempt a comprehensive survey of prophetic expectations. But we shall see the main strands of expectation which prophets announced and which gave shape to Israel's hopes.

Prophets whose books appear in the Old Testament began to emerge at a time when Israel's faith had become focused largely on the past. People looked back to the exodus from Egypt, back to the reign of David and to the building of the Temple in Jerusalem. Amos, in the middle of the eighth century B.C., took them by the scruff of the neck and insisted that the event which they most needed to reckon with lay in the future—the day of the Lord. And that day would be darkness, not light (Amos 5:18–20). Indeed, the new feature which Amos brought to prophecy was his 'preaching of a judgment which meant the end of Israel as the people of Yahweh'.[4] Probably it was this startling new emphasis on total doom which caused Amos's message to be preserved in writing. As other prophets appeared over the next three centuries, their messages too were written down.

The first element, then, in the prophets' proclamation about the future was their *denunciation of all false hopes*. At a time of national prosperity in the northern kingdom, Israel, Amos announced imminent catastrophe because of widespread social injustice, moral decay and religious unfaithfulness.

The Lord says, 'The people of Israel have sinned again and again, and for this I will certainly punish them. They sell into slavery honest men who cannot pay their debts, poor men who cannot repay even the price of a pair of sandals' (Amos 2:6).

How terrible it will be for you who long for the day of the Lord! What good will that day do you? For you it will be a day of darkness and not of light (Amos 5:18).

Stop your noisy songs; I do not want to listen to your harps. Instead, let justice flow like a stream, and righteousness like a river that never goes dry (Amos 5:23f.).

Isaiah mocked the attempts of Judah to find security in alliances with the super-powers, without reference to God:

The Lord has spoken: 'Those who rule Judah are doomed because they rebel against me. They follow plans that I did not make, and sign treaties against my will, piling one sin on another. They go to Egypt for help without asking my advice.'

The Sovereign Lord, the holy God of Israel, says to the people, 'Come back and quietly trust in me. Then you will be strong and secure.' But you refuse to do it! Indeed, you plan to escape from your enemies by riding fast horses. And you are right—escape is what you will have to do! You think your horses are fast enough, but those who pursue you will be faster! (Isaiah 30:1f., 15f.).

For Jeremiah a century later it is no different:

I remember how faithful you were when you were young, how you loved me when we were first married . . . (Jeremiah 2:2). [But now] People of Jerusalem, run through your streets! Look around! See for yourselves! Search the market-places! Can you find one person who does what is right and tries to be faithful to God? (Jeremiah 5:1).

And with pathetic self-deception, the people of Jerusalem treat the temple like an impenetrable fall-out shelter where they can worship in safety, protected from the attack of God himself:

Stop believing those deceitful words, 'We are safe! This is the Lord's Temple, this is the Lord's Temple, this is the Lord's Temple!' Change the way you are living and stop doing the things you are doing. Be fair in your treatment of one another. Stop taking advantage of aliens, orphans, and widows. Stop killing innocent people in this land. Stop worshipping other gods, for that will destroy you. If you change, I will let you go on living here in the land which I gave your ancestors as a permanent possession (Jeremiah 7:4–7).

This exposure of false hopes, this insistent message of God's opposition to all attempts to find satisfaction and security in anything less than himself and his will for mankind, runs right through the prophetic writings. And yet, sure and catastrophic though the judgment is, for the prophets it is never God's final word. The crashing of false hopes becomes the Lord's way of pointing his people to a fresh beginning. Until false hopes are put aside, there is no chance for real hopes to be grasped.

But why should there be any new beginning? Logically, Israel's persistent failure to live in obedience to God should have meant the end of her relationship with him. Amos says as much:

> Listen, people of Israel, to this funeral song which
> I sing over you:
> Virgin Israel has fallen,
> Never to rise again!
> She lies abandoned on the ground,
> And no one helps her up (Amos 5:1–2; cf. 8:1–2).

So does Hosea. His children were named—on God's instructions—'Jezreel' (because in the valley of Jezreel God would soon punish Israel for crimes earlier committed there), 'Unloved' (because God would cease to show love to Israel), and 'Not-my-people' (because God now ceased to regard Israel as his people) (Hosea 1:4, 6, 9).

17

Why, then, is hope still held out to God's people? For Hosea, such hope is based on *God's burning love*. The love which has kept the people going ever since the exodus from Egypt cannot give up now.

> How can I give you up, Israel?
> How can I abandon you?
> Could I ever destroy you as I did Admah,
> Or treat you as I did Zeboiim?
> My heart will not let me do it!
> My love for you is too strong.
> I will not punish you in my anger;
> I will not destroy Israel again.
> For I am God and not man.
> I, the Holy One, am with you.
> I will not come to you in anger (Hosea 11:8f.).

Later, when Jerusalem lay desolate after the exile of 587 B.C., the author of Lamentations pinned his hope on this same characteristic of God:

> My hope in the Lord is gone . . .
> Yet hope returns when I remember this one thing:
> The Lord's unfailing love and mercy still continue,
> Fresh as the morning, as sure as the sunrise,
> The Lord is all I have, and so I put my hope in him.
>   (Lamentations 3:18, 21–24)

For Isaiah, the renewal of hope rested on God's *faithfulness* to his promise, his commitment to the dynasty of David and to the Temple. In face of the threat of Assyrian invaders about 700 B.C. God's word was 'I will defend this city and protect it, for the sake of my own honour and because of the promise I made to my servant David' (Isaiah 37:35). For Ezekiel, the reason for hope was God's *concern for his own honour*. The Jews were in exile in Babylon and seemed to have brought an end to their national life and to have discredited the name of Yahweh among the nations. But God was about to give his people a fresh beginning:

18

'What I am going to do is not for the sake of you Israelites, but for the sake of my holy name, which you have disgraced in every country where you have gone. When I demonstrate to the nations the holiness of my great name—the name you disgraced among them—then they will know that I am the Lord' (Ezekiel 36:22f.; cf. Isaiah 48:11).

A fourth reason why the prophets had confidence that God would make a new beginning with his people is that God is *creative*. It is simply inconceivable that the God who made Israel and the whole world should allow catastrophe to be the final word. The unknown prophet of the exile who speaks in Isaiah 40–55 makes this link between God as creator and as the deliverer of Israel from her despair:

> Israel, the Lord who created you says,
> Do not be afraid—I will save you.
> I have called you by name—you are mine
> (Isaiah 43:1; cf. 40:27–31).

A further motive for God's action is also prominent in Isaiah 40–55: he will restore Israel's fortunes because they still have to carry out his promised task of bringing blessing to the Gentiles:

> 'I have a greater task for you, my servant.
> Not only will you restore to greatness the people of Israel who have survived,
> but I will also make you a light to the nations—
> so that all the world may be saved' (Isaiah 49:6).

The original promise to Abraham still stood. God would find a way to fulfil it through the renewal of Israel.

If these are the reasons why hope was possible, what forms did the hopes of Israel take? Since the basis of hope was the character and purpose of God as he had revealed them in the past, it is not surprising that hope was expressed

CHRIST WILL COME AGAIN

in terms of *renewal* of Israel's past. The rich variety of expectations can be summarised in the following way:

There was hope of a *new David*—a descendant of the great king who would rule in justice and peace. Partly in confidence that God would keep his promise to David of a 'throne for ever' (2 Samuel 7:12–16), partly in disappointment at the feebleness and wickedness of some kings under whom the nation had suffered, the prophets saw God's deliverance as coming through 'David's greater son'.

> A child is born to us!
> A son is given to us!
> And he will be our ruler.
> He will be called, 'Wonderful Counsellor',
> 'Mighty God', 'Eternal Father', 'Prince of Peace'.
> His royal power will continue to grow;
> his kingdom will always be at peace.
> He will rule as King David's successor,
> basing his power on right and justice,
> from now until the end of time.
> (Isaiah 9:6f.; cf. 11:1–9; Jeremiah 33:15f.; Zechariah 9:9.)

Linked with the expectation of a new David are the prophecies of a *new Jerusalem*, or a renewed status for *Mount Zion* in Jerusalem. This theme also is prominent in Isaiah, who foresaw a day when Jerusalem would cease to be threatened by enemy armies and would become the focus of the nations' worship:

> In days to come
> the mountain where the Temple stands
> will be the highest one of all,
> towering above all the hills.
> Many nations will come streaming to it,
> and their people will say,
> Let us go up the hill of the Lord,
> to the Temple of Israel's God (Isaiah 2:2–4).

Not only *worship* (cf. Isa. 12:5f.; Zech. 14:16ff.), but also *peace and safety* would characterise the new Jerusalem: The people of Judah and of Jerusalem will be rescued and will live in safety. The city will be called 'The Lord Our Salvation' (Jeremiah 33:16; cf. Zechariah 14:11; Isaiah 65:17–25).

And it would become a place of *plenty and prosperity*:

> Everyone will live in peace
> among his own vineyards and fig-trees,
> and no one will make him afraid,
> The Lord Almighty has promised this.
>   (Micah 4:4; cf. Isaiah 65:21; Ezekiel 47:12; Joel 3:18; Amos 9:13–15)

These hopes for Jerusalem were further developed in Ezekiel's vision of a *new Temple* (chapters 40–48). Previously, in chapter 10, the prophet saw the glory of God depart from the Temple because of his people's rebellion against him. Now, in the final section of his book, Ezekiel has a vision of the future Temple, built in perfect symmetry on Mount Zion. And returning to it there comes 'the dazzling light of the presence of the God of Israel' (Ezekiel 43:2). Instructions are given for a purified priesthood and a renewed system of animal sacrifices and religious festivals (Ezekiel 43–46). Land is to be redistributed and injustice driven out (Ezekiel 45; 47:13–48:29). And from beneath the Temple a stream flows down to the Jordan valley and the Dead Sea: 'the stream will make the water of the Dead Sea fresh, and wherever it flows, it will bring life' (Ezekiel 47:9). Here, then, we have a picture of God's perfect plan for his restored people, where worship and service will be all-important, and blessings will flow to the barren places of the earth. But the most central fact of all—which the Temple imagery is designed to convey—is the permanent presence of the Lord with his people. Ezekiel ends his book: 'The name of the city from now on will be, "The-Lord-is- Here!"' (Ezekiel 48:35).[5]

Despite the centrality of Jerusalem in these expressions of hope, it is often stressed in the prophets that God's action in the future will involve his whole people in a new relationship with him. They speak of a *new Israel*, a chastened and repentant people which will emerge from the batterings of divine judgment and exile:

But the time will come when the people of Israel will once again turn to the Lord their God, and to a descendant of David their king. Then they will fear the Lord and will receive his good gifts (Hosea 3:5).

> The time is coming!
> I will bring your scattered people home;
> I will make you famous throughout the world
> and make you prosperous once again.
> The Lord has spoken.
> (Zephaniah 3:20; cf. Isaiah 1:4, 25–27; Jeremiah 30:8f.; Amos 9:11–15; Micah 4:6f.)

One way in which the prophets express their hope for a renewed Israel is by speaking of a *new relationship with God*. Hosea, for example, faced by the idolatrous people of the northern kingdom and their abandonment of the God of Israel, announces the promise of God:

So I am going to take her into the desert again; there I will win her back with words of love. I will give back to her the vineyards she had and make Trouble Valley a door of hope. She will respond to me there as she did when she was young, when she came from Egypt. Then once again she will call me her husband—she will no longer call me her Baal . . . Israel, I will make you my wife; I will be true and faithful; I will show you constant love and mercy and make you mine forever' (Hosea 2:14–16, 19).

Jeremiah speaks of this new relationship as a *new*

covenant—the old covenant made with Moses at Mount Sinai is to be transposed into a new key:

> The Lord says, 'The time is coming when I will make a new covenant with the people of Judah. It will not be like the old covenant that I made with their ancestors when I took them by the hand and led them out of Egypt. Although I was like a husband to them, they did not keep that covenant. The new covenant that I will make with the people of Israel will be this: I will put my law within them and write it on their hearts. I will be their God and they will be my people. None of them will have to teach his fellow-countryman to know the Lord, because all will know me, from the least to the greatest. I will forgive their sins and I will no longer remember their wrongs. I, the Lord, have spoken' (Jeremiah 31:31–34).

In Ezekiel the same promise occurs in different words— God will give his people *a new heart*:

> I will sprinkle clean water on you and make you clean from all your idols and everything else that has defiled you. I will give you a new heart and a new mind. I will take away your stubborn heart of stone and give you an obedient heart. I will put my spirit in you and I will see to it that you follow my laws and keep all the commands I have given you. Then you will live in the land I gave your ancestors. You will be my people, and I will be your God (Ezekiel 36:25–28; cf. 18:30–32).

In such ways the prophets affirm that the over-riding purpose of God is that men and women should be in whole-hearted and obedient relationship to him. He will not rest until that goal is achieved. But, lest it be thought that God's work is a purely internal, 'spiritual' thing, the prophets also announce God's new activities in history and in the world.

The sixth-century prophet known as Second Isaiah encourages the Judeans in exile with the promise of a *new exodus* (the theme is already anticipated in Hosea 2:14ff. and Ezekiel 20:33ff.). If God liberated Israel from slavery in Egypt and carried her across the Red Sea and through the wilderness, he will surely achieve an even more remarkable deliverance for his people in exile. Their return to Palestine will not be a hurried affair like the original exodus: it will be deliberate, majestic, triumphant:

> This time you will not have to leave in a hurry; you will
> not be trying to escape.
> The Lord your God will lead you and protect you on
> every side (Isaiah 52:12).
>
> The Lord says,
> 'Do not cling to events of the past
> or dwell on what happened long ago.
> Watch for the new thing I am going to do.
> It is happening already—you can see it now!
> I will make a road through the wilderness
> and give you streams of water there. . . .
> (Isaiah 43:18f.; cf. 40:1–11, 48).

This marvellous event will come about because God will use the pagan king of Persia, Cyrus, as his agent: Cyrus will conquer Babylon and send the exiles back to their homeland (Isaiah 45:1–8). The God of Israel is Lord of history, Lord of the nations, whether or not they acknowledge him.

But even after the return from exile has begun, the thrust towards the future continues. The last part of the book of Isaiah (chapters 56–66), which reflects the situation in Palestine after the return of the exiles, is full of hope not only for God's action in history but also for '*a new earth and new heavens*' (Isaiah 65:17). The whole cosmos is the sphere of God's activity, the transformation of the cosmos is his ultimate goal. But we must be careful about jumping too readily to conclusions about Isaiah's meaning here. Since he goes on to speak of childbirth (65:20), of building homes and planting vines (65:21f.), he seems not to be expecting the destruction of the present universe and its replacement by something totally new. It is a vision of events on the plane of history. But what events! There will be a universal new beginning, a radically new era characterised by joy, peace and security, freedom from oppression, and the permanent blessing of God.

The prophets, then, were men with a vision of the future. The God whom they experienced and served in the present time had far-reaching plans for his people and for the world. From what we have surveyed so far we may draw three general conclusions about their convictions and expectations. First, it was fundamental to their thinking that *God acts in history and controls history*. He was responsible not only for the deliverance of Israel from Egypt, but also for the migrations of Philistines and Syrians. And if the northern kingdom is conquered, it is the Lord who is destroying it for its sinfulness (Amos 9:7f.). He uses the Assyrians to chastise Judah, though the Assyrians in their turn will be punished for their tyrannical oppression (Isaiah 10:5–15). It is Second Isaiah above all who exudes this conviction of God's sovereignty in world events, God working his purpose out through the ebbs and flows of history. Referring to Cyrus's role in the restoration of the Jews to their land, God declares:

Who was it that brought the conqueror from the east,
and makes him triumphant wherever he goes?
Who gives him victory over kings and nations? . . .
Who was it that made this happen?
Who has determined the course of history?
I, the Lord, was there at the beginning,
and I, the Lord, will be there at the end
  (Isaiah 41:2, 4).

It is because they discern God's purposeful activity in past and present events that the prophets can declare God's intention of doing something new, and can be certain that he will carry out what he announces (see Isaiah 42:9;

43:18f.). And that is why Second Isaiah in particular can kindle hope in the despairing people of the exile. Because the Lord controls history, 'no one who waits (hopes) for my help will be disappointed' (Isaiah 49:23). Hope for this prophet does not mean retreating into a private spiritual world to be cushioned from the crises of history. Rather it means looking to God to direct the course of history and to *do* something about the oppression of his people. But they must realise, too, that God does not act for them *at the expense of* other nations. Since God rules *their* history, there is hope for them too:

> I give my teaching to the nations;
> my laws will bring them light.
> I will come quickly and save them;
> the time of my victory is near.
> I myself will rule over the nations.
> Distant lands wait for me to come;
> they wait with hope for me to save them
> (Isaiah 51:4f.).[6]

The second fundamental conviction of the prophets is that there is both *continuity and discontinuity* between God's action in the past and in the future. There is discontinuity, because God as Lord of history is not imprisoned in the past. He will do new things, surprising and dramatic things—even, for example, calling the pagan king Cyrus his 'anointed' (Isaiah 45:1). He will bring to his people such blessing and security as they have never known before (see, for example, Amos 9:11–15; Isaiah 65:17–25, referred to above). The only way to describe such things is in language which suggests a radical break with people's present experience of the world:

> Wolves and sheep will live together in peace,
> and leopards will lie down with young goats.
> Calves and lion cubs will feed together,
> and little children will take care of them . . .
> On Zion, God's sacred hill,

there will be nothing harmful or evil.
The land will be as full of knowledge of the Lord
as the seas are full of water. (Isaiah 11:6, 9; cf. 65:25).

The word 'new', to which we have drawn attention in our survey of prophetic hopes, sums up this sense of discontinuity. God's salvation will be fresh, glorious and permanent. It will bring an end to present anxieties, injustices and imperfections, because God—so often disobeyed and dimly perceived in the present—will be in clear focus.

But the prophets' ways of speaking about the future also imply continuity. The very choice of concepts like 'new covenant' and 'new exodus' implies a continuity with the past. Although God is expected to do new things, his purpose for the world is to be worked out not in an arbitrary way but in a way consistent with his acts in the past. That is why in Israel the past must at all costs be remembered:

The Lord says,
'Listen to me, you that want to be saved,
you that come to me for help.
Think of the rock from which you came,
the quarry from which you were dug.
Think of your ancestor, Abraham,
and of Sarah, from whom you are descended.
When I called Abraham, he was childless
but I blessed him and gave him children.
I made his descendants numerous' (Isaiah 51:1f.).

The God who will reveal himself in the future, in the ultimate salvation of mankind, already reveals himself within Israel's history. Therefore we should expect elements both of discontinuity and of continuity in the prophets' understanding of God's future activity. Any treatment of biblical hope which ignores either of these elements is suspect.[7]

The third point is that the prophets envisage the future in terms of *expanding horizons*. Since, as we have seen, they are constantly expecting God to do *new* things, it is inconceivable to them that his word of promise should be strait-jacketed in a rigid pattern of precise prediction and literal fulfilment. The very variety of their ways of expressing God's plan for the future bears witness to their understanding of how God works in history. Because he desires to reveal his constant love and justice to Israel and the nations, he interacts with human affairs in a way which does not necessarily fulfil the letter of previous prediction or expectation, but does maintain the forward movement towards fulfilment of his overarching intentions. For example, we find in Second Isaiah two examples of 'messianic' expectation which would certainly have surprised his predecessors in the prophetic tradition. In the first place, he gives the title 'anointed' ('messiah') to the Persian king Cyrus, because through him deliverance is to be brought to God's people (Isaiah 45:1). And secondly, the original promise to David, that through him God's power would be shown to the nations, is now to be fulfilled in the whole nation of Israel. God says to the people:

I will make a lasting covenant with you
and give you the blessings I promised to David . . .
Now you will summon foreign nations. . . .
    (Isaiah 55:3–5).

Since God's purposes develop and expand in interaction with human events, an over-literalistic approach to them can be misleading. In Jeremiah's day it is the 'literalists' who are out of step with God. Clinging to the hundred-year-old promises of God's protection for Jerusalem, originally uttered by Isaiah, they chant, 'We are safe! This is the Lord's temple, this is the Lord's temple, this is the Lord's temple!' But those, says Jeremiah, are deceitful words, because God's protection for the city has been removed because of his people's persistent rejection of his will (Jeremiah 7). It is the 'literalist' Jonah who complains that God has changed his mind when the people of Nineveh repent at Jonah's prophecy of the city's destruction (Jonah 4). But he earns God's rebuke for his failure to see the broadening horizon of God's purposes. The prophetic books, then, bear witness to a God who acts in faithfulness to his declared intentions, *and yet* does new, unexpected things which invite his people to widen their vision of where he is leading. We shall need to look again at this issue in chapter 4, when we study some ways of interpreting prophecy.

These words of hope among the prophets—hope for new and renewing acts of God—can be summarised in three phrases. They are phrases favoured by the prophets to express their conviction that at the heart of every hope is God himself. Each phrase is taken up and developed in the New Testament.

First, they say, *God will come*. He will come at 'the day of the Lord' to bring judgment on all who challenge his sovereignty: 'When the Lord comes to shake the earth, people will hide in holes and caves in the rocky hills to try to escape from his anger and to hide from his power and glory' (Isaiah 2:21; cf. 2:10–21; 26:21; 63:1–6; Zechariah 14:3, 5). But God's coming will also bring deliverance to those who turn to him: 'I will come to Jerusalem to defend you and to save all of you that turn from your sins' (Isaiah 59:20; cf. 35:4; 40:9; Zechariah 2:10–13).

And some prophets declare that the coming of God will cause Gentiles to belong to his people: The Lord said, 'Sing for joy, people of Jerusalem! I am coming to live among you!' At that time many nations will come to the Lord and become his people (Zechariah 2:10f.; cf. Isaiah 66:18ff.).[8]

Secondly—and this follows naturally from his coming— *God will be with his people*. References to God's coming are often couched in the dramatic language of battle and cosmic upheaval. But the positive intention of his coming is that he should be amongst his people. The God who so often seems to have hidden himself or to have abandoned Israel because of her unfaithfulness (see, e.g., Lamentations 5:17–22), will establish permanent residence in their midst:

A day is coming when people will sing, . . .
'Let everyone who lives in Zion shout and sing!
Israel's holy God is great,
and he lives among his people'
(Isaiah 12:6; cf. Ezekiel 37:27f.; 43:1–9; 48:35; Joel
2:27; 3:16f.; Zephaniah 3:14–20).

Thirdly, the prophets assert that *God will rule*. Of course, there is a sense in which God the creator of the universe already rules, always and everywhere.

I, the Lord almighty, am king.
I am the living God (Jeremiah 46:18).

God's universal rule is celebrated constantly in Israel's worship (Psalm 24; 29:10; 47:2; 93; 96:10; 97; 99). And it is a source of comfort and hope to Israel in the face of catastrophe, such as the devastation of Jerusalem during the exile (Lamentations 5:19). In a more particular way, God is said to rule over Israel, for he has chosen her as his special people and they, at least partially, acknowledge his kingship over them:

I am the Lord, your holy God.
I created you, Israel, and I am your king
(Isaiah 43:15; cf. Numbers 23:21; Deuteronomy 33:5).

But the rule of God has a future tense which expresses the prophetic expectation. They knew all too well that God's rule was only imperfectly realised in the past and present experience of Israel, and so they looked forward to a day when God's rule would be fully acknowledged and its blessings fully experienced. The coming rule of God was the object of hope.[9] Sometimes the prophets associate this new era with the coming of the earthly ruler descended from David (the 'messiah'): God will rule through his appointed agent. But sometimes the era of God's rule is described without any allusion to an earthly 'messianic' figure (notably, in Isaiah 40–66). The important thing is that God will establish his rule, in a fresh and total way. Six characteristics of this future rule of God stand out in the prophets' descriptions.

1. *God's rule will be righteous*. In welcome contrast to the injustice and corruption of so many national leaders of their own day, the prophets declared that right and justice would mark the rule of 'David's greater son':

> He will rule his people with justice and integrity
> (Isaiah 11:5; cf. 11:2–5; 9:7).

In Jeremiah 23:5f. there may be a biting comment on Judah's current double-dealing king, Zedekiah, whose name means 'Yahweh is my righteousness'. Your hope must lie, says the prophet, not in such dubious examples of kingly power, but in the future king of God's choice: 'That king will rule wisely and do what is right and just throughout the land. When he is king, the people of Judah will be safe, and the people of Israel will live in peace. He will be called, "The Lord is our righteousness"' (Jeremiah 23:5f.).

All the warnings of God's judgment on human wickedness, which embarrass so many readers of the prophets, must be seen as the necessary prelude to the righteous kingdom of God. You cannot have one without the other. If righteousness is to pervade the sphere of God's rule, unrighteousness must first be rooted out—either by repentance and forgiveness, or, failing that, by condemnation of the unrepentant. The prophetic preaching alternates, as we have seen,

31

between the threat of judgment and the promise of forgiveness. This tension is resolved in the ultimate kingdom of righteousness (Isaiah 2:2–4; 29:18–21; Ezekiel 36:25–32).

2. *God's rule will be peaceful.* In contrast to the wars and insecurity of Israel's historical experience, God's kingdom will bring peace and security. The great powers

> will hammer their swords into ploughs and their spears into pruning-knives. Nations will never again go to war, never prepare for battle again. Everyone will live in peace among his own vineyards and fig-trees, and no one will make him afraid. The Lord almighty has promised this (Micah 4:3f.; cf. Isaiah 2:2–4).

And the Davidic king will be known as 'Prince of Peace' (Isaiah 9:6). 'Peace' in the Old Testament means much more than merely the absence of war. It means the positive experience of well-being in right relationship to God and man.

3. *God's rule will be permanent.* The promise is not simply that Israel's fortunes will be restored, but that they will be restored 'for ever' (Micah 4:6f.). Once God's rule is established, there will be no going back to the vulnerability of subjection to other regimes. I heard an exile from President Amin's Uganda say how, when he and his wife began to live in America, he heard her saying, 'Tomorrow we will go shopping.' He realised that while in Uganda they had not dared to use the word 'tomorrow'. Under the rule of God such uncertainty will be a thing of the past. Of the messianic king Isaiah says:

> His royal power will continue to grow;
> his kingdom will always be at peace.
> He will rule as King David's successor,
> basing his power on right and justice,
> from now until the end of time (Isaiah 9:7).

4. *God's rule will be universal*. The time is coming, say the prophets, when the nations will acknowledge Israel's God as their own God, and when Israel will acknowledge that the knowledge of God is to be shared with all peoples. Isaiah has a picture of the Lord preparing on Mount Zion a banquet for all the nations of the world (Isaiah 25:6–9). Zechariah looks forward to the day when 'ten foreigners will come to one Jew and say, "We want to share in your destiny, because we have heard that God is with you"' (Zechariah 8:22f.; cf. 14:9, 16–19; Zephaniah 3:9f.; Isaiah 44:5).

Sometimes the role of the nations is seen in terms of their *serving* Israel in the coming age (Isaiah 60:10ff.; 61:5), or at least *coming* to Jerusalem in order to find salvation (Isaiah 2:1–4; 56:1–8; 66:19–21). But also there is Second Isaiah's vision of Israel as a *witness* to the nations, a people with a mission to bring 'light to the nations, so that all the world may be saved' (Isaiah 49:6; cf. 42:6f.; 43:10). And in those passages where the 'messianic' king comes into the picture, it is said that 'people all over the earth will acknowledge his greatness' (Micah 5:2–5), and 'he will rule . . . to the ends of the earth' (Zechariah 9:10).

5. *God's rule will be on earth*. Whatever our own assumptions may be about the kingdom of God and the destiny of his people, the prophets consistently state or assume that God's purposes will be worked out on earth. This can be seen in many of the passages quoted earlier. Because this world is God's world, salvation does not mean escaping from the world and from man's place as a creature within it. Rather, the world will share in the transformation of man under God's rule. Admittedly, the world itself will need transforming if it is to be fitted for the permanent and peaceful rule of God over his creatures. Thus there are references to 'new earth and new heavens' (Isaiah 65:17); it is said that God will 'shake heaven and earth, land and sea' (Haggai 2:7); 'the waste land will become fertile' (Isaiah 32:15), and 'wolves and sheep will live together in peace' (Isaiah 11:6–9). But still the picture of the new order is a

fundamentally earthly one, with little hint that the whole human race has been transferred to a totally different sphere of existence. There is, as we saw earlier, continuity as well as discontinuity.[10]

6. *God's rule will be a cause of worship and rejoicing.* We have already seen how Ezekiel's vision of the new Temple indicates the centrality of worship in God's kingdom. Other prophets express the same message in various ways. Isaiah 25 depicts God's rule as a banquet where Jew and Gentile together rejoice in God and his salvation. Isaiah 12 proposes songs of celebration to be sung when the day of deliverance arrives (cf. Zephaniah 3:14–20; and the note of joy in Isaiah 9:7; 52:7–9). Zechariah asserts: 'Then the Lord will be king over all the earth; everyone will worship him as God and know him by the same name' (Zechariah 14:9).

Zechariah in fact has a passage which sums up all six points we have made about the coming rule of God (except that its permanence is not made explicit). He foresees the messianic king coming to establish God's rule:

Rejoice, rejoice, people of Zion!
Shout for joy, you people of Jerusalem!
Look, your king is coming to you!
He comes triumphant and victorious,
but humble and riding on a donkey—
on a colt, the foal of a donkey.
The Lord says,
'I will remove the war-chariots from Israel
and take the horses from Jerusalem;
the bows used in battle will be destroyed.
Your king will make peace among the nations;
he will rule from sea to sea,
from the River Euphrates to the ends of the earth'
(Zechariah 9:9f.; cf. Psalm 72, which in similar language expresses Israel's longing for God's ideal king).

34

When will it happen?

It may seem that so far I have been covering up a problem raised by the prophets' expressions of hope. Or at least I have ignored a vital question. What sort of time-scale were they using in their messages about the future? In the passages to which we have referred, were they *really* talking about God's ultimate establishment of his rule, or about some more mundane event in the immediate future of their nation? And how do we cope with the fact that Zephaniah, for example, announced the nearness of the day of the Lord, when he would not only 'punish the people of Jerusalem', but also 'destroy everything on earth' so that no survivors would be left (Zephaniah 1:2–4; cf. the whole chapter)? Or how do we reconcile Second Isaiah's triumphant declarations of the establishing of God's rule, through the Jews' return from exile, with the historical reality which followed—a rather pathetic trickle of people back from Babylonia to a depressed situation in Palestine, requiring frequent bucking up from later prophets like Haggai, Zechariah and Malachi? This problem invites a three-fold response.

First, it is misguided to expect a sharp distinction in the prophets' minds between immediate and ultimate fulfilment of their prophecies. For them, the future always stands in tension with the present. They do not create visions of God's ultimate goals in a detached way, but speak of the future as it relates to the present situation of their people. So Zephaniah does not distinguish in time between the immediate fate of Judah and the final, universal judgment: he sees both as though they are one Day of the Lord. The prophets 'were able to view the immediate historical future against the background of the ultimate eschatological goal, for both embodied the coming of Israel's God to judge and to save his people. The focus of attention is the acting of God, not the chronology of the future.'[11]

It need not puzzle or embarrass us that sometimes

prophets speak of God's ultimate salvation as though it were just round the corner. They can speak like that because each crisis in history, each act of deliverance, each judgment and each blessing in the experience of God's people is an anticipation of the ultimate struggle between right and wrong and the ultimate victory of God. The God who will reveal himself at the end of time reveals himself already in the immediate crises of history. The God who fulfils within history the promises and warnings of the prophets will one day bring a final and total fulfilment to their messages of judgment and salvation.

Secondly, when the fulfilment of a prophecy within history seems to be only a pale reflection of the prophet's confident prediction, we should recognise that prophecies are not necessarily fulfilled all at once. After a prophet such as Ezekiel or Second Isaiah spoke in glowing terms of the return from exile as the ultimate saving act of God, there was *real* fulfilment but *not total* fulfilment. There was a return from exile and a partial restoration of Israel's fortunes, but the road to the kingdom of God turned out to be longer than anticipated. This pattern of partial but not complete fulfilment was already recognised in Israel's earlier history. The promise of the land given to Abraham was fulfilled when Israel conquered Palestine under Joshua, yet that settlement in the land was not regarded as a complete fulfilment. The book of Deuteronomy is well aware that, although peace was promised as a result of Israel's entry into the land (Deuteronomy 12:9), that peace remained elusive and the possibility of great discomfort was all too real (Deuteronomy 28:65–68). G. von Rad describes this pattern:

> Promises which have been fulfilled in history are not thereby exhausted of their content, but remain as promises on a different level, although they are to some extent metamorphosed in the process. The promise of the land was proclaimed ever anew, even after its fulfilment, as a future benefit of God's redemptive activity.[12]

36

Such was the prophets' sense that God has a future goal for his people towards which he is moving. Every sign of progress, every little victory along the way is not itself the final blessing. But it is a pointer to the ultimate 'promised land'. It is an indication that hope is not in vain.

Thirdly, we must recognise the close link between the prophets' vision for the future and their ethical concern. They do not predict a fixed future with a predetermined timetable. They are concerned with the moral impact of the future upon the present. They speak of the nearness of the day of the Lord, not so much to instruct in chronology as to urge repentance. For the people confronted with this exhortation to change their lives in the face of divine judgment, the imminent crisis has a final quality. Compared with that, our modern questions about chronology are technical niceties which are only possible from a detached viewpoint. For the prophets, the wonder is not that the chronology of God's plans can be accurately predicted, but that God can actually change his plans in response to repentance. This is what Jeremiah learnt at the potter's house (Jeremiah 18:1-12). This is what Jonah struggled to come to terms with:

> Lord, didn't I say before I left home that this is just what you would do? That's why I did my best to run away to Spain! I knew that you are a loving and merciful God, always patient, always kind, and always ready to change your mind and not punish (Jonah 4:2).

These, then, were some of the ways in which the prophets expressed their hopes. We shall return in chapter 4 to the question of what Jesus and the New Testament writers made of their hopes. For the moment we simply acknowledge the breadth of their vision and their crucial importance for the development of Israel's faith. They were men convinced that God always has something new to do.

The apocalyptic literature

'Apocalyptic' is the literature of crisis. It is a type of literature which flourished in Judaism from the second century B.C. to about A.D.100—a period of seemingly endless oppression for the Jewish people, or at least for some groups within Judaism. 'Apocalyptic' (from the Greek word for 'revelation') is our term for a group of writings which claim to reveal the hidden purpose of God and his plans for the new creation. Only one of these writings is in the Old Testament—the book of Daniel—though in fact some passages in the Old Testament prophets, such as Isaiah 24–7, Ezekiel 38–9 and Zechariah 9–14, already have some of the characteristics of apocalyptic literature.[13]

Scholars have frequently given lists of distinctive features of apocalyptic, noting for example their pessimism about the present course of history, their sense that history is predetermined, and their stress on the nearness of the end of this age. The trouble with this approach is that no one apocalyptic book exhibits all these features, and the book of Daniel is different from the others in some important respects. I shall refer only to Daniel in this section.

But why all this fuss? Why do we single out Daniel as being different from the prophetic books of the Old Testament? If (as I believe) apocalyptic arose out of prophecy, what is the difference between prophecy and apocalyptic? It is partly a matter of the clothing in which the message is dressed; the elaborate dreams and interpretations, and the strange imagery of statues and monsters, goes beyond what we find in the prophets. But the emphasis of the message itself is different. The difference is usually put in the following way. The prophets saw God working out his purposes *in history*, through the work of individuals and nations. But the apocalyptists believed that evil had become so powerful in the world that only by a direct intervention of God from *beyond history* could evil be brought to an end and God's righteous rule be established.

So the apocalyptic writers stressed the radical *discontinuity* between the present age and the age to come. I believe this distinction between prophecy and apocalyptic can be over-stated. After all, the prophets stressed that it is *God* who causes his people to be restored and his rule established, and the book of Daniel stressed that God is sovereign in the present course of history as well as in his future kingdom (Daniel 2:21, 37; 4:17, 25, 32; 5:21). Nevertheless, there *is* a difference of atmosphere and emphasis, and it is important to look at Daniel's special contribution to the Old Testament hope.

The book's *setting* is the Jewish exile in Babylonia in the sixth century B.C. It tells of Daniel, a loyal Jew at the court of king Nebuchadnezzar. But its *purpose* seems to be to encourage oppressed Jews about 165 B.C, when Antiochus IV Epiphanes of Syria (part of the Greek empire established by Alexander the Great) was attempting to impose Greek culture by force on the Jews, and forbade Jews to worship God. In face of this unbearable pressure the book of Daniel would urge Jews to stand firm against alien culture, proclaiming that the evil regime of Antiochus was about to be squashed by the arrival of the kingdom of God. The book's message about the future can be outlined as follows:

In chapter 2, king Nebuchadnezzar has a dream about a giant statue, with a head of gold, chest and arms of silver, waist and hips of bronze, legs of iron, and feet of iron and clay. A stone shatters the statue and it becomes a huge mountain. Daniel interprets the dream to represent a sequence of four world empires, beginning with Nebuchadnezzar's own Babylonian empire. The fourth empire will be destroyed by God's kingdom, which will last for ever. The book itself does not say, but probably the four empires are the Babylonian, Median, Persian and Greek empires, this last being embodied in Antiochus.[14]

In chapter 7 Daniel himself has a dream about four terrible beasts which appear one after another, and are eventually destroyed. Then 'what looked like a human being' (RSV, 'one like a son of man') comes to 'One who had been living for ever', and receives from him authority to rule over all people for ever. It is explained to Daniel that the four beasts represent four empires. The one who 'looked like a human being' represents the people of God, who will receive permanent royal power—but only after a vicious campaign of persecution lasting three and a half years.

The four-empire scheme in fact follows a pattern well known in Greek, Latin and Persian literature, where four successive ages are symbolised by metals of decreasing value. The author of Daniel in fact knows that there are not two separate Median and Persian empires in between the Babylonian and the Greek, but rather one Medo-Persian empire. But he uses the familiar four-empire scheme in order to assert his faith in God's sovereignty over the course of history. Even the degeneration from one age to another is under his control. The ragings of the final empire do not take him by surprise. He knows how long he will let them last before he gives the kingdom to his people.

In chapter 8 Daniel has a vision of a ram which is over-powered by a goat. The goat grows increasingly arrogant, especially when a 'little horn' grows out of its head and extends its power 'towards the south and east and towards the promised land'. It even defies the commander of the heavenly army, stopping the daily sacrifices in the Temple. Daniel is told the Temple will be desecrated for 1,150 days, and then it will be restored. The interpretation given to Daniel is that the ram represents the kingdoms of Media and Persia, which are overthrown by the Greek empire (the goat). The 'little horn' (cf. Daniel 7:8) is the vicious king—surely Antiochus—who will defy God and his Temple, until he is destroyed by God, and the period of Greek domination is brought to an end.

In Daniel 9:24–27 the angel Gabriel offers Daniel an explanation of Jeremiah's prophecy that Jerusalem would lie in ruins for seventy years (see Daniel 9:2; Jeremiah 25:11; 29:10). The explanation is in fact allusive and obscure. In essence, it interprets the seventy years as 'seven times seventy years'. The number seven frequently symbolises perfection in the Bible, and the 490 years seems to represent the period from the exile in 587 to the time of Antiochus in the second century. Rather than giving us a chronologically precise calculation, it tells us that the time is under God's control. The seven times seventy years are divided into three stages. First, seven times seven years— the Babylonian period. Secondly, seven times sixty-two years, beginning with the coming of 'an anointed one' (TEV 'God's chosen leader'—? Cyrus, as in Isaiah 45:1), and ended with the killing of 'an anointed one' (?Onias, the legitimate high priest murdered in 171 B.C.). This period would be the Medo-Persian period, and the Greek period until the rise of Antiochus to power. Then there is a final period of seven years, during which an invading king (Antiochus?) will work havoc in Jerusalem and its Temple. For the last half of this seven year period (that is, for three and a half years) he will suspend the Temple sacrifices and place the 'Awful Horror' (a pagan image) in the Temple, until he 'meets the end which God has prepared for him'. Again, then, the message is that the oppressed people of God should keep faith, in confidence that God is Lord of history and is about to bring Antiochus's reign of terror to a decisive end. [15]

In chapters 11–12 an angel offers Daniel 'a vision about the future' (Daniel 10:14). He gives a detailed summary of the history of the Greek period down to Antiochus's attempt to destroy the Jews' religion and his setting up of the 'Awful Horror'. He says that some of the Jews will fight back (a reference to the Maccabean resistance fighters), though many will pay with their lives for their devotion to God. 'This will continue until the end comes, the time that God has set.' Then 'God will do exactly what he has planned' (Daniel 11:35f.). So the faithful people among the Jews will be saved. And God's justice requires that the persecuted and the persecutors who have not received their proper reward or punishment 'will live again: some will enjoy

41

eternal life, and some will suffer eternal disgrace' (Daniel 12:3).

When Daniel asks when the end will come, he is told that the persecution will last three and a half years—or again, 1,290 days or 1,335 days—from the time when the Temple sacrifices are stopped and the 'Awful Horror' is set up (Daniel 12:7, 11f.). The fact that these numbers are similar but not identical (cf. 1,150 days in 8:14), and correspond roughly to half of seven years, suggests that their significance is symbolic and not literal. God's people must persevere to the end in trust that God will not long delay the end of suffering and the coming of his rule.

How, then, may we summarise the message of Daniel? What convictions are the basis of its author's hope? He is a man grappling with acute crisis: How can God be said to be working out his purposes, he asks, when the subjection of his faithful people goes on unabated? This was no academic question. It pressed for an answer, and Daniel's answer is in terms of God's sovereign control of history. His visions of the four empires, his use of numbers, affirm that the story of men and nations is in God's hands. Often the book says that the enemies of the Jews only do their evil work because God permits it (Daniel 2:21; 4:25, 32, 35; 7:12; 8:24). And in his good time he will bring their power to an abrupt end (7:22, 26; 8:25; 9:27; 11:35). Even in the darkness he can be trusted. This stress on God's control of history, expressed in terms of fixed times and periods, is certainly different from the more flexible approach of the prophets, according to whom God makes continually fresh decisions (Jeremiah 18:7–10). But it is quite different again from the resignation to Fate which can be found in many pagan writers of the period—and of all periods. It is an expression of faith in the *grace* of God, countering despair in the face of the tragedies of history and of personal experience.

Because his present experience is so dark, the author of Daniel stresses the discontinuity between the present age and the future rule of God. If evil powers are to be defeated and a kingdom of peace and righteousness is to be established, it can only happen by a supernatural, world-transforming act of God. From the crucible of painful experience, Daniel gives the lie to all optimistic and simplistic assumptions about men 'building the kingdom of God'. The book in fact says very little about the future kingdom of God—only that his people will rule for ever over the nations, and God alone will bring this about (7:14, 25f.; 8:25). His expectation that the Temple worship will be restored seems to presuppose that the kingdom will be on earth.

Daniel also declares that the purposes of God are worked out on a level which goes beyond the limits of the Jews' present experience. The salvation of his people will involve resurrection to a new life beyond death (12:3)—an idea foreshadowed in a handful of earlier passages such as Isaiah 25:8 and 26:19, which becomes increasingly important in the apocalyptic literature. God's sovereignty in history involves all nations, not merely the Jews (4:34f.; 7:27). The battle between good and evil is fought out on a superhuman scale, for it involves angels as well as men (chapter 10). This sense of the cosmic scope of God's plan is one of the major contributions of the apocalyptists to the faith of Jews and Christians.

A further dominant note in Daniel is the imminence of the end. Three and a half years, and the troubles will be over. This poses the same problem as we encountered with the prophets—the problem of non-fulfilment. True enough, the time from Antiochus's suspension of the Temple sacrifices in 167 B.C. to the Jews' deliverance and the rededication of the Temple in 164 *was* about three and a half years. But the course of history continued. No world-transforming act of God took place. Some interpreters have tried to cope with this by suggesting that at some point in the narrative (for example, after the sixty-ninth week of years in Daniel 9:26, or towards the end of chapter 11), there is a 'prophetic gap' where the point of reference leaps forward from the crisis under Antiochus to the end of the world in the distant future. But it is indeed hard to find any hint in the text that such a gap is intended. The problem is surely to be handled in the same way as we handled it in the prophets. The Jews' deliverance from Antiochus was a notable deliverance, a realisation within history of God's ultimate establishment of his rule.

Finally, Daniel makes it quite clear what God requires of his people when they are confronted by oppression and are tempted to believe that God has abandoned them. They are to offer him obedience and to exalt his honour. They are to go on praying to him, even if a royal decree declares that the penalty for this is an extra item on the lions' menu (chapter 6). They are to refuse to compromise their faith, like Daniel's three friends who addressed Nebuchadnezzar:

> Your Majesty, we will not try to defend ourselves. If the God whom we serve is able to save us from the blazing furnace and from your power, then he will. But even if he doesn't Your Majesty may be sure that we will not worship your god, and we will not bow down to the gold statue that you have set up (3:16–18).

'*Even if he doesn't*'. Those are the crucial words. Even without guarantees of divine protection against extreme suffering, real hope remains true to its vision of God and the triumph of his purposes.

Ecclesiastes, 'The Philosopher'

There is, however, another voice in the Old Testament—the voice not of hope but of questioning. It is the voice of The Philosopher, and he also must be listened to. Not for him the soaring visions and uncompromising faith of the apocalypist. Like many a modern person, he hovers between faith and doubt, between hope and despair, between enjoyment of life and puzzlement about life's meaning.

He knows that man is a creature who finds himself

impelled to press beyond the present, to plan for the future: God 'has given us a desire to know the future' (Ecclesiastes 3:11). Man is hungry for hope. Yet the Philosopher has also discovered that God keeps the future to himself. The future is unpredictable, and we may as well accept that God keeps his plans dark, and make the best of the present (3:11–13). Again, he has reached the conclusion that 'there is nothing new in the whole world' (1:9). And when you say that, you have given up on hope. You have imprisoned yourself in a treadmill world, with nothing to look forward to.

The Philosopher has searched for meaning in life. He has tried to find it in the pursuit of pleasure (2:1ff.), of wisdom (2:12ff.; 8:16f.), and of money (5:10, 12; 2:1ff.). He has sought satisfaction in hard work (2:10f., 18, 22; 4:4–8). And he knows that these things have value: 'The best thing a man can do is to eat and drink and enjoy what he has earned' (2:24). But they offer no ultimate answers, because 'Useless, useless, said the Philosopher. It is all useless.' (12:8; cf. 1:2). This word 'useless' or 'vanity', which occurs over thirty times in Ecclesiastes, means a vapour, a puff of wind, something without substance. And why is that dismissive slogan to be written across the whole of life? Because evil, uncertainty and above all death cast their mocking shadow across every search for meaning. Evil is everywhere: 'Then I looked again at all the injustice that goes on in this world. The oppressed were weeping, and no one would help them. No one would help them, because their oppressors had power on their side' (4:1; cf. 7:20; 9:3). The uncertainties of life make a mockery of conventional wisdom: 'I realised another thing, that in this world fast runners do not always win the race, and the brave do not always win the battle. Wise men do not always earn a living, intelligent men do not always get rich, and capable men do not always rise to high positions. Bad luck happens to everyone' (9:11).

But death is the hardest fact of all. It comes like the tide which destroys the sandcastle and makes it as though it had never existed. It comes to man and animal, wise man and fool, the righteous and the wicked alike (2:14–16; 3:19f.; 9:2). It comes in its own time, and it is 'a battle we cannot escape; we cannot cheat our way out' (8:8). We do not always see justice prevailing in this life—evil men prosper and good men suffer (8:9–14). But there is no point in looking for justice beyond death. A dead saint is no better off than a dead villain (9:1–10). The Philosopher does once entertain the possibility that death may be the doorway to a better life, but he dismisses it. For 'how can anyone be sure that a man's spirit goes upwards while an animal's spirit goes down to the ground?' (3:21).

So the Philosopher can see no answers to the ultimate questions of life. The future of the world is hidden from us; our own death brings an abrupt end to all our longings and achievements. We can enjoy the present and all the things that God gives us (3:12f.). But our pressing towards the future, our search for a clear purpose in life and for a hope beyond death, are doomed to frustration.

The Philosopher is a man like ourselves, full of questions about the complexities and uncertainties of life, expressing doubt because so often God *seems* not to be involved in the unfolding of events. And yet there is a difference between the Philosopher and many modern doubters. As Robert Short puts it, Ecclesiastes knows God exists, but is confronted by God's *hiddenness*. Modern man, however, feels himself confronted by the *non-existence* of God.[16] Camus speaks of 'that hopeless encounter between human questioning and the silence of the universe'. Because of this basic difference of starting point, the possibilities of discovering the meaning of life are different. Modern man can only ask, 'What do I do until the undertaker comes?' But the Philosopher could ask, 'What do I do until the Messiah comes?—*if* he comes?'. It is a question full of hesitation, and of course Ecclesiastes does not express it in those words. But he belonged to a people who were still looking forward, a people for whom, even if God were hidden, there was still a hope for some new act of self-disclosure and salvation by God.

The modern Christian must not point people to Christ as 'the answer' to human questions before he has himself felt deeply the force of those questions. But having felt them, he must invite his modern neighbour to listen again to the word of hope which came to the Jews and to the world in Jesus. Because of Jesus there can be a rekindling of hope for the world, a renewal of purpose for men and women in the face of both life and death. To the significance of Jesus we now turn.

Notes to chapter 1

1. *Uniting in Hope* (WCC, Geneva, 1975), p. 7.
2. Cf. J. Bright, *Covenant and Promise* (SCM, London, 1977), pp. 20–4.
3. See the illuminating discussion of 'Promise and History' in J. Moltmann, *Theology of Hope* (Eng. tr., SCM, London, 1967), pp. 95ff.
4. R. E. Clements, *Prophecy and Covenant* (SCM, London, 1965), p. 40 (Yahweh is the normal Old Testament name of God).
5. On the interpretation of Ezekiel 40–48, see J. B. Taylor, *Ezekiel* (IVP, London, 1969), pp. 250–4.
6. On God's control of history in Second Isaiah, see W. Zimmerli, *Man and his Hope in the Old Testament* (Eng. tr., SCM, London, 1971), pp. 130–5.
7. The balance between continuity and discontinuity is prominent in G. E. Ladd, *The Presence of the Future* (SPCK, London, 1980), chapter 2. I draw out some of its implications below, pp. 109f., 172f., 181, 235.
8. For a brief discussion of 'the God who comes', see Ladd, *The Presence of the Future*, pp. 48–52. 'The coming of God' is transformed in the New Testament into 'the coming of Jesus' as Son of Man. See below, pp. 72ff.
9. The 'rule of God' or 'kingdom of God' is a phrase which does not occur in the Old Testament. But the idea of God's rule appears frequently.
10. On the idea of an earthly hope in the prophets, see further Ladd, *The Presence of the Future*, pp. 59–64.
11. Ladd, *The Presence of the Future*, p. 68. On this whole issue see his discussion on pp. 64–70, 74f.
12. *The Problem of the Hexateuch* (Eng. tr., Oliver & Boyd, Edinburgh, 1966), p. 93.

13. I wish not to be dogmatic about the dating of Daniel, but I am inclined to accept the view that it was written at the time of the Maccabean crisis around 165 B.C., for reasons given by J. E. Goldingay in 'The Book of Daniel: Three Issues', *Themelios* 2.2, January, 1977, pp. 45–9. I have discussed several issues concerning apocalyptic in my article 'The Value of Apocalyptic', *Tyndale Bulletin* 30 (1979), pp. 53–76; and in *Christian Hope and the Future of Man* (IVP, Leicester, 1980), chapters 2–4.

14. I am following the interpretation summarised by Goldingay (see n. 13). See also his *How to Read the Bible* (Oliphants, London, 1977), pp. 121–6.

15. For a survey of interpretations of this passage, see J. G. Baldwin, *Daniel* (IVP, Leicester, 1978, pp. 172–8).

16. *A Time to be Born—a Time to Die* (Harper, New York, 1973), pp. 80f. The whole of the present paragraph is indebted to Short, and the words from Camus are cited by him on p. 80.

Chapter 2   The Hope of Jesus

Jesus Christ is 'the Yes pronounced upon God's promises, every one of them' (2 Corinthians 1:20, NEB). That was Paul's verdict, expressed about twenty-five years after Jesus's death. It is a staggering statement. And yet many readers of Paul's letter pass over it without a second thought—like someone who spots a diamond in the road and dismisses it as a worthless piece of broken glass. But how did it come about that an amateur rabbi who challenged the Jewish establishment and died a criminal's death should be hailed as the one in whom all the promises of God and the longings of God's people reach their goal? One answer of course is the retort of the Roman governor Festus when Paul, his prisoner, offered him a dose of Christian interpretation of prophecy—'Paul, you are mad; your great learning is turning you mad' (Acts 26:24). But before we come to that conclusion we should see whether Paul's reasons for understanding Jesus in this way have a solid basis. Most importantly, we must ask how Jesus himself understood his place in God's purposes. What was the hope of Jesus, for his own destiny, and for the world?

The rule of God

If there is one thing that is generally agreed amongst the scholars, it is that the central theme of Jesus's message was the kingdom of God. To understand his message of the kingdom is to understand what he was all about. But it is crucial to understand it correctly, because what a man thinks about the kingdom of God has far-reaching effects on what he thinks about everything else. For example, to regard the kingdom as a wholly future or a wholly other-worldly phenomenon normally leads to a conservative attitude towards social change, and to a narrow view of the church's mission in terms of rescuing individuals out of a fallen world. By contrast, those who stress that the kingdom of God is already at work in the world are likely to argue for radical social change and for a view of mission which refuses to limit its scope to the spiritual deliverance of individuals out of the world into the safety of the church. As this book proceeds I shall try to make clear what I think the kingdom of God implies for Christian life and thought. That is why I must get the foundations right. It is in fact notoriously difficult to expound Jesus's teaching about the kingdom without falling prey to one's own predetermined theological viewpoint. Twentieth-century scholarship is strewn with presentations of Jesus's message which betray this built-in bias of the scholar. R. H. Hiers wrote a vigorous survey of them, arguing (in an allusion to Luke 16:16) that 'everyone forces the kingdom of God violently into his own theological traditions.'[1] Despite the risk, I offer the following survey, believing that it represents the authentic message of Jesus.[2]

Just before launching into it, we should consider whether it is worth the effort. After all, the term 'kingdom' is today suspect, associated as it is with traditional patterns of government. In some countries kingship implies despotic rule. In some there are 'royalist' parties fighting to preserve the status quo, or to restore past privileges of a ruling elite. So is it not best to abandon Jesus's term, and look for something more suitable for the atmosphere of our times? In response, I would say three things. First, if we are to take Jesus seriously, we must first try to understand him in his own terms, however we try to interpret those terms for our own day after we have understood them.

Secondly, we must remember that Jesus and his Jewish predecessors spoke of God's kingdom in a context where kingship was frequently associated with tyranny, injustice and incompetence. Old Testament prophets unleashed their anger against rulers who failed to practise justice and

THE HOPE OF JESUS

care for the weak (e.g., Isaiah 1:23; Micah 3:1, 9; Ezekiel 22:6–12; 34). God's kingship, however, involved his demonstrating precisely those qualities of which Israel's kings were so lamentably short (see, e.g., Psalm 146). So the proclamation of God's kingship was not at all a piece of nostalgia for traditional patterns of government. To announce God's kingdom was to offer a revolutionary hope: when God rules in perfect love and justice all earthly kings are cut down to their proper size. It is that very contrast between God's kingship and human rulers which impels us to take Jesus's kingdom language seriously.

The third point is that the language of the kingdom has in fact been making a come-back. Christians in many countries have grown to recognise that traditional language of 'salvation' and 'eternal life' focuses mainly on the individual's relationship to God, and on spiritual experience within the church. There was a need to discover a biblically-based theological framework for understanding and engaging with the increasingly complex world of politics and social need. Such a framework was found in the concept of the kingdom. It has been a constant theme amongst writers—such as the Latin-American exponents of liberation theology—who aim to relate the Christian gospel to the great issues of injustice, oppression and social change. Indeed, the current danger in some quarters is that a few mentions of the word 'kingdom' in any theological document will be enough to guarantee that it be received with uncritical enthusiasm.

What, then, did Jesus mean by 'the kingdom of God'? As we saw in chapter 1, the Old Testament prophets looked for the time when God would begin to rule in a new and decisive way, removing the imperfections of the world and demonstrating his total care for mankind by guaranteeing peace and justice, security and joy in his presence. When Jesus announced, 'The right time has come, and the Kingdom of God is near!' (Mark 1:15), he was declaring the fulfilment of that hope. 'The kingdom of God' on Jesus's lips referred to God acting powerfully to bring in this new era. Or it referred to the blessings experienced by God's people in this new era, or to the realm within which those blessings may be experienced. It is difficult to give a precise definition, for the richness of the concept ensures that it constantly overflows all attempts to define it with precision. And we should not expect 'kingdom' to mean exactly the same in every instance, any more than we expect 'grace' or 'glory' or 'hope' or 'faith' always to have exactly the same meaning. But 'kingdom' for Jesus does not mean an area of land, and so it is preferable to speak of God's rule or reign.

God's rule has begun!

The new thing about Jesus's message was his announcement that God's rule was no longer merely an object of hope: the longed-for day had arrived. The Jewish scholar David Flusser says Jesus 'is the only Jew of ancient times known to us, who preached not only that men were on the threshold of the end of time, but that the new age of salvation had already begun'.[3] Jesus declares this in a host of images. The wedding has begun, the bridegroom has come, it is a time for feasting, not fasting. New wine has appeared, which old wineskins cannot contain (Mark 2:19, 22). Harvest-time has arrived, and Jesus sends out his disciples to gather the harvest (Matthew 9:38).

Apart from such well-known Jewish images for the time of salvation, Jesus makes specific reference to *Scripture*. When John the Baptist sent messengers from his prison cell to ask if Jesus was indeed God's chosen deliverer, Jesus's reply was:

Go back and tell John what you are hearing and seeing: the blind can see, the lame can walk, the lepers are made clean, the deaf hear, the dead are raised to life, and the Good News is preached to the poor. How happy is he who has no doubts about me! (Matthew 11:2–6).

His allusions are to Isaiah 35:5ff., 29:18f., and 61:1f.—time-honoured descriptions of the era of salvation, when God would remove sorrow and suffering. And the fact that the lepers and the dead appear in Jesus's list, despite their absence from Isaiah, suggests that the fulfilment which Jesus brings goes beyond all expectations.

As this allusion to Scripture has already illustrated, Jesus not only announced the arrival of God's rule in images, but also demonstrated it by his *deeds*. For he brought not just a new message, but a new reality, a new experience of God's saving power. His healing miracles are not so much proofs of his divinity or of his messiahship as demonstrations of the kingdom of God at work. Those Old Testament promises that people would be made whole were actually coming true in the lives of real, specific suffering people. And it is clear that Jesus saw his miracles as a central part of his activity from his warning to the people of Capernaum, Bethsaida and Chorazin:

> How terrible it will be for you . . . For if the miracles which were performed in you had been performed in Tyre and Sidon, long ago the people there would have put on sackcloth, and sprinkled ashes on themselves to show they had changed their ways! (Matthew 11:20–24).

Here Jesus makes no mention of his preaching, but only of his miracles. They in themselves are sufficient to show the kingdom's presence and to challenge people to take sides.

Jesus's exorcisms in particular indicate that God's rule has begun. In response to those cynical critics who claimed that his success at exorcism must be due to Satan himself, Jesus retorted, 'No, it is God's Spirit who gives me the power to drive out demons, which proves that the Kingdom of God has already come upon you' (Matthew 12:28). It is the Spirit who makes the difference, and the Spirit is the long-awaited sign that the time of salvation has arrived. There were other exorcists in those days, both Jewish and pagan, and neither Jesus nor the gospel-writers deny it. The distinctiveness in Jesus's exorcisms was this spiritual power and authority which ensured not only that evil powers were driven out, but also that the people exorcised found their broken personalities restored and transformed by the Spirit of the new age. They were not only emptied of demons, but also filled with God. Thus Jesus showed that the beginning of God's rule meant the breaking of the grip of evil over people's lives. The strong man was bound and his house plundered (Matthew 12:29). And when he sent out his followers to announce the coming of God's kingdom, the result was the same. Their success in subduing evil powers caused him to exclaim, 'I saw Satan fall like lightning from heaven' (Luke 10:17).

The presence of the Spirit

The powerful work of the Holy Spirit, then, was evidence of the kingdom's presence. For in Jewish expectation the Spirit was to be a dominant feature of the coming age (e.g., Joel 2:28f.; Ezekiel 36:26f.). Jesus's intense sense of being the bearer of the Spirit is clear from his declaration about driving out demons by the power of God's Spirit (Matthew 12:28). It is clear too from his warning that 'whoever says something against the Holy Spirit will not be forgiven—now or ever' (Matthew 12:32). Anyone who deliberately suppressed the plain evidence of his eyes, that the Spirit of God himself was at work in Jesus's exorcisms, put himself beyond the reach of God's forgiveness.

Or again, deep in Jesus's consciousness lay the conviction that *he* was the one to fulfil the prophecy of Isaiah 61 which spoke of the prophet of a new age, anointed by the Spirit:

> The Sovereign Lord has filled me with his spirit.
> He has chosen me and sent me to bring good news
> to the poor . . .

Jesus alludes to this passage as the meaning of his ministry not only in Luke 4:18f. (the fullest quotation), but also in Matthew 11:2–6 (already cited). There is a further allusion in the beatitudes of Matthew 5:3ff. and Luke 6:20f., where the references to 'the poor' and 'those who mourn' ('weep' in Luke) echo Isaiah 61:1, 3.

So Jesus saw himself as the one endowed with the Spirit to bring in the new age. The drought of the Spirit, which began when the line of Old Testament prophets came to an end, was now over. The floodtide of the Spirit had come. And when did Jesus receive this unique sense of being the bearer of the Spirit? At his baptism, when he saw heaven opening and the Spirit coming down on him like a dove. And he heard a voice from heaven: 'You are my own dear Son. I am well pleased with you' (Mark 1:10f.). The age of God's rule is the age of the Spirit, and it was Jesus's empowering with that Spirit which enabled him to demonstrate God's saving power in people's lives.[4]

Some difficult sayings

Jesus, then, saw his own ministry as the time of decisive fulfilment. A new power was at work in history, prompting him to say to his disciples, 'How happy are you, to see the things you see! For many prophets and kings, I tell you, wanted to see what you see, but they could not, and to hear what you hear, but they did not' (Luke 10:23f.). So even before we come to his more direct teaching, we find that Jesus's use of images and his deeds show that the rule of God has begun. The meaning of these 'direct sayings' has in fact been hotly disputed amongst scholars. Through most of the twentieth century there has run a debate between those who argue that Jesus spoke of the kingdom of God as already present ('realised eschatology') and those who insist that for Jesus the kingdom was not present but coming in the near future ('futurist' or 'thoroughgoing eschatology').[5] In my judgment, the following disputed passages all indicate that the rule of God is in some sense present: Mark 1:15: 'The right time has come, and the Kingdom of God is near. Turn away from your sins and believe the Good News.' The dispute turns on whether the phrase 'is near' (literally, 'has drawn near') refers to something which still lies in the near future, or to something which has actually arrived. In practice, the difference is small, and weight must be given to the emphasis on fulfilment in the phrase 'the right time has come.' Jesus is not so much urging people to mend their ways in view of an imminent crisis—that was John the Baptist's message. Rather, Jesus is declaring good news because of what God has now begun to do. As Gunther Bornkamm puts it, 'between these two and their preaching there is a difference like that between the eleventh and the twelfth hours. For Jesus calls: the shift in the aeons is here, the kingdom of God is already dawning.'[6]

Matthew 11:12: 'From the time John preached his message until this very day the Kingdom of heaven has suffered violent attacks, and violent men try to seize it.' The precise meaning of the saying is notoriously difficult to decide. The Greek words here translated 'the Kingdom of heaven has suffered violent attacks' *could* mean 'the Kingdom of heaven exercises its force.' That interpretation would bring it close in meaning to Luke's parallel saying in Luke 16:16. But the reference to violence in both halves of the saying supports the GNB translation. Jesus is referring to the violent opposition to the kingdom of God which has been experienced ever since John the Baptist heralded the kingdom's coming. Opposition from whom? Perhaps from Satan, or from Herod Antipas, who had imprisoned and executed John, or from Zealots, who try to bring in the kingdom by using violence against the Romans. If this is the meaning, it is important in showing that Jesus accepted that the coming of the kingdom inevitably involved conflict and sometimes setbacks, even though ultimate victory was assured.[7] But whatever the exact meaning of the saying, its importance for our purposes is clear. Whether the kingdom of God is 'exercising its force' or 'suffering violent attacks', it must be already present. Such things could not be said of a purely future phenomenon.

Luke 17:20f.: 'Some Pharisees asked Jesus when the Kingdom of God would come. His answer was: "The

Kingdom of God does not come in such a way as to be seen. No one will say, 'Look, here it is!' or, 'There it is!'; because the Kingdom of God is in your midst" ' (the last phrase is not in GNB, which has 'is within you'). Here Jesus denies the possibility of calculating a date for the coming of God's rule. Such calculation is impossible because the kingdom's coming is not to be deduced from observing wars or earthquakes or heavenly bodies, nor is it to be seen in the arrival of messianic pretenders claiming to tell people where it is located. And such calculation is irrelevant, because in fact the kingdom is already present in the midst of those who witness the activity of Jesus.[8]

Good news to the poor

In Jesus's mind, then, there was no doubt that God's rule was present. His actions and his teaching point clearly to the fact that in him the saving activity of God was present in a new way. But in his own estimation the supreme sign of the kingdom's presence was not healings or exorcisms, but his preaching good news to the poor. *That* is what stands as the climax of his quotation from Isaiah—'the blind can see, the lame can walk, the lepers are made clean, the deaf hear, the dead are raised to life, and the Good News is preached to the poor' (Matthew 11:5).

Who are 'the poor'? Although in the Old and New Testaments the term often referred to those who were materially poor, it came to have a broader meaning. In the Isaiah 61 passage, the term 'poor' is explained by a whole series of parallel phrases: 'the broken-hearted', 'captives', 'those in prison', 'all who mourn'. This makes it clear that the poor are those who are oppressed in a quite general sense, those who are powerless, as compared with others who are in a position to dominate or despise them. These are the ones who cast themselves on God's mercy, because they have nowhere else to go. They are empty, and therefore open to what God may do for them. Thus in the Psalms, for example, 'the poor' is often a way of describing those who are faithful and open to God (e.g., Psalms 70:14; 40:17; 109:31).

In Jesus's mind the poor included those who were powerless in face of the religious establishment. There were people who stood no chance of salvation because they did despised jobs. These included the sexually immoral, such as prostitutes, and those notorious for dishonesty, such as gamblers or tax-collectors. All such people were commonly lumped together under the label 'sinners', and placed firmly beyond the scope of God's care. In Jewish terms, there was no practical way out for the sinner. Theoretically, a prostitute could be made clean by repentance, purification and atonement. But that would cost money, and her ill-gotten gains could not be used for it. So what chance did she have? She was predestined to inferiority, disgrace and condemnation.

Again, for Jesus the poor were the sick, the widows, the orphans, who only survived by dependence on other people's charity. There was a saying: 'Four things are compared with a dead man: the lame, the blind, the leper and the childless' (b.Ned. 64b Bar.). To such people Jesus brought good news. To those whom others called dead, he offered new life (Luke 15:32). Those whom others denounced as sinners were the very ones he had come to call (Mark 2:17). Those whom others despised and shut out from consideration, Jesus called 'lost' and gave them hope of being found (Luke 15). Whereas other religious teachers laid intolerable burdens on those already weighed down by poverty, guilt and despair, Jesus offered his invitation: 'Come to me, all of you who are tired from carrying your heavy loads, and I will give you rest' (Matthew 11:28).

What, then, is the good news for the poor? In its simplest form it is there in the first beatitude: 'Happy are you poor: The Kingdom of God is yours' (Luke 6:20). The nobodies of Jewish society are the first to know the blessings of God's saving presence. The kingdom of God is for them! No wonder the religious establishment and the respectable people of society were furious with Jesus. We see this clearly from the whole gospel story, but also from Jesus's words which we have already looked at: 'The Good News is preached to the poor. How happy is he who has no doubts about me' (or 'is not scandalised by me') (Matthew 11:5f.). But for the poor, hope is kindled. Jesus's preaching that the kingdom of God is for the poor is itself the supreme sign that the kingdom is present. For in the very act of preaching, things begin to change. That is because of the nature of the message, which we may explain under three headings:

The character of God's rule

First, the King in this kingdom is a *Father*. It was from Jesus's own experience of the character of God that everything in his life and message flowed. Never before had any Jew dared to address God as Jesus did—'Abba' (Mark 14:36).[9] As is well known, this was an everyday, Aramaic word, in contrast to the ancient, liturgical Hebrew language normally used in prayer. And it was an intimate, family word used by an infant in addressing his father (though it was sometimes also used by grown-up sons and daughters to their father, or by younger people to any older, respected man). Even today, if you sit on the beach at a popular Israeli resort such as Netanya on the Mediterranean coast, your peace will be disturbed by the excited cries of 'Abba' as little children call to their fathers (in modern Hebrew). Jesus used this way of addressing God for precisely the reason which made other people avoid it: it expressed the intimacy of relationship, as well as the totality of obedience, which other people thought blasphemous or presumptuous, but which for Jesus was the consuming reality of his spiritual experience. More than any other single word, it expressed what the dawning of God's kingdom entailed.

It is true, of course, that Jesus did not speak openly about God as Father to every passer-by. To know God as Father was to him a deep personal experience not to be spoken of lightly. Yet he did say to his disciples, 'Do not be afraid, little flock! For your Father is pleased to give you the

Kingdom' (Luke 12:32). And he taught them to pray, 'Our Father . . . May your Kingdom come' (Matthew 6:9f.)—alluding to that future coming of the kingdom which we shall consider below. Apart from these actual instances of the word 'Father' on Jesus's lips, the character of God as a father seeking relationship with his creatures pervades Jesus's preaching of the kingdom. The poor to whom the good news comes may raise their heads and their expectations, because—contrary to what the religious authorities would have them believe—it is this fatherly God who comes near to them in Jesus.

The second aspect of the kingdom message is that it is good news of *forgiveness*. To the paralysed man who came to him through the mud roof of a crowded house, Jesus declared, 'My son, your sins are forgiven' (Mark 2:5). And to underline his authority to forgive he healed the man's paralysis as well. For this was no mere talk about forgiveness: Jesus conveyed an experience of forgiveness. And it was no mere promise of future forgiveness at death or at the last judgment: it was forgiveness, acceptance in the sight of God *now*. 'The Son of Man has authority *on earth* to forgive sins' (Mark 2:10). Numerous parables convey this news of God's forgiveness. God is like a king who wrote off the debt of a servant, even though he owed him millions of pounds (Matthew 18:23–35). With joy he welcomes the person who comes to him for forgiveness, as a woman rejoices when she finds her lost coin, or a shepherd his sheep, or a father his son (Luke 15). Even the wretched tax-collector who dares only to stand in the outer court of the temple and say, 'O God, have pity on me, a sinner!', goes home with his prayer heard and his sins forgiven (Luke 18:9–14).

Jesus enacted God's forgiveness as well as declaring it, by sharing his meal-table with sinners. In the east to share a meal with someone was no mere social or gastronomic convenience. It was an expression of trust and brotherhood, an offer of forgiveness, even an expression of fellowship before God. So in a society dominated by rules about ritual uncleanness and by commands to keep away from 'sinners',

Jesus's action was of deep and shocking significance. After calling Levi the tax-collector to follow him, he was joined by other outcasts for a meal in Levi's home. Then—

> Some teachers of the Law, who were Pharisees, saw that Jesus was eating with these outcasts and tax collectors; so they asked the disciples, 'Why does he eat with tax collectors and outcasts?' Jesus heard them and answered: 'People who are well do not need a doctor, but only those who are sick. I have not come to call the respectable people, but the outcasts' (Mark 2:15–17).

And when Jesus speaks of 'calling', he means that he is inviting people to the banquet of salvation—for God's final kingdom was often pictured in terms of a banquet or a wedding-feast (cf. Matthew 8:11). Jesus's eating with sinners was a foretaste, an acted promise, of a share in that feast. It was forgiveness made real, an acceptance that could be felt.

Try to imagine what this would mean to those lonely, despised people. By accepting them in friendship and sealing that friendship with a meal, Jesus took away their shame, their guilt. He showed that they mattered. All this is made clear in the incident at the home of Simon the Pharisee (Luke 7:36–50). Jesus was having dinner at Simon's invitation, when a prostitute came in and poured on Jesus her perfume and her tears. When Simon objected, Jesus told the story of two debtors. One of them owed a moneylender five thousand pounds, the other owed him five hundred. Since neither could pay, he cancelled the debts of both. 'Which one, then,' asked Jesus, 'will love him more?' 'The one who was forgiven more, I suppose,' replied the Pharisee. 'Exactly,' said Jesus, 'and the same is true of this woman. She has washed my feet with her tears, dried them with her hair, kissed my feet, covered them with perfume. I tell you, then, the great love she has shown proves that her many sins have been forgiven.' And to the woman he said, 'Your faith has saved you; go in peace.' In contrast to Simon's well-meaning but misguided correctness, Jesus welcomes the woman into the fellowship. Without embarrassment he allows her to touch him and to lavish on him her simple expressions of penitence and gratitude. Shame and remorse give way to acceptance, forgiveness, faith, a new start, and joy at the overwhelming generosity of God.

World upside-down

The third part of the good news was the announcement of *a new order of things*. We have seen that in the Old Testament the reign of God was expected as a time when he would demonstrate his total care for the world and his sovereignty over it by removing evil and all its consequences, and by establishing justice and peace, wholeness and joy in his presence. Jesus's announcement of the dawn of God's rule involved declaring the dawning of this new order of things. Not only forgiveness and an individual relationship with God as Father, but also a whole 'new world' was implied by Jesus's message. Because his message was supremely 'good news for the poor', he spoke often of the reversal of fortunes which the kingdom brings.

> Happy are you poor: the kingdom of God is yours! Happy are you who are hungry now: you will be filled! Happy are you who weep now: you will laugh! . . . But how terrible for you who are rich now: you have had your easy life! How terrible for you who are full now: you will go hungry! How terrible for you who laugh now: you will mourn and weep! (Luke 6:20f., 24f.).

God reveals his truth not to the theologians but to the simple (Matthew 11:25f.). He opens the kingdom to children (Mark 10:14; Matthew 18:3). The nobodies of society fill the banqueting hall, whilst the invited guests refuse to come (Matthew 22:1–10). Lazarus is welcomed to Abraham's side whilst the rich man suffers in hell (Luke 16:19–31). The first become last, and the last first (Luke 13:30). It is all summed up in Mary's song about the meaning of Jesus's coming: where the kingdom is present, the attitudes and power-structures of the present age are reversed—

He stretched out his mighty arm
and scattered the proud people with all their plans.
He brought down mighty kings from their thrones,
and lifted up the lowly.
He filled the hungry with good things,
and sent the rich away with empty hands
   (Luke 1:51–53).

Such insistence on the reversal of conditions in the kingdom of God carries a clear promise that the coming of Jesus was to affect much more than the spiritual lives of particular individuals. It implied the transformation of social conditions, the arrival of that elusive justice and harmony for which the prophets longed. No wonder the poor hung on Jesus's words, and the self-satisfied were horrified by him. Yet it would be quite wrong, on the strength of this part of Jesus's teaching, to see him as a conventional political revolutionary figure. For he was not calling people to rebel against the established power; he was telling them what *God* is doing. And despite his magnificent bias in favour of the poor, Jesus was not *against* other people. There is a gospel for them, too. The same love of God which reaches to the outcast reaches out to the wealthy, the secure, the influential—if they will hear. God's care is undiscriminating: he gives sun and rain to the good and the bad alike, and 'he is good to the ungrateful and the wicked' (Matthew 5:45; Luke 6:35). And Jesus was as ready to eat with a Pharisee as with a tax-collector. He healed the daughter of a synagogue official (Mark 5:21–43). His followers included some wealthy women who met some of his financial needs (Luke 5:3). And his final lament over Jerusalem bears witness to his agonised longing that all its people should know the blessings of God's rule: 'O Jerusalem, Jerusalem! You kill the prophets and stone the messengers God has sent you! How many times have I wanted to put my arms around you people, just as a hen gathers her chicks under her wings, but you would not let me!' (Matthew 23:37).

So Jesus was not setting out to stir up class conflict when he announced good news to the poor. But he was declaring a new order of things which was rich with promise for the poor, and deeply threatening to those who found their security in the prevailing social and religious structures. The kingdom of God involved a social revolution which would mean nothing less than the reclaiming for God and his will of every area of human life. His actions are all of a piece with this intention. In his miracles he overcame disease, death, demon-possession, even shortage of food. He restored the leper to human society. He tore down the barriers of a caste system to which the regulations of religion lent legitimacy. He attacked the commercial exploitation of the Temple. His cleansing of the Temple was more than that, however. It implied a new approach to the worship of God—in fulfilment of the visions of Ezekiel 40–48.[10] And since it brought to mind the word of Zechariah 14:21, that when the day of the Lord arrived 'there shall no longer be any merchant in the house of the Lord Almighty', Jesus's action was an assertion that the day of the Lord, the kingdom of God, had indeed come (cf. Malachi 3:1–3). Jesus also challenged the religious establishment by his attitude to their restrictive interpretations of the Law. His healings on the sabbath, for example, showed that God is concerned to make people whole and to liberate them, not to shackle them with a complex legal system. Finally, Jesus sowed the seeds of a new society in a diverse group of twelve imperfect men, to whom he taught the nature of life under God's rule. We shall consider some implications of this in the final chapter.

The presence of God's rule, then, may be described in these three ways: it is the rule of a father, it conveys forgiveness, it involves a new order of things. To summarise it in a word, we could use Paul's word 'grace'. For Jesus's message was that God accepts people as they are, because of his all-embracing love. Those who have nothing to offer him but their sins need not despair, because their forgiveness, their beginning afresh depends on him and his gift of the kingdom's blessings. And for precisely the same reason those who think they have every credential for claiming God's approval must recognise that, unless they cease their self-satisfaction and self-congratulation, they have no part in his kingdom. Behind the whole message stands the character and activity of God himself. He is the God exemplified, for example, in the parable which we in our folly have called the parable of the prodigal son, though it is really about the *God* who is prodigal—that is, lavishly generous—with his love (Luke 15:11–32). He is the God portrayed in the parable about the owner of the vineyard, who pays his workers a full day's wage, whether they have worked for the whole day or merely for an hour. When those who had worked all day complained at this arrangement, the owner answered, 'If I want to give this man who was hired last as much as I have given you, don't I have the right to do as I wish with my own money? Or are you jealous simply because I am generous?' (Matthew 20:14f.). That the workers who began near the end of the day received a full wage is entirely due to the owner's generosity. And God's kingdom is like that; he lavishes his love on the most undeserving cases. Those who argue that this is improper have completely failed to understand what God is like and what he is doing in the coming of his kingdom through Jesus.

The demands of God's rule

We have seen that when Jesus spoke of the kingdom of God he was referring sometimes to God's action in bringing the kingdom, sometimes of the blessings which the kingdom involves. Jesus also spoke of God's kingdom as a realm to be 'entered', a gift which has to be grasped. 'Remember this! Whoever does not receive the Kingdom of God like a child will never enter it' (Mark 10:15). The presence of the kingdom demands a response. The gift is there, but it must be received; the door is open, but it must be entered. And how is it to be entered? What response does the kingdom demand? At its simplest the demand was: repentance and faith.

'The right time has come and the Kingdom of God is near! Turn away from your sins and believe the Good News!' (Mark 1:15).

'Turn away from your sins.' To all his hearers Jesus urged the need to make a break with wrongdoing, whether they were 'obvious' sinners like Zacchaeus the tax-collector or the woman caught in the act of adultery, or 'respectable' sinners like teachers of the Law who 'take advantage of widows and rob them of their homes, then make a show of saying long prayers!' (Luke 20:47).

Every ordinary person has this challenge to face. When told about some Galileans whom Pilate had butchered, Jesus exclaimed, 'Because these Galileans were killed in that way, do you think it proves that they were worse sinners than all the other Galileans? No! I tell you that if you do not change your ways, you will all die as they did' (Luke 13:2f.). The fact that certain people suffered such a fate does not prove that they were worse sinners than anyone else: let everyone realise that unless he repents a far worse fate awaits him at God's final judgment. Can you not see, says Jesus, that you are like an accused man at the very door of the law-court, whose case is hopeless? Settle quickly with your accuser, before it is too late (Matthew 5:25f.).

But repentance is not only a turning from the past. It involves following Jesus—going with him, identifying with his life-style, doing his will. And that is a very radical demand indeed. 'If anyone wants to come with me, he must forget himself, carry his cross, and follow me. For the man who wants to save his own life will lose it; but the man who loses his life for me and for the gospel will save it' (Mark 8:34f.). Jesus said this would involve renunciation of every-thing which might hinder entry into God's kingdom. Hence

66

his warning, that if a hand or a foot or an eye tempts one to sin, it should be removed. 'It is better for you to enter the Kingdom of God with only one eye [or hand, or foot] than to keep both eyes and be thrown into hell' (Mark 9:47). Picturesque language, of course—for if one eye is a cause of temptation the other one is bound to be equally dangerous! But the starkness of the warning cannot be side-stepped simply by labelling it 'picture-language'. This renunciation might involve money (Mark 10:17–31), all earthly security (Matthew 6:24–34), prestige (Matthew 23:5–12), even family and friends (Luke 14:26). It would certainly involve the limitless demands of self-giving love (Luke 6:27–36). That is what it means to follow the Son of Man who 'has no place to lie down and rest' (Luke 9:58), who 'must suffer much, and be rejected' (Mark 9:31), who 'did not come to be served; he came to serve and to give his life to redeem many people' (Mark 10:45).

Consider two parables of Jesus:

The Kingdom of heaven is like a treasure hidden in a field. A man happens to find it, so he covers it up again. He is so happy that he goes and sells everything he has, and then goes back and buys the field. Also, the Kingdom of heaven is like a buyer looking for fine pearls. When he finds one that is unusually fine, he goes and sells everything he has, and buys the pearl (Matthew 13:44–46).

Whether we find the blessings of the kingdom after a long stretch, or stumble across them, as it were, by accident, the issue is clear. The kingdom's blessings are a treasure of infinite value, but they demand all that we can give. Total offer, total demand.

The other part of the kingdom's demand is Jesus's call for faith or trust. Welcoming the children brought to him for blessing, he said, 'Let the children come to me! Do not stop them, because the Kingdom of God belongs to such as these. Remember this! Whoever does not receive the Kingdom of God like a child will never enter it' (Mark

10:14f.; cf. Matthew 18:1–5). To receive the kingdom like a child, or to become like a child, means to live in trustful dependence on God as 'Abba'. As Jeremias puts it, 'repentance means learning to say *Abba* again, putting one's whole trust in the heavenly Father, returning to the Father's house and the Father's arms' (cf. Luke 15:11—32). 'In the last resort, repentance is simply trusting in the grace of God.'[11] To believe the good news is to unravel one's reliance on all systems of earthly security, whether they are religious or material, and to entrust oneself to the care of the Father.

The radical nature and the directness of Jesus's demand is seen clearly enough from the reaction of those who ranged themselves against him—those who derived prestige from their place in the religious establishment, those whose adherence to the Law convinced them of their own righteousness, those whose wealth was too precious to abandon. Having too much to lose, they were deaf to the offer of God's grace. Unable to share God's compassion for people, they met with Jesus's blunt condemnation: 'The tax collectors and prostitutes are going into the Kingdom of God ahead of you' (Matthew 21:31—where 'ahead of you' means 'and not you').[12]

Has God's rule fully come?

We have seen that, according to Jesus's proclamation, God's rule was already present. It was a fact within history, evidenced in his actions and in the influence of God's Spirit on people's lives. It was there whether people acknowledged it or not. And yet, paradoxically, it was present in a sense only for those who acknowledged it and responded to Jesus's demands. The paradox can be seen in Jesus's reply to John the Baptist, with its list of signs of the kingdom's presence followed by the ominous saying, 'How happy is he who has no doubts about me!' (Matthew 11:2–6). The kingdom leaves its mark in history, yet it must become real for each individual if he is to be included within the scope of its blessings. The same paradox is there in the passages where Jesus warns of judgment to those who witness the signs of the kingdom yet do not repent. In an objective sense, 'the Kingdom of God has come near you!' Yet if that message is not welcomed, 'on the Judgment Day God will show more mercy to Sodom than to that town!' (Luke 10:11f.; cf. 11:31f.).

This paradox was there because God's rule had not yet fully come. The kingdom was present in the sense that the blessings of the new age were already being experienced through Jesus's ministry. Yet its full realisation—in the sense of God's total triumph over the powers of evil and his establishing of a realm of permanent justice and peace—remained an object of hope for the future. The kingdom was present, but hidden. Although a new power had been unleashed in the world, there were many who were not touched by it, many who failed to recognise it. But the day would come when doubt and opposition and hiddenness would give way to the full and perfect realisation of God's rule. Thus Jesus taught his followers to pray, 'May your kingdom come' (Matthew 6:10). He spoke of a future realm where 'people will come from the east and the west, from the north and the south, and sit at the table in the Kingdom of God' (Luke 13:29).

How, then, did Jesus envisage the future, and the coming of God's kingdom in that future? In the first place, he spoke of the *growth* of the kingdom. Several parables highlight the contrast between the kingdom's small and hidden beginnings and its ultimate open success. It is like when a farmer scatters seed, which eventually—without his understanding it or doing anything about it—produces a great harvest. It is like the tiny mustard seed which becomes a great shrub, or the small piece of yeast which has extraordinary results on a large lump of dough (Mark 4:26–32; Matthew 13:33). Modern scholars are right to call such parables 'parables of contrast' rather than 'parables of growth', which has been their traditional name. Nevertheless, the contrast implies the growth, and it is growth which is attributed to God. He, rather than human effort or human ingenuity, is responsible for the ultimate triumph of his purposes.

Other sayings, too, imply a progressive coming of God's kingdom. The much-debated saying of Mark 9:1 seems to me to fit best in this context. 'Remember this! There are some here who will not die until they have seen the Kingdom of God come with power.' This saying is often interpreted as a clear-cut prediction of the 'second coming' of Jesus within a generation of his lifetime—a prediction which turned out to be mistaken. But this fails to reckon with the flexibility of the term 'kingdom' for Jesus, or to recognise that he expected events such as his resurrection and the fall of Jerusalem, which he saw as key points in the fulfilment of God's sovereign purposes. In the saying, Jesus is declaring that 'some' of those listening to him—that is, the disciples as opposed to the uncommitted crowd who are looking on (Mark 8:34)—will, before they die, recognise the powerful presence of God's rule through his action in historical events. Jesus was unspecific about what such events might be, but we with hindsight might point to his death and resurrection, the events of Pentecost, the amazing growth of the church under the control of God's Spirit, the fall of Jerusalem in A.D. 70 as the seal of his judgment on unresponsive Israel. And the transfiguration of Jesus, which follows immediately in Mark's account (Mark 9:2–8), was surely seen by the gospel-writer as a foretaste of that glory which would belong to Jesus through the coming of the kingdom 'with power'.

God will act!

Secondly, Jesus insisted that the kingdom would come by *God's gracious act*. When he spoke of growth, he assumed that God would grant the growth. When he spoke of the kingdom coming with power, it was God's power which he had in mind. When his disciples needed reassurance, his message was, 'Do not be afraid, little flock! For your Father is pleased to *give* you the kingdom' (Luke 12:32). This stress on God's action does not rule out the call for people to co-operate with God's purpose in trustful obedience. But it does rule out the idea that the kingdom can be 'spread' or 'built' by sheer human effort. It also rules out the option, adopted by the Zealot movement in Jesus's day, of seeking to establish God's rule by armed resistance to the occupying Roman forces. Such revolutionary action might conceivably have restored the kingdom of Israel (if the revolutionaries were persistent and the Romans were continually and miraculously incompetent!). But it could not create the new order of universal, God-centred peace and justice which the kingdom of God was to be.

Far from it. For, thirdly, Jesus anticipated that God would bring in his final kingdom through his own *suffering and death*. He spoke of his death as a cup which must be drunk, a baptism which must be undergone—it was part of the destiny of suffering which God had laid upon him in order to achieve his purpose (Mark 10:38; Luke 12:50). When he was warned that King Herod Antipas planned to kill him, his reply showed that he regarded his dying, even more than his healing, as the means through which the kingdom of God would be revealed. 'Go tell that fox, "I am driving out demons and performing cures today and tomorrow, and on the third day I shall finish my work." Yet I must be on my way today, tomorrow and the next day; it is not right for a prophet to be killed anywhere except in Jerusalem' (Luke 13:32f.). Most of all, Jesus spoke of his death in terms of the 'Son of Man'—that mysterious figure from Daniel 7 who leads and represents the suffering people of God, and through his suffering attains to royal power. And 'his authority would last for ever, and his kingdom would never end' (Daniel 7:14).[13] Jesus saw himself as fulfilling the pattern followed by the 'one like a son of man' in Daniel's dream. Hence the famous 'passion predictions' of Mark 8:31; 9:31; 10:33f.

The vindication of the Son of Man

But these passages immediately lead us on to a further expectation of Jesus—and here we approach the heart of his hope for the future. Jesus expected not only to die, but also to be *vindicated by God*. As in Daniel 7, the Son of Man's destiny was to suffer, and beyond his suffering to receive God's public approval of his work. Sometimes, as in the passion predictions, this vindication is expressed in terms of resurrection: 'The Son of Man will be handed over to men who will kill him; three days later, however, he will be raised to life' (Mark 9:31). Elsewhere, vindication is expressed in terms of the Son of Man's coming again to earth in the future. 'If, then, a man is ashamed of me and of my teaching in this godless and wicked day, then the Son of Man will be ashamed of him when he comes in the glory of his Father with the holy angels' (Mark 8:38). Again, in response to the high priest's question whether he was the Messiah, Jesus said, 'I am, and you will all see the Son of Man seated at the right side of the Almighty, and coming with the clouds of heaven!' (Mark 14:62. Other references to the Son of Man's 'coming' include Mark 13:26; Matthew 10:23; 24:44; 25:31; Luke 18:8). Two problems immediately arise. First, it has been forcefully argued that, since there is no saying in the gospels in which Jesus speaks of 'Kingdom of God' and 'Son of Man' in relationship to each other, he cannot in fact have used both these terms. One set of sayings must be inauthentic. And since Jesus certainly spoke of the kingdom of God, it must be the 'Son of Man' sayings which are inauthentic—inventions of Jesus's followers. The absence of any saying where Jesus speaks of 'Kingdom of God' and 'Son of Man' in the same breath is certainly a remarkable fact. But the conclusion drawn from this fact, that Jesus cannot have spoken of himself as Son of Man, can surely be disposed of. 'Son of Man' and 'Kingdom of God' are closely related to each other in Daniel 7, in such a way that the one implies the other. So when Jesus used one or other of these terms he did not need to expound it in

72

relation to the other term; to use both terms in any one saying would convey no more meaning than was implied by using one term.

The second problem is that, whilst Jesus expected vindication and spoke of it sometimes in terms of resurrection and sometimes in terms of a future 'coming', there is no saying where he speaks of 'resurrection' and 'coming' in the same breath. Does this suggest that for him there is no distinction between these two events, that they are alternative ways of referring to the same thing? And might that imply that Jesus anticipated vindication by God in terms of resurrection from death, but did not foresee a 'second coming' as it has traditionally been understood among Christians? Five comments are relevant here. First, it need not surprise us that Jesus was imprecise about the timing of events which lay beyond his death, or about the relationship between his 'rising' and his 'coming'. Right through the Bible, prophecy has a way of asserting its faith in the future in such a way that the time-distinctions between events only become clear after they have begun to be fulfilled. Jesus had no timetable of future events comparable to the 'diary of forthcoming events' distributed by the local tourist information office. His confidence that he would be vindicated by God was a triumphant, visionary expression of faith, and faith operates by trust in the purposes of a loving God, not by timetables. It is quite natural that, once his resurrection had happened, his followers should be able to see more clearly than he had himself seen that the ultimate act of vindication, his coming from heaven, still lay in the future.

The second comment is this. Although Jesus was not explicit about it, his sayings about the Son of Man's coming in glory *assume* that it will be the coming of one already exalted. In other words, the Son of Man who comes will be the Son of Man who was raised from death after three days, even though Jesus never specifically made this connection. This may be seen, for example, in Mark 14:62 (quoted above), where Jesus tells his hearers that they will see the Son of Man already enthroned before he comes with the clouds. Those who judged Jesus on earth will one day see the Son of Man vindicated and exalted by God, and coming to pass judgment on *them*.[14]

Thirdly, we may see that Jesus implicitly distinguished between his rising and his coming from the fact that he spoke in different ways about the outcome of these two events. When he spoke of the coming of the Son of Man, he associated with it the final judgment of all men and the full and final establishment of God's perfect kingdom (see, for example, Mark 8:38; 13:26f; Matthew 25:31–46; Luke 21:36). But Jesus did not refer to his resurrection as the moment of the final establishing of God's kingdom: it was to be the moment of his *personal* vindication, rather than the vindication of all God's purposes and of God's people.

Fourthly, if Jesus did not imply some distinction between his resurrection and his coming, it is hard to explain how the early Christians came to such a clear-cut viewpoint so early and so consistently. The distinction is there in one of Paul's earliest letters, where he summarises the gospel he has learnt to preach: '. . . to wait for his Son to come from heaven—his Son Jesus, whom he raised from death, and who rescues us from God's wrath that is to come' (1 Thessalonians 1:10). And in a sermon in Acts, widely regarded by scholars as preserving a piece of extremely early Christian tradition, Peter says, '. . . that he may send Jesus, who is the Messiah he has already chosen for you. He must remain in heaven until the time comes for all things to be made new' (Acts 3:20f.).

The fifth comment links closely with this. The time-interval between resurrection and coming is not only asserted by apostles, it is also presupposed in a variety of ways by Jesus himself. An interval of some length is assumed in Jesus's saying that, whilst his disciples do not fast during his ministry, they will fast 'when the bridegroom is taken away from them' (Mark 2:18–20), and in his declaration that, although God's people will for a time cry to him night and day without apparently getting any response, he will soon vindicate them at the coming of the Son of Man

(Luke 18:7–8). The same expectation of an interval under-lies Jesus's command to his followers to repeat the last supper (Luke 22:19; Corinthians 11:25), along with his saying, 'I tell you, I will never again drink this wine until the day I drink it new in the Kingdom of God' (Mark 14:25). And his promise that after being raised to life he would go before his disciples to Galilee (Mark 14:28) implies a relationship between the risen Lord and his disciples while they remain in their present earthly circumstances. Jesus's predictions of persecution for his followers (e.g., Mark 10:35ff.; Matthew 10:28, 38), his references to gospel-preaching among the Gentiles (e.g., Mark 13:10; 14:9), and several parables (e.g., the image of the waiting servant in Luke 12:35–40 and the parables of Matthew 25) confirm this conclusion.[15]

Now it might be argued that passages such as these are evidence for Jesus's expectation of an interval between his *death* and his second coming, but not necessarily of an interval between his *resurrection* and his coming. But we have already found reason to believe that Jesus was aware of a distinction in time between his rising and his coming. It would therefore be extremely odd to argue that the interval presupposed by the passages we have just looked at was the 'short time' (this is the meaning of 'three days' in Jesus's predictions) between death and resurrection, rather than the more indefinite period between the resurrection and the second coming. Also, to argue in this way would be to ignore completely the relevance of the words of the *risen* Jesus recorded in the gospels. Why should we adopt a total scepticism towards the words of the Lord already risen, who in Matthew 28, Luke 24 and John 20–21 commissions his followers to do his work through the continuing course of history, and assures them of his help 'to the end of the age' (Matthew 28:20)?

The shape of history

Jesus, then, expected as Son of Man to die, to be vindicated by God through resurrection from death, and ultimately to come again so as to bring God's purposes for the world to their complete fulfilment. The final part of this chapter will be concerned with how Jesus envisaged that climax, and what events he anticipated in the intervening time.

In the first place, Jesus foresaw catastrophe for the Jewish nation. Having resisted God's ongoing purposes so often, the nation's doom was now sealed by its failure to respond to his urgent pleas for a change of heart. Approaching Jerusalem on his final journey there, he wept, saying:

> If only you knew today what is needed for peace! But now you cannot see it! For the days will come upon you when your enemies will surround you with barricades, blockade you, and close in on you from every side. They will completely destroy you and the people within your walls; not a single stone will they leave in place, because you did not recognise the time when God came to save you! (Luke 19:42–44).

And of Herod's magnificent temple he said, 'You see these great buildings? Not a single stone here will be left in its place; every one of them will be thrown down' (Mark 13:2). Jesus said nothing about a national restoration of the Jewish people, nothing about the establishment of a self-governing Jewish state. He promised a share in the kingdom of God to any Jew who would receive his good news. But for the nation as a whole the only promise was one of doom for its persistent resistance to God. Within a generation the Jewish revolt was met by the crushing power of Rome, and Jerusalem and its Temple lay in ruins.

But, secondly, Jesus expected an alternative to doomed Israel—the church. It is often disputed by scholars whether Jesus anticipated the emergence of the church. And we certainly must not assume that he expected the kind of church which has in fact developed through history. But it seems clear from the following facts that he planned for his followers to fulfil the role of being God's people, the true

Israel, which national Israel had failed to be. He appointed twelve men—parallel to the twelve tribes of Israel—to form the nucleus of a new community, and he sent them out as heralds of the kingdom of God. He spoke of himself as shepherd of a flock (John 10; Luke 12:32), just as, in the Old Testament, God, or a leader of his people such as Moses, was shepherd of Israel (Genesis 49:24; Isaiah 63:11; Ezekiel 34). At the last supper he enacted the beginning of a new covenant—a new relationship between God and his people—and instructed his disciples to repeat that symbolic meal as the focus of their worshipping life. And this 'new Israel' (Jesus himself did not use this term) would include not just Jews, but anyone from any race who responded to the good news of the kingdom. Jesus envisaged a day when 'many will come from the east and the west and sit down at the table in the Kingdom of heaven with Abraham, Isaac, and Jacob', whilst 'the sons of the kingdom' would remain in the darkness outside (Matthew 8:11f.).

Thirdly, Jesus foresaw conflict between his followers and the forces ranged against them—conflict which is itself one aspect of the universal battle between God and the forces of evil and chaos. This is the theme of Mark 13, which speaks not only of the destruction of Jerusalem, but also of wars, earthquakes, famines, false messiahs, persecutions. Although often interpreted as 'signs' that the final coming of the Son of Man is just around the corner, the dominant note of the chapter is not one of calculating dates, but of warning and exhortation: 'Be on your guard! I have told you everything ahead of time' (Mark 13:23). The purpose of this teaching is not to give timetables of the End, but to forearm God's people with understanding of the pressures they will face. If they have Jesus's word about it, they will know that the situation is not beyond God's control, that they can 'hold out to the end and be saved' (verse 13), and that beyond these troubles lies the Son of Man's triumphant coming (verses 24–27).

This leads us to the fourth point. Jesus expected not merely the existence of the new Israel, not merely their suffering, but also their vindication. Just as Jesus himself would be vindicated by God, so his faithful followers would find that God would accept them and show their decision to follow Christ to be the right one. Having lost their lives for Jesus and the gospel, they would find themselves delivered (Mark 8:35). Having acknowledged Jesus before other people, they would find themselves acknowledged in the presence of God (Matthew 10:32). Though weak and defenceless, they would receive the kingdom (Luke 12:32). The language of 'reward' underlines this vindication, yet in a context which removes all danger that the reward would be sought out of mere selfish desire: 'Happy are you when men hate you, and reject you, and insult you, and say that you are evil, because of the Son of Man! Be happy when that happens, and dance for joy, for a great reward is kept for you in heaven' (Luke 6:22f.).

The coming climax

Fifthly, there was to be the Son of Man's coming itself—the moment at which the vindication of his people would take place. Jesus spoke of his coming in the language of cosmic catastrophe and transformation, and the Son of Man's appearing in the clouds (a regular Old Testament symbol for the presence of God).

The sun will grow dark, the moon will no longer shine, the stars will fall from heaven, and the powers in space will be driven from their course. Then the Son of Man will appear, coming in the clouds with great power and glory. He will send out the angels to the four corners of the earth and gather God's chosen people from one end of the world to the other (Mark 13:24–27).

The language is extraordinarily restrained and allusive, when one compares it with the detailed, often grotesque imagery of Jewish apocalyptic literature. The stress is on the triumphant and public completion of God's purposes,

78

in contrast with the obscure and humiliating pattern of Jesus's earthly life. And Jesus's concern is with the reason for this final coming, rather than with the manner of it.

For the purpose of his coming will be to raise his people to the new life of his kingdom (Mark 12:18–27) or to gather them into his presence from all over the world (Mark 13:27). It will involve judgment on the lives of all people (Matthew 25:31–46), a judgment whose outcome will be division between those who have entered God's kingdom and those who have chosen to remain outside (Matthew 24:40f.; Mark 9:33–48). Satan and all his works will be totally destroyed (Matthew 25:41). The world will be renewed (Mark 13:31), and God's people will enter his final and perfect kingdom. Jesus gave no detailed description of what this final state would be like, but he denied that it would simply be a continuation of earthly life on a rather superior level. For example, when provoked by critics, he said that those who rise from death will not marry, but will be like angels in heaven (Mark 12:25). Rather than describe the details, Jesus offered a series of pictures, a rich source of inspiration for the imagination of faith. The people of God will enter into joy in his presence (Matthew 25:21, 23). It will be like the joy of a wedding celebration (Matthew 25:10). There will be laughter and dancing, and the hungry will be filled (Luke 6:21, 23). They will see God (Matthew 5:8). Christ the bridegroom will be the centre of attention (Matthew 25:1–13). The community of his people will be together at worship (cf. the imagery of the new Temple in Mark 14:58). Their joyful excitement will be like that of a group of pilgrims who finally reach their destination after a long and testing journey (this is implied in Luke 16:9, where Jesus speaks of 'the eternal tents'—the ultimate and permanent counterpart of the ever-moving 'tent of meeting' where God met with his people during their wanderings in the wilderness between Egypt and the promised land).[16] Best of all, perhaps, is the news that this community will bring together Jew and Gentile in one harmonious fellowship. There would be Gentiles among those to whom the

King would say: 'You are blessed by my Father: come! Come and receive the kingdom which has been prepared for you ever since the creation of the world' (Matthew 25:34). People from every corner of the earth would feast in the kingdom of God with Abraham, Isaac and Jacob (Matthew 8:11). The grace of God sets no limits beyond which it refuses to reach.

This, then, was the hope of Jesus—a visionary insistence that the God whose rule was already at work through Jesus's ministry would bring his plan to its final goal in the Son of Man's coming in glory. Then the Old Testament's picture of a kingdom of peace and righteousness, already anticipated in part in Jesus's ministry and in the life of his people, would reach its complete fulfilment. Meanwhile we are faced with the challenge to give the kingdom first place (Matthew 6:33), to give up everything for it (Mark 10:16–31), to pray for its coming (Luke 11:2). We may do this in confidence because the God of the kingdom is one who cares fully and gives freely.

Notes to chapter 2

1. 'Eschatology and Methodology', *Journal of Biblical Literature*, 85, 1966, pp. 170–184 (p.183).
2. I shall not go into detail on questions of the authenticity of particular verses, since I have discussed many of them in *Christian Hope and the Future of Man* (IVP, Leicester, 1980). My general stance on the critical issues is similar to that found, for example, in C. E. B. Cranfield, *St. Mark* (Cambridge University Press, 2nd edition 1963), and I. H. Marshall, *The Gospel of Luke* (Paternoster, Exeter, 1978).
3. *Jesus* (Eng. tr., Herder, New York, 1969), p. 87. In what follows I have drawn much on J. Jeremias, *New Testament Theology*, vol. 1 (Eng. tr., SCM, London, 1971), pp. 96ff.
4. On the significance of the Spirit in Jesus's experience see J. D. G. Dunn, *Jesus and the Spirit* (SCM, London, 1975), pp. 41–67.
5. See my discussion in *Christian Hope and the Future of Man*, chapters 1 and 5.
6. *Jesus of Nazareth* (Eng. tr., Hodder, London, 1960), p. 67.
7. See the discussion in W. G. Kümmel, *Promise and Fulfilment* (Eng. tr., SCM, London, 1957), pp. 121–4.

8. For this interpretation, see N. Perrin, *The Kingdom of God in the Teaching of Jesus* (SCM, London, 1963), pp. 174–8; and *Rediscovering the Teaching of Jesus* (SCM, London, 1967), pp. 68–74.

9. On 'Abba' see Jeremias, *New Testament Theology*, pp. 61–8. He shows that this Aramaic word underlies the use of 'father' as an address to God in Jesus's other prayers in the gospels. Dunn points out the use of 'father' in Ecclesiasticus 23:1, 4; 51:10 (*Jesus and the Spirit*, p. 23), but the usage there seems to me more formal, less intimate.

10. See above, p. 21.

11. *New Testament Theology*, p. 156.

12. Jeremias, *The Parables of Jesus* (Eng. tr., SCM, London, revised edition 1963), p. 125.

13. Recent discussions of 'Son of Man', arguing that Jesus did refer to himself as Son of Man and that the gospel sayings are substantially authentic, include I. H. Marshall, *The Origins of New Testament Christology* (IVP, Leicester, 1976), pp. 63–82, and M. D. Hooker, 'Is the Son of Man problem really insoluble?', in E. Best and R. McL. Wilson, eds., *Text and Interpretation*: Studies in the New Testament presented to Matthew Black (CUP, Cambridge, 1979), pp. 155–168.

14. *In Christian Hope and the Future of Man*, pp. 79–82, I have given my reasons for rejecting the view that Jesus's 'coming' in this verse is another way of describing his exaltation.

15. On this question of the interval before the second coming, see further W. G. Kümmel, *Promise and Fulfilment*, pp. 64–83, and I. H. Marshall, *Eschatology and the Parables* (Tyndale, London, 1963).

16. Jeremias, *New Testament Theology*, p. 249.

Chapter 3   Christ our Hope

God's rule was the dominant theme of Jesus's message, the object of his mission. Yet when we come to the writings of his followers, we find surprisingly few references to God's rule. Instead of the kingdom of God, they proclaim Jesus as Lord. Instead of calling people to 'receive' or to 'enter the kingdom', they speak about 'being saved' or 'having eternal life'. Instead of the 'coming of the Son of Man' they expect the 'coming of the Lord Jesus Christ'. But all this is not a distortion or a new message. It was the almost inevitable outcome of two facts. First, now that the death and resurrection of Jesus had been accomplished, it was natural that Jesus's implicit teaching about his own role in the achievement of God's purposes should be transformed into explicit teaching about Jesus as the focus of hope, the one in whom all God's promises find their fulfilment (cf. 2 Corinthians 1:20). Secondly, as the church and its message spread into the Greek and Roman world, the message had to be understood and communicated in terms which would make sense in the new situation. The Gentiles did not share Israel's tradition of speaking about God as king. Nor had they any concept of a messiah. Indeed, the best sense a Greek could make of the Greek word 'christos' (which means 'anointed one'—the equivalent of the Hebrew 'messiah') would be to assume that it referred to someone who had just been to the massage parlour at the public baths, and been massaged or 'anointed' with olive oil. So in the non-Jewish world 'Christ' tended to become a proper name, and 'Lord' took over as the most popular title of Jesus. And to translate the idea of 'kingdom' as the blessings of God's rule, Christians began increasingly to use terms such as 'salvation' and 'eternal life', which made more sense among Gentiles. That such terms were meant to convey the same meaning as Jesus's language about the kingdom can be seen from Mark 10. There in the story of the rich young ruler these various terms are used interchangeably ('inherit eternal life', verse 17; 'enter the kingdom of God', verses 23–25; 'be saved', verse 26; 'in the age to come eternal life', verse 30). Granted these changes in terminology and the new perspective arising from what God had already done in raising Jesus from death, we can see that the basic structure of Paul's hope follows from Jesus's own preaching. It is Paul's letters we shall look at for the next few pages.

The hope of Paul

The main elements in Paul's expectation about Jesus can be found in four passages: 1 Thessalonians 4:13–5:11; 2 Thessalonians 1:3–2:12; 1 Corinthians 15:20–28; and Romans 8. I will now sketch briefly the teaching of these passages (listed in the order in which Paul wrote them), though some points mentioned here will come up for fuller discussion later.

In 1 Thessalonians 4 Paul has to deal with a question about the destiny of Christians at Thessalonica who have already died. Will they miss out on the fullness of God's blessings which he has promised to give to his people at the future coming of Jesus? It seems that in his brief stay at Thessalonica Paul had led the new church there to believe that Jesus would come soon to usher in God's final kingdom and to welcome his people into his presence. The death of some of their number before this great event came as a puzzling shock. In response to their concern, Paul elaborated his teaching. No, he says, those already dead before Jesus's coming will not lose out in comparison with those still alive when it happens. When Jesus comes from heaven—appropriately heralded by an archangel's shout and a trumpet fanfare—both dead and living believers will meet with Christ, and so will experience for ever his life and his presence.

As for the timing of the Lord's coming, it will be sudden and unexpected, like a thief in the night. But though it will take unbelievers by surprise, Paul's friends at Thessalonica are prepared for it (5:1–4). They belong already to the day which is about to dawn. Their life is characterised not by mere waiting for the end to come, but by the faith, love and hope of people who *already* know the Christ who is to come, and already experience the power which raised him from death (5:5–11).

Several things are worth noting about this passage. First, Paul has three terms for the coming of Jesus. It is *the day of the Lord* (5:2). This familiar Old Testament term for the expected day of God's judgment and deliverance has been taken over by Paul for Jesus's coming. This is because he is the Lord, the one who does the work of God and has the status of God, and because his coming will in fact be the moment of God's final act of judgment and salvation. Paul also refers to Christ's coming as a *parousia* (4:15). This word means 'presence' or 'arrival'. It was used in the Greek world to describe the visit of a ruler to a city, with all the festive atmosphere which surrounded such a visit.[1] Often a party of civic dignitaries, or even the whole population, would go out to meet the ruler as he approached the city. It was a day of festival. Similarly, says Paul, Christ's people will meet him as he comes, amid much rejoicing. Paul's other way of describing Jesus's coming is to talk about his *coming down* from heaven (4:16); and with this we should couple the reference to clouds in verse 17. This clearly echoes the language already familiar to us from Jesus's teaching. We saw how in Mark 14:62 Jesus, using the picture from Daniel 7, spoke of the Son of Man's coming with the clouds of heaven—clouds being a common Old Testament symbol of the glorious presence of God, either to protect his people (Exodus 13:21f.) or to judge those who oppose him (Psalm 97:2f.). Paul's description here is a 'translation' of Jesus's own language.

Secondly, whatever we make of the details of Paul's description, we can see that his emphasis lies on the *purpose* of Christ's coming; it is so that 'we will always be with the Lord' (4:17). That is the issue about which the church at Thessalonica as asked him, and that is the climax of his reply.

The third point to note is that Paul writes as if he fully expects to be alive when Jesus comes. He assumes (rather than argues) that the Lord's coming will not be long delayed. Yet at the same time he stresses the suddenness and unpredictability of his coming. It cannot be the object of calculation. We shall return to this problem later in this chapter.

The fourth point follows from this. Whether we are alive or dead at the time of Christ's coming is a matter of indifference, because Christ has already come, and we are already united with him in his death and resurrection (5:10). Paul's whole attitude to the future, with all its unknown features, springs from his confidence in the Christ who has come and rules as Lord now.

Fifthly, this confidence in what Christ has already done is also the basis of Paul's exhortation to his readers. When he urges them to live responsibly, and to exercise faith, love and hope, this appeal is based not so much on the need to be on top form when Jesus appears, as on the need to practise the new life which Christ through his death and resurrection has already conveyed to them. For people who already belong to the light of day, the life-style which characterises the darkness ought to be out of the question.

Finally, we may underline the fact that Paul's concern is pastoral. His teaching is not given to tickle the brain, or to be consigned to a filing cabinet. It is given to meet needs, to assure his readers that Christ's care embraces all their lives: it goes with them through death, it controls the unknown future right through to its finale. For that reason, it gives encouragement and comfort (4:18; 5:11).

2 Thessalonians

In his second letter to Thessalonica, Paul adds further features to what we have learnt. Conscious that the

Thessalonians face the pressure of persecution, he assures them that God will bring them through suffering to his kingdom (1:5, one of a dozen or so instances of this word in Paul). And he stresses two features of Christ's coming. First, it will demonstrate God's justice, in that he will pass judgment on those who refuse to respond to the gospel, including those who persecute the people of God. Secondly, Paul speaks of Christ's coming as his 'being revealed' or 'appearing' (Greek *apokalypsis* 1:7). This description, like the equivalent word for 'appearing' (*epiphaneia*) in 2:8, repeats a theme which we have already noticed in Jesus's teaching. One of the purposes of Chirst's coming will be to reveal what is now hidden, to make clear-cut what is now open to doubt, to demonstrate the glory of Christ in contrast to the 'incognito' element in his first coming.

In 2 Thessalonians 2 Paul reminds his readers of something he had often told them whilst he was with them (2:5). Even though the time of Jesus's coming cannot be calculated, nevertheless certain things must take place before he comes. What Paul is alluding to is extremely obscure to us—he only needs to allude, because his readers, unlike us, know well enough what he is talking about. But the general picture is of an intensifying conflict between good and evil, and the individuals and institutions which embody them before Christ asserts the final triumph of God and his will.

1 Corinthians 15

1 Corinthians 15:20–28, like the passage in 1 Thessalonians, is concerned with resurrection from death. Paul responds to the doubts of some of his readers by appealing to the resurrection of Jesus, claiming that his resurrection is the first instance, within history, of the resurrection to be experienced by all God's people at the end of history. Like the 'first-fruits', the first sheaf of corn which guarantees that the rest of the harvest will follow, so Jesus's resurrection guarantees that those who are united with him will also be resurrected. Their resurrection will take place at his coming.

And the coming of Christ will have two further features. It will mark the completion of his victory over *all* the forces of evil and destruction which threaten his authority and cause havoc in human life. When death, the 'last enemy', is destroyed at that final resurrection, there will be no further enemies left to subdue. And that victory will lead into the final, eternal stage of God's plan for the world. Christ will 'hand over the Kingdom to God the Father', and 'God will rule completely over all' (verses 24, 28). Thus will God's creation reach the goal which was always his loving purpose for it.

Romans 8

In Romans 8 we come to the high-point of Paul's greatest letter. Here he does not speak of the second coming of Christ specifically, but the chapter is infused with the sense of living between the two comings of Christ, and moving from the one towards the other. Because Christ has already come and has been raised from death, we can experience now the blessings of God which Jews associated with God's final kingdom. In the present time we have a right relationship with God ('justification', verse 10). He has given us his Spirit, who enables us to express this new relation to God as we call him 'Abba, my Father'. He delivers us from feeling afraid of God and enables us to live before him with the kind of trustful freedom which should characterise a child's relationship to his father (verses 14–16). The Spirit also enables us to steer clear of wrongdoing, and fills us with life and peace (verses 4–11). And he helps us in our prayers, so that—with all our weakness—we have a foretaste of what God's ultimate kingdom is like. For the Spirit is the first-fruits—a foretaste of that kingdom. Paul's image is the same image which he used to describe Jesus's resurrection in 1 Corinthians 15:20. The Spirit as we experience him in our present life is a foretaste—partial, yet real—of the full blessing of God to be received in the life to come.

Yet alongside this joy in present experience which

pulsates through Romans 8, there is another perspective. We suffer (verse 18), we wait (verses 18, 23), we groan with a sense of the incompleteness of our salvation (verse 23). For we have been saved in *hope*, and who needs to hope for something which he already sees (verse 24)? The day when we shall be fully set free to enjoy all that it means to be children of God lies in the future. But it is not only we Christians who wait eagerly for that day. For, Paul says, the whole of creation is involved in this longing for perfection! The whole universe is subject to change, decay and imperfection, and will itself share in that transformation to perfection which God's people will experience at the last day (verses 19–23). Renewed people will need a renewed environment, fitted for the eternity of God's kingdom.

With this magnificent vision, Paul can see the sufferings and ambiguities of the present life in the right light. Assured of God's creative and loving purpose, we have the resources to face the conflicts and disappointments which are the necessary features of this time before Christ comes again.

> Faced with all this, what can we say? If God is for us, who can be against us? . . . For I am certain that nothing can separate us from his love: neither death nor life; neither angels nor other heavenly rulers or powers; neither the present nor the future; neither the world above nor the world below—there is nothing in all creation that will ever be able to separate us from the love of God which is ours through Christ Jesus our Lord (Romans 8:31–39).

Such, then, is the structure of Paul's hope. Its foundation is God's work in Christ, who died and was raised to life. Its goal is the perfection of God's people, in a renewed environment, in the presence of Christ. Its lifestyle is living in the power of God's Spirit, sharing in the suffering which 'cannot be compared with the glory that is going to be revealed to us' (Romans 8:18). Sometimes with other words, or with other emphases, the rest of the New Testament joins in the same affirmations—all of them springing ultimately from the message and work of Jesus himself. But the pattern is not without its problems, to which we must now give some attention. The issues to be examined in the rest of this chapter involve the questions When? How? and Why? When will Jesus come? How can we conceive of such an event? What is the purpose of his coming?

Delayed or cancelled?

I stood at the bus stop in the snow. I looked impatiently at the timetable and then at my watch, wondering if the cold was playing tricks with its accuracy. How much longer must I go on waiting? Ten minutes? Twenty minutes? Was the bus delayed by the weather conditions, or had the bus company in its wisdom decided to cancel it altogether?

For the last hundred years New Testament scholars have agonised and argued over a similar problem. Did not Jesus and the early Christians have a kind of timetable which expected his coming again within a generation of Jesus's death? Since it has not yet happened, is not the conviction bound to grow that it must be relegated to an irrelevant remote future, or that it is not going to happen at all? And can we not detect, in the New Testament, signs that the early Christians were busy trying to adjust to the non-occurrence of the great event, covering up their disappointment and looking for alternative objects of Christian faith and hope? Rudolf Bultmann aired the problem, and implied his answer when he wrote, 'The mythical eschatology is untenable for the simple reason that the parousia of Christ never took place as the New Testament expected. History did not come to an end, and, as every schoolboy knows, it will continue to run its course.'[2]

The problem is raised particularly by three sayings of Jesus:

There are some standing here who will not die until they have seen the Kingdom of God come with power (Mark 9:1).

When you see these things happening, you will know that the time is near, ready to begin. Remember this! All these things will happen before the people now living have all died (Mark 13:29f.).

I tell you, you will not finish your work in all the towns of Israel before the Son of Man comes (Matthew 10:23).

In Paul's letters, apart from his apparent assumption in 1 Thessalonians that he will be alive when Jesus comes, there are texts such as: 'The moment when we will be saved is closer now than it was when we first believed. The night is nearly over, the day is almost here' (Romans 13:11f.; cf. 1 Corinthians 7:29; Philippians 4:5). The same expectation is there in other writers: 'Keep your hopes high, for the day of the Lord's coming is near' (James 5:8). 'The end of all things is near' (1 Peter 4:7). And almost the last word of the New Testament is the word of the risen Jesus, 'I am coming soon!' which evokes the response 'So be it. Come, Lord Jesus!' (Revelation 22:20; cf. also Hebrews 10:25; 1 John 2:18).

It appears, then, that Jesus and his first followers expected the end of this age and the coming of the Lord within a generation or so. How are we to handle this problem? Should we agree with those who deny that Jesus ever said such things, and so lay the problem at the door of the early Christians rather than that of Jesus himself? Or with those who say Jesus did expect the end soon, and was wrong about the date, and yet was gloriously right in his fundamental assertions about God and his purposes? Or with those who argue that Jesus predicted an imminent end, and that its non-occurrence provoked a crisis of faith in first-century Christians, whose attempts to grapple with this disappointment can be seen all over the New Testament?[3]

A possible solution

My own approach to the problem involves the following three points: First, we must recognise that, alongside the promises of an imminent second coming, Jesus and the New Testament writers also speak sometimes about its being delayed, and sometimes about its date being unknown. For example, in his correspondence with the Christians at Thessalonica Paul warns that the timing of Jesus's coming is as sudden and unpredictable as the arrival of a burglar (1 Thessalonians 5), *and* that certain events must take place before the end will come (2 Thessalonians 2). In Romans 13 he speaks of the nearness of the end, even though in chapters 9–11 his discussion of the destiny of Israel seems to presuppose a period of history, possibly a long period, during which God's purposes will be worked out. And the same tension is present in Jesus's own teaching. We saw in the previous chapter that Jesus expected an interval between his death and his coming again. The imagery of some parables (e.g., the faithful or unfaithful servant in Matthew 24:45–51) speaks of 'delay'—a motif which need not be dismissed as inauthentic except by those who have already decided to regard the delay of Jesus's coming as a problem for the early church. In Mark 13, on which much of the debate focuses, Jesus declares not only the nearness of the end (verses 29f.), but also his ignorance of its date (verse 32). And on the basis of this ignorance he urges his followers to be watchful and alert (verses 33–37). In view of this paradoxical variety of emphasis—nearness, unknown date, and interval or delay—any interpretation of the 'nearness' sayings which presses their meaning too literally is surely suspect.

Secondly, Jesus denounced the fascination for calculating the date of God's final triumph. When some Pharisees asked him when the kingdom of God would come, his answer was, 'The Kingdom of God does not come in such a way as to be seen' (Luke 17:20). Probably this means that the kingdom's appearance is not foreshadowed by signs which make calculation possible. Jesus is rejecting the view, widespread amongst Pharisees, that the coming of the Messiah could be precisely dated with the help of numerical data from the book of Daniel. It is clear that such predictions had great influence and caused much confusion amongst Jews, as we see from the rare protest of Rabbi Jonathan (about A.D. 220): 'May the bones of the end-time calculators be scattered who, when the date of the end comes without the Messiah arriving, say, "He will never come at all." Rather, tarry for him as it is written, "If he delays, tarry for him." '[4]

Against such a background, Jesus's resistance to the date-fixing mentality makes powerful sense, and it fits naturally with the stress on the sudden, unpredictable, thief-in-the-night nature of his coming which we have already observed.

It does, however, appear to be at variance with the passages (mainly Mark 13) where Jesus offers a series of signs which must appear before the end comes. The difference is so striking that scholars have frequently denied that both types of saying could have sprung from the same mind—with the result that Jesus is credited with the rejection of signs (Luke 17:20), and the early church is blamed for letting the signs-sayings (Mark 13) get into the gospel-accounts of Jesus's teaching.[5] Such dismissal of Mark 13 is unwarranted, once we recognise that the 'signs' described in Mark 13 are not given to make calculation possible, and are too unspecific for that purpose, anyway.

Earthquakes, famine, political upheaval, false messiahs, persecution and gospel-preaching, and the fall of Jerusalem —these things are not the kind of events which will pinpoint a particular moment of history when the Son of Man will come. They are the kind of things which characterise the whole period between Jesus's first and second comings (though the fall of Jerusalem in A.D. 70 was of course a particular, 'one-off' event). Jesus warned his followers of them not so that they would know the date of the end, but so that they could understand the nature of the conflict which would surround them and thus be forearmed to endure it. Unlike the Jewish apocalyptic writings, much of Mark 13 is cast in the form of commands. For example: 'Watch out' (verses 5, 9, 33). 'Don't be troubled' (verse 7).

'Do not worry' (verse 11). 'Be on your guard! I have told you everything ahead of time' (verse 23). 'Keep awake!' (verses 35, 37). This highlights the fact that Jesus's purpose is to encourage not speculation but watchfulness—to strengthen faith and to forewarn his disciples what will be their lot as his followers. If this assessment of Mark 13, with its series of 'signs of the times' is fair, then the two strands of Jesus's teaching—the 'sudden' strand and the 'signs' strand—are not contradictory but complementary. And we see the same two strands in Paul: the 'sudden' strand in 1 Thessalonians 5, the 'signs' strand in 2 Thessalonians 2.[6] New Testament teaching about 'signs' in no way undermines Jesus's rejection of attempts to calculate dates. And if that is so, his conviction about the nearness of the coming climax cannot be understood in precise chronological terms. His language is visionary, poetic more than chronological. I am reminded of those lines in 'Stand up, stand up for Jesus':

> . . . the strife will not be long;
> This day the noise of battle,
> The next the victor's song.

When we sing that hymn, do we mutter under our breath that it is not true, that we sang it a month ago and still we are waiting for the day of the victor's song? No. We treat it as what it is—a poetic and imaginative assertion of the certainty that the triumph of the crucified Christ *will* one day be complete. Surely it is not unreasonable to see the same kind of poetic flexibility in Jesus's own statements about 'nearness'.

Thirdly, we should recognise that the problem of imminence in the message of Jesus is the same problem as is found right through biblical prophecy and biblical apocalyptic. Old Testament prophets often expressed hopes of deliverance or warnings of judgment in a way which suggested that the day of their fulfilment was just around the corner. Daniel saw the kingdom given to Israel within a declared number of days. Paul sometimes wrote as though he assumed the Lord would come soon. The Christ of

John's Apocalypse addressed the church at Sardis as though his second coming were imminent (Revelation 3:3). In a literal and final sense, none of these prophecies was fulfilled. But the fact that this pattern is frequently repeated in the Bible suggests that to label the prophecies as mistaken is too simple a solution. It is preferable to see each crisis, each judgment, each deliverance which followed the words of the prophet as a partial realisation within history of the ultimate triumph of God. In Mark 13, for example, the fall of Jerusalem and the final appearance of the Son of Man are mingled together precisely because they are theologically related to each other. The destruction of Jerusalem which, as Jesus spoke, lay 'just around the corner', was a kind of anticipation or preliminary form of the judgment which will take place at the end of history. So Jesus's talk about the nearness of the Son of Man's coming was a declaration that the age of decisive fulfilment had really dawned, the kingdom of God was exerting its power there and then, and those present manifestations of God's rule were a guarantee of God's ultimate victory through Christ. It is in the very nature of prophecy to have such a vivid vision of God's purposes that chronological time-spans are shortened in this way, because their vision is a vision of God and his goals rather than a clairvoyance of timetables for the future. The fact that these visions of 'nearness' are in formal contradiction with Jesus's statements about delay or about ignorance of dates should preserve us from too wooden and prosaic an understanding of them.[7]

Whilst I have argued that Jesus's sayings about the nearness of his coming are not to be taken with excessive literalness, I am not of course saying that Jesus or the early church would have seriously reckoned with the continuation of history for thousands of years. Such a long interval between the inauguration of God's rule and its final complete coming would no doubt have surprised them. Nevertheless, we find in the New Testament that early Christian thinkers were coming to terms with the lengthening period between Christ's earthly life and his return.

What might at first have seemed like a period of waiting quickly became a period of fulfilment. Life was not to be a matter of killing time, like waiting for a late bus, but of using time, recognising it as God's gift and enjoying God's presence within it. Different writers expressed the significance of this interval in different ways. But each of them was drawing out what was already implicit in Jesus's own message.

There is a purpose in the delay

One type of response to the delay was to say, 'It is a matter of waiting for God to bring the present period of suffering to an end, but waiting is something we can cope with.' In response to scoffers who laugh at Christians because the Lord's coming seems delayed interminably, 2 Peter quotes Psalm 90: 'There is no difference in the Lord's sight between one day and a thousand years' (2 Peter 3:8). The delay which from our perspective seems so long is not long from God's perspective. Indeed, the delay allows even the scoffers a chance to turn to God. For 'he is patient with you, because he does not want anyone to be destroyed, but wants all to turn away from their sins' (2 Peter 3:9). We can cope, because God has a purpose in the delay, and he sustains us with 'precious and very great promises' (2 Peter 1:4). In Revelation 6:10 the martyrs cry out, 'Almighty Lord, holy and true! How long will it be until you will judge the people of earth and punish them for killing us?' And they are told to wait a little longer until the full number of martyrs is made up—in other words, in God's sovereign purpose there *is* a limit to the period of suffering and martyrdom. But the author of Revelation takes us a stage further in our understanding. For he places the suffering of the church in the context of the suffering of the Lamb. Because Jesus, 'the Lamb who was killed' (5:12), won the victory over death and evil, his followers too may face with confidence the suffering which delay inevitably brings, knowing that their suffering has creative power.[8]

The writer to the Hebrews, also, is confronted by the needs of Christians under pressure of persecution. They cannot see an end to it, and are tempted to go back into the security of Judaism. The whole letter urges upon them the folly of going backwards, since God is in front of them, beckoning them forwards. He quotes Habakkuk: 'Just a little while longer, and he who is coming will come; he will not delay' (Hebrews 10:37). He reminds them of the 'large crowd of witnesses' who endured against impossible odds because their faith was fixed on 'the city which God has designed and built, the city with permanent foundations' (Hebrews 11:10). Above all, he reminds them of Jesus, who 'did not give up because of the cross . . . Think of what he went through, how he put up with so much hatred from sinful men! So do not let yourselves become discouraged and give up' (Hebrews 12:2f.). But it is not only the example of others which sustains them: they have already 'tasted heaven's gift and received their share of the Holy Spirit'. In their own experience they have 'felt the powers of the age to come' (Hebrews, 6:4f.).

Paul's message: in Christ you are already rich!

But it is Paul most of all who expounds this conviction that our present experience of God is the key to a positive understanding of the interval before the coming of Christ. The present life of the Christian, he says, is determined by two facts. First, the expected messiah has already come, has died and has been raised to life by God. The resurrection of Christ is the pivot on which the whole plan of God turns: the future coming of Christ in glory is not a totally new event, but the completion of the reign which began at his resurrection. What Christ gives to his people then will not be compensation for what they lack now, so much as the full experience of what they now know in part. Every page of Paul breathes this atmosphere of fulfilment. 'When the right time finally came, God sent his own Son' (Galatians 4:4). He has introduced a new covenant, superior to the covenant with Moses (2 Corinthians 3). Since he is risen from death for ever, 'when anyone is joined to Christ he is a new being: the old is gone, the new has come' (2 Corinthians 5:17). Already, God has 'rescued us from the power of darkness and brought us safe into the kingdom of his dear Son, by whom we are set free and our sins are forgiven' (Colossians 1:13f.).

The second fact to which Paul appeals is the gift of the Holy Spirit. He knows that the Spirit—promised in Joel 2:28f. as God's gift when 'the day of the Lord' comes—is already part of the Christian's present experience. The Christian life is a matter of 'living by the Spirit', and knowing the Spirit's control over our lives (Galatians 5:25). The Spirit is *the* distinguishing mark of the Christian, so that 'whoever does not have the Spirit of Christ does not belong to him' (Romans 8:9). The Spirit is the 'first-fruits' (Romans 8:23), 'the guarantee that we shall receive what God has promised to his people' (Ephesians 1:14). The effect of this two-fold emphasis in Paul is to show that the present time, between Christ's two comings, is not a time of frustrated waiting but of experiencing the gifts of God made available because Christ has come. Consequently, the length of the interval ceases to matter greatly. The Christian is more like the child who has learnt to enjoy last year's Christmas present than he is like the child who 'can't wait' for next Christmas to come. And yet at the same time it matters greatly to Paul that there remains a future consummation of what the Christian has begun to experience. The present interval, however long it may last, *is* an interval, until the Christ who now reigns comes to demonstrate, publicly and triumphantly, that God's purposes have reached their goal.

Luke and Acts: continuing history is God's history

Two gospel-writers add further insights by the way in which they present the story of Jesus. Luke puts out of court any idea that Christians are to see themselves as a sect cocooned from the world and waiting for Christ to come and rescue them from it. He stresses Jesus's relationship with Israel—for example, by showing in chapters 1–2 how Jesus's birth fulfils the hopes of loyal Jews. He places the life of Jesus in the context of secular history—for example, by dating the beginning of his ministry in relation to Roman and Jewish government (3:1f.). But the most striking thing about Luke, of course, is his production of a two-volume work, telling the story of the church as well as the story of Jesus. This in itself indicates that Luke came to terms with the continuation of history and the possibility of a long interval before Jesus comes again. No one writes church history, or any kind of history, if he is convinced that the world is about to end. So Luke, by writing the Acts of the Apostles, gave positive significance to the period of the church, the period between Christ's resurrection and his coming. How the period of the church should be viewed is indicated at the very beginning of Acts: 'In the first book, O Theophilus, I have dealt with all that Jesus began to do and teach, until the day when he was taken up' (Acts 1:1f., RSV). Luke's Gospel tells what Jesus *began* to do and teach, and Acts reports what he continued to do and to teach in the church through his Spirit.[9]

This, then, is Luke's way of underlining the positive meaning of the present time: it is a time when Jesus is active in the world to bring salvation to mankind. And the demand he makes of his followers during this interval is set out in a parable found only in Luke 19:11–27, the parable of the pounds. Jesus's audience, Luke tells us, thought the kingdom of God was just about to appear (verse 11). So he told them the story of a nobleman who, before departing to a far country where he was to receive kingly power, gave to ten of his servants a gold coin each and told them to trade with it. When the nobleman returned as king he discovered that the first two servants had made substantial profits. And they were suitably rewarded. But a third, who had simply hidden his coin in a handkerchief, was condemned. He took no chances. He typifies the disciple who—though called by his master to put his faith to the test by a creative sharing of the kingdom-treasures entrusted to him—risks nothing. He confines the good news to the safe-deposit of tradition, and is thus a living denial of the radical nature of the kingdom itself. He is like the football team which plays for a 0–0 draw in its away matches, and thereby kills the game.[10]

John: the time is now

John's Gospel, more than the other gospels, emphasises that the present time is loaded with eternal significance. 'The time is coming, and now is' is a constant refrain through the Gospel. Divine judgment is not something which waits till after death. For 'whoever does not believe has already been judged, because he has not believed in God's only Son' (John 3:18). Equally, eternal life is to be experienced now by those who believe in Jesus: 'Whoever believes in the Son *has* eternal life' (John 3:36). These two things—judgment and eternal life—which were commonly regarded as future events, are shown to be facts of present experience. Judgment takes place in the response a person makes when he is confronted by the claims of Christ. Eternal life is a quality of life, a relationship with God which begins the moment a man opens his life to Jesus.

But John has a further thing to say. In his account of the 'farewell discourse' (John 14–16), Jesus speaks of his 'coming again' in words which sound at first to be a reference to his final coming. But he turns out in fact to be promising that after his resurrection he will come and dwell in the believer through the Holy Spirit.

There are many rooms in my Father's house, and I am going to prepare a place for you . . . And after I go and prepare a place for you, I will come back and take you to myself, so that you will be where I am . . .

I will ask the Father, and he will give you another Helper, the Spirit of truth, to stay with you forever . . . I will not leave you alone; I will come back to you . . .

Whoever loves me will obey my message. My Father will love him, and my Father and I will come to him and live with him (John 14:2f., 16, 18, 23).

This is not to say that the idea of Jesus's final coming is absent from John's Gospel. It is to say that John shows more clearly than the other gospels the unity of all Christ's work. The Christ who will come finally for the resurrection and judgment of all men (John 5:25f.; 6:39f.; 11:23–27; 12:48; 21:20–23) is the Christ who comes today to those who love him. So the time before the end is not a time for lamenting Jesus's absence and kicking one's heels until he comes. It is a time for loving and obeying him, for seeing him with the eye of faith, and for drawing on the power of his Spirit, who is 'another Helper'—another one like Jesus (John 14:16).

In these various ways, then, New Testament writers saw positive meaning in the lengthening interval between Jesus's first and final comings. They came to see that the nearness of the end in terms of dates and times was less important than the fact that God was moving his purposes towards a declared goal. The source of their hope was what God had *already* done in the life, death and resurrection of Jesus Christ. His coming again, whenever it might be, would mark the completion of the plan begun in those events.

The nature of the second coming

We now reach the second main question of this chapter: *how* will Jesus come? What will it be like? Should we, for example, take the biblical language quite literally, as many Christians do, and formulate a detailed description of how it will all happen? Here are two newspaper reports to think about. In 1978 American newspaper editors were asked to say what they considered to be the most sensational headline they could ever write. *The People's Almanac* which gave the results of the poll, recorded 'Jesus returns to earth' as the most frequently suggested headline among the editors who took part. But will Jesus's return be the *kind* of event that can be reported in a newspaper? And will there still be newspapers after it has happened?

Or consider the case of Ernest Digweed. According to *The Times* of 21st January, 1977, Mr. Digweed died in 1976, leaving his estate of £26,107 in trust to be paid to Jesus Christ at his second coming. The will says the whole estate should be invested for eighty years. 'If during those eighty years the Lord Jesus Christ shall come to reign on earth, then the Public Trustees, upon obtaining proof which shall satisfy them of his identity, shall pay to the Lord Jesus Christ all the property which they hold on his behalf.' The will also states that if Christ has not returned within eighty years the whole estate shall go to the Crown. Again, questions are raised by the assumptions underlying Mr. Digweed's will. Will money be of any relevance when Jesus comes? And how will public trustees establish his identity? Or will his coming be such an earth-shattering event as to render quite bizarre the suggestion that anyone would need proof of his identity?

I shall say more in chapter 4 about the type of approach to the Bible which seems to underlie such views. For the time being, let it be said that we must resist the temptation to assert too much about the nature of Christ's coming. For if we take one biblical author, Paul, and study the ways in which he speaks about the Christian hope, we find such variety of expression that we are led to the conclusion that his teaching contains a large measure of picture-language. To understand it all as literal and detailed description of Christ's coming leads to confusion and contradiction. In 1 Thessalonians 4, as we have seen, Paul envisages the following sequence: Jesus will descend, the Christian dead will rise to meet him, and then living Christians will join them in the clouds to meet the Lord in the air, and so all will be with him for ever. But nowhere else does Paul mention clouds or the air: in 1 Corinthians 15 he says nothing about the location of Christ or of his resurrected people. And whereas 1 Corinthians 15:20–28 seems to suggest a certain logical sequence in the events associated with Christ's coming, 1 Corinthians 15:51f. declares that the whole event will be completed 'in the twinkling of an eye'. Again, in Romans 8:18–23 he can express hope for the full salvation of God's people and the transformation of the world without a mention of the personal coming of Jesus.

Or again, we may ask about the tension in Paul's letters between the passages which say that Christians will experience resurrection at Jesus's coming and those which promise that they will be with Christ immediately following their death. To look for a neat way of removing the contradiction may be to lose sight of the complementary truths which the two types of statement aim to safeguard. Or what are we to make of the assumption behind our two examples from the newspapers that, when Jesus comes, earthly life will continue largely as before? It is surely a very dubious assumption, in view of Paul's vision in Romans 8 of a transformed world, delivered from its 'slavery to decay', and his sharp contrast in 1 Corinthians 15 between our present physical bodies and our future 'spiritual bodies', when in the new environment of God's kingdom we 'will wear the likeness of the Man from heaven' (1 Corinthians 15:49).

We must, then, resist the temptation to assert too much. We must recognise that 'our life is a matter of faith, not of sight' (2 Corinthians 5:7), and that it is no part of mature Christian faith to claim more sight than God has in fact given. What matters most is that over our future and the future of the world stands the risen Christ who says, 'Don't be afraid! I am the first and the last. I am the living one! I was dead, but look, I am alive for ever and ever. I have authority over death and the world of the dead' (Revelation 1:17f.).

But we must be equally careful not to assert too little about the coming of Christ. In much modern theology the hope of a genuinely future coming has been so modified as to become something quite different from the New Testament message. For example, Rudolf Bultmann's 'demythologising' programme removed the expectation of Christ's coming by arguing that for twentieth-century people it 'really means' that Christ 'comes to me' now in my moment of decision to respond to the gospel message. Such an interpretation goes much further than simply 'making sense' of the New Testament message. For it abandons the New Testament's emphasis on God as active in the past, present and future, and concentrates on the individual's understanding of himself. It underplays the biblical view of salvation as a social rather than a merely individual experience; it ignores the fact that the New Testament hope involves not only human beings, but also the whole world. It abandons the tension, characteristic of the New Testament, between what we *already* experience in Christ, and what we do *not yet* experience before the end of this age.[11]

Why the second coming is important

What, then, may we assert about Christ's coming? To begin with, we must comment on two difficulties. First, is it proper to speak of the 'second coming' at all? It is not a New Testament term, and it suggests that Jesus came once, is now absent, and will one day return, like a rent-collector or a travelling salesman. The earliest Christian writer to refer explicitly to the two comings of Jesus—his incarnation and his future coming in glory—was Justin Martyr in the second century (*Apology* I.52.3; *Dialogue* 14.4; 118.2). But the term is almost there in Hebrews 9:28: 'Christ also was offered in sacrifice once to take away the sins of many. He will appear a second time, not to deal with sin, but to save those who are waiting for him.' This, together with the widespread New Testament language about a final and glorious coming of Jesus, surely justifies our speaking of his 'second coming'. This does not prevent us speaking about Jesus coming in the intervening period—his coming through the Spirit at Pentecost, for example, or his coming to pass judgment on an unfaithful church or to restore a penitent church (Revelation 3:3, 20), or his coming into the life of an individual person. Nor must we think of Jesus as being absent from the world between his two comings—indeed, Matthew's version of his final words to his disciples precludes that: 'Remember! I will be with you always, to the end of the age' (Matthew 28:20). Through his Spirit, Jesus is present in the lives of his people. But the distinctive thing about his final coming is that it will mark the end of this period when his presence is spiritual, hidden, disputed. When he comes there will be no room for doubt. Faith will give way to sight, and Jesus will be the undisputed and permanent focus of his people's service and worship.

A second question is, Can the biblical hope be reconciled with what we know from science about the world? Suppose, for example, that we follow some scientists in the view that, by the law of entropy (the dissipation of heat and energy) the universe will eventually 'run down', so that life as we know it ceases to be possible. How does this fit in with the traditional picture of a sudden, final catastrophic end to the present world when Jesus comes? I think here we must recognise a certain similarity between the way the Bible talks about the end, and the way it talks about the beginning. We have learnt to say that the biblical accounts of creation are not in conflict with scientific theory because they are concerned more with God's *purpose* in creation and with his relationship to the world than with the *manner* in which the world came into being. We can allow scientists to debate the various theories about the origin of the universe, and maybe to come up with an agreed conclusion, without feeling that this is going to rock our faith in God as Creator. Can we say something similar about the end? Can we say that it does not matter for Christian faith how the world will end—whether it is by collision with another heavenly body, or by nuclear explosion, or by millions of years of 'running down'? What matters is that Jesus Christ rules as Lord over the world God has made and over the destiny of all his creatures. The New Testament hope is about God's *purpose* for his creation and his relationship to it through Christ, rather than about the *manner* in which his purposes will be brought to their goal. For this reason the New Testament is remarkably restrained about *how* the end will be: one passage speaks of the destruction of the universe, followed by 'new heavens and a new earth' (2 Peter 3:12f.), while another suggests that the present universe will be used up in the creation of a new transformed order (Romans 8:19–21). The emphasis falls repeatedly not on how but on *why* Jesus will come, and on the fact that it is *Jesus* who holds the key to the future. It is not Fate or horoscopes that rule the universe and human lives. It is God, whose loving purposes are already disclosed to us in Jesus.

We must now turn to a further question. What, theologically, is the significance of Christ's second coming? Why cannot we simply affirm that Christ has already come to reveal God and to achieve salvation, and that people proceed at death into a closer union with him? Can we not say all that is essential without insisting on the importance of Christ's return?

The hope of Christ's coming at the end of history is the logical and necessary outcome of our faith that God has already acted for our salvation in the historical events of Jesus's life, death and resurrection. To remove the hope of a final consummation of what Jesus Christ began in history is to undermine the whole idea of God acting in history. God's plan of salvation worked out through history is left with a beginning and no end. As Emil Brunner puts it, 'this thought of the future is anything but superfluous mythology . . . Faith in Jesus without the expectation of his Parousia is a cheque that is never cashed, a promise that is not made in earnest. A faith in Christ without the expectation of a Parousia is like a flight of stairs that leads nowhere, but ends in the void.'[12]

Jesus's death, resurrection and coming again are all of a piece. We misunderstand his second coming unless we see it as the completion of what was done in Gethsemane and at Golgotha and on the third day. And those events in Jerusalem need the vindication and triumph of the second coming if they are to be seen in their full light. It is a matter not just of our future or the future of the world, but the future of Jesus himself. The coming of Jesus means not only the triumph of his cause, but also the triumph of his own person. Christian hope is focused not on something but on him. We do not know in any detail *what* to expect, but we know *whom* to expect. And that is enough. But we cannot say *less* than that, if we are to retain faith in God's saving action in history.

However, it is important not to regard the second coming as 'merely' a historical event, like the battle of Hastings or the American War of Independence. It will be an event marking the climax of our present historical order, but will itself be beyond history in the sense that it will introduce a new order, God's eternal kingdom, which will not be subject to the limitations of our present experience of time and space. We already see a foreshadowing of this in Jesus's resurrection. The resurrection was a historical event in the sense that it involved an empty tomb and transformed disciples—and these could be investigated by a historian. But it was also an event beyond history in that Jesus was raised to a new level of life—an eternal, supernatural level—which is not discernible to the historians' study, but only to faith.

Having considered why the return of Christ is a necessary part of the Christian's faith, we now turn to the reasons for his return and the actions associated with it.

The purpose of Christ's coming

First, his coming will complete the work of rescuing mankind which God began in Jesus Christ. On that day he will be revealed in his triumph and glory. The New Testament language about 'power and glory' (e.g., Mark 13:26) emphasises the contrast between his first coming in obscurity and weakness and his final coming as a public, triumphant, unmistakable event. Apparent absence will give way to impressive presence, hiddenness will give way to open manifestation of the character and splendour of Jesus. There is no biblical basis for any idea that when Jesus comes there will be room for doubt about who he is or whether he really has come.

Secondly, his coming will mean the 'unveiling' not only of what is at present hidden about Christ, but also of what is at present hidden about us human beings. This is the process of judgment about which we shall think in some detail in chapter 6. In the New Testament, judgment on men's lives is stressed as one of the main purposes of Jesus's coming. 'Final judgment must wait until the Lord comes: he will bring to light the dark secrets and expose the hidden purposes of men's hearts. And then every man will receive from God the praise he deserves' (1 Corinthians 4:5). On that day the ultimate issues of life will be laid bare. The ambiguities, the excuses will vanish like soap bubbles. And it is when we recognise this fact, and realise that God has already revealed his ultimate will and purpose for us in Jesus, the 'last Adam' (1 Corinthians 15:45), that we are able to discern the more clearly what are the crucial issues and decisions of our lives *now*. God's ultimate disclosure of his will and purpose in Jesus (cf. Hebrews 1:1f.) challenges us to decide whether we will seek what is of lasting value, or whether we will reject it and find ourselves fighting against God.

Thirdly, it follows that Christ's coming will mark his final conquest over all that is evil. 'Christ will overcome all spiritual rulers, authorities, and powers, and hand over the Kingdom to God the Father. For Christ must rule until God defeats all enemies and puts them under his feet' (1 Corinthians 15:24f.). And in the Revelation to John we find his vision of the lake of fire, swallowing up the devil, and death, and all who have chosen to work against God (Revelation 20:7–15). This is no place to go into the great problem for faith posed by the presence of evil and tragedy in the world. But we must say that, without the biblical vision of a final victory over evil, the problem is insoluble. The coming of Christ will mean the removal of physical suffering and the end of every evil action and situation which prevents a person growing to his full potential in Christ. It will mean the vindication of those who suffer 'for righteousness' sake', and the unmasking of every power-hungry oppressor of his fellow-men. As Reinhold Niebuhr put it, 'when history confronts God, the differences between good and evil are not swallowed up in a distinctionless eternity.'[13] Evil will be dealt with, finally. And, as with other aspects of Christian hope, this expectation is not a piece of foolhardy optimism, but a confidence based on what God has already done in Christ. We see evil already being conquered in his healings and exorcisms, his resurrection and the transformation which he brings to sinful people, both during his earthly ministry and ever since.

Fourthly, when Jesus comes he will gather his people into his presence, bringing resurrection to those who have died before his coming. This we shall study in chapter 5.

But, fifthly, he will not only transform human beings in their resurrection to eternal life. Also there will be a transformation of the universe, a 'new creation', a 'new heaven and new earth' (2 Peter 3:13; Revelation 21:1). God's purposes embrace more than the private destiny of human beings: there was always this hope, says Paul, 'that creation itself would one day be set free from its slavery to decay, and share the glorious freedom of the children of God' (Romans 8:21). We cannot begin to imagine what this might mean in detail. And it is significant that Jesus never described in specific terms the nature of God's ultimate kingdom. What he did was to teach—largely in parables—about the spiritual dynamics of the kingdom. He spoke about God's care for his people, about the quality of relationships in the kingdom, about the radical cost of entering the kingdom. But this imagery of a transformed universe does tell us that God's plan for his world is something different from what we now observe. God can and will bring about a different order of things, and the difference will be great and surprising. It will be perfect—'new heavens and a new earth, where righteousness will be at home' (2 Peter 3:13).

The New Testament describes this new world both in terms of continuity with the present world, and in terms of discontinuity. Continuity is expressed in the Romans 8 passage quoted in the previous paragraph: the new world will be the present world brought to that perfection of which all our present experience of God and his creative goodness is a foretaste. Discontinuity is the emphasis of 2 Peter 3:12, which speaks of the day when 'the heavens will burn up and be destroyed' to make way for the new order. This implies the radical difference between the future order and the present world. It will be eternal rather than transitory, perfect rather than ambiguous, God-centred rather than dyed with the deeds of people desiring to be like God. From time to time in this book we shall make use of this tension between continuity and discontinuity.

Meaning in history

The sixth implication of Jesus's coming concerns our understanding of history. His coming will mark both the end of history and the goal of history. The course of history is not circular, as was widely believed in the ancient world. Nor is it aimless, as many people assume today. Nor is the present course of history everlasting. The Bible presents history as a movement towards a goal: the perfect kingdom of God. It sees God as acting in history towards the fulfilment of his purposes. In his book *Christ the Meaning of History*, Hendrikus Berkhof argues that people today have lost the sense of history. Europeans have abandoned their biblical roots, which inspired the belief that history is directed towards a goal, and that it is important to take part in history, to plan and make sacrifices for the future. Marxism, using a secularised form of this biblical hope, is very confident about the meaning of history: the class struggle drives history onwards until the means of production fall into the control of the proletariat, and so the 'kingdom' of justice, peace and perfection will be established. But because Marxism derives the meaning of history from *within* history, and is prepared to sacrifice human lives and values for the sake of that future utopia, the meaning it gives to history is a wrong meaning. Meanwhile Eastern religions think of history either as circular or as illusory. So modern man has the uncomfortable choice between wrong meaning and no meaning—unless he can discover the biblical meaning.[14] The Bible sees history not as a struggle between classes but as a struggle between good and evil, leading to the ultimate triumph of God and good. For the meaning of good and evil is determined not by chance or by cultural convenience, but by the will of God.

At that climax of history there will be an end of all opposition to God and to his will. This is not because an 'inevitable' progress of mankind through history will have led us to a point where all opposition to God has been voluntarily abandoned. The Bible's realistic view of evil does not encourage such optimism. The idea of a perfect earthly utopia achieved by human progress—whether it is a Marxist or a humanist utopia—is hostile to the biblical view of God's purposes and of human experience. Because God alone can establish his perfect, eternal kingdom, there must be a discontinuity between our present experience of history and what lies beyond Jesus's coming. But there is continuity, too. Because the will of God is, in part, done in history, and because the power of the risen Christ is already at work in history, the climax of history will mark the consummation of God's purposes in history. Both continuity and discontinuity are expressed in John's vision of the new Jerusalem: 'The greatness and the wealth of the nations will be brought into the city. But nothing that is defiled will enter the city.' (Revelation 21:26f.).

In the Bible, historical events are constantly looked at in the light of the End. Amos prophesied the fall of the northern kingdom in terms of the Day of the Lord and his judgment. Jesus related the fall of Jerusalem to his final coming in judgment (Mark 13). In a similar way the people of God today would be wise to look at what happens to us as individuals and as a church as part of the ongoing struggle

110

between God's will and the powers of evil which goes on until the End.

But we must be careful about generalising from this, for the Bible is concerned primarily with God's specific purposes for his people Israel (in the Old Testament) and the 'new Israel' (in the New Testament). We are not entitled to take from the Bible any very specific promise or threats about the history of Israel and turn them into statements about the history of other nations—about the decline of the British Empire, for example, or the Vietnam war or the Gulag Archipelago. What we can suggest is that there is some principle of morality woven into the fabric of existence, which tends towards the vindication of goodness and the punishment of evil. That is not something confined to God's unique relationship with Israel, for the creation-story in Genesis reminds us that there is a moral dimension built into the structure of man's life before God.

Problems in history

However, as soon as we state a general principle such as this, we are up against problems. How is goodness vindicated, we ask, in the Soviet invasions of Czechoslovakia and Afghanistan? Or in the subduing of the North and South American Indians? Or in the forced exile of the Banabans of Ocean Island so that Britain can exploit their phosphate? Or in the sufferings of noble souls in Siberia? Do not the authors of such wickedness simply get away with it? Four brief comments may be appropriate here.

First, whilst governments as governments may impose their evil will because of the power at their disposal, the individuals of whom governments consist will not 'get away with it'. 'All of us must appear before the judgment seat of Christ, so that each one may receive what he deserves, according to what he has done, good or bad, in his bodily life' (2 Corinthians 5:10). In the end each man must answer to God himself for his treatment of his fellow-men.

Secondly, societies do experience in their common life a

111

kind of 'inbuilt retribution' similar to that which individuals experience. For the individual, 'the penalty for selfishness is being a selfish person; the punishment for materialism is to drown in possessions; the reward of lechery is the coarsening of sexual response.'[15] Similarly, a society has to reap the consequences of its own actions. Thus, for example, the racial problems of British and American society can be traced back to the inhumanity of the slave trade. The class divisions in British society are the result of centuries of mistrust, mismanagement and false belief about the value of people.

Thirdly, this process of cause and effect takes time to operate. There are many examples of the sins of the fathers being visited upon the children—and before we complain at the injustice of that let us at least remember that what is true of the fathers' sins is true of their right deeds and wise decisions. In the mid-1980s we could not dream how judgment would come upon the Soviet oppression of dissidents or upon apartheid in South Africa. But now we know.

The fourth point is the Christian insight that God's involvement in history follows a pattern of crucifixion and resurrection. In human terms the life of Jesus was a waste, a defeat, but from God's viewpoint it was the most powerful, the most creative event in all human history. This warns us that we shall only see God's hand in human affairs if we can look at them in the light of this paradoxical pattern, whereby service is the very essence of greatness, suffering is creative, and misdirected force is ultimately self-destructive.

The paradox is present in its full force in the book of Revelation, with its extraordinary contrast between what *appears* to be the case and what is *really* happening. Rome appears to have absolute power to do what it likes, and that includes persecuting God's people. But in reality Jesus Christ is 'the ruler of the kings of the earth' (Revelation 1:5). The book's vision of history (chapter 5) begins with the Lamb's opening the book of history. He not only explains it, he is its beginning and end. When castastrophes come, that is ultimately because he allows them. For although they are the work of evil forces, they only have power because (in John's often-repeated phrase) 'power was given them'. And we can see God's hand behind these calamities in that they are constantly restrained. For example, oil and wine are not harmed (Revelation 6:6); only a third of the world is destroyed (8:7ff.; 9:15), and this in the hope that the rest might repent (9:20). 'The message of Revelation is that God's kingdom is active in our midst through suffering and judgment, restraint and triumph.'[16]

There is one final thing to add about history. Because it is not yet completed, our historical future remains open. It is not predetermined by God, by fate or by anyone else. The biblical understanding of prophecy does not commit us to the view that events are rigidly determined and nothing can be changed. Often in the Old Testament we find prophecies which are clearly conditional. In Jeremiah 7, for example, the prophet declares that, because of the wickedness of Judah, 'the land shall become a desert' (7:34). Yet he also says that if only the people will change their ways, then God will 'let you go on living here, in the land which I gave your ancestors as a permanent possession' (7:7). And Jonah's worry about announcing to the people of Nineveh God's plan to destroy their city was that they might repent at his preaching and so avert the city's destruction. The progress of history, then, remains open, undecided, and therefore not clear. The conflict of history goes on. Under God, we are called to be involved in history, to engage with people and events in the light of God's will.

The Triumph of God

As we draw to a close this review of the purpose and character of Christ's coming, we must note that what we are talking about is 'the kingdom of *God*'. This reminds us that we are dealing with God's purpose, God's sovereignty, God's action. An understanding of Christianity which attempts to take seriously the *grace* of God as the basis of all relationships between man and God must never give in to

113

the notion that the coming of the kingdom is a human achievement or a matter of inevitable progress. The coming of God's kingdom in Christ is an act of his grace and power.

Our confidence in its coming derives from the grace and power already demonstrated in Jesus's resurrection and in our own present experience of them through relationship with the living Christ. We long for the coming kingdom not so much because we look for compensation for the pain and deficiencies of life on earth, but because we look for the fullness of what we already joyfully experience in Christ. And many of the pictures we use for the future kingdom reflect this. We know the Holy Spirit as the 'first fruits' of our future life (Romans 8:23). We celebrate the Lord's Supper as a foretaste of the heavenly banquet (1 Corinthians 11:23–26). We are 'redeemed'—like slaves enjoying their liberation—and Jesus's coming will bring with it an even fuller liberation (Romans 8:21).

Notes to chapter 3

1. For an interesting discussion of this, see L. Cerfaux, *Christ in the Theology of St. Paul* (Eng. tr., Herder, New York, 1959), pp. 31ff.
2. 'New Testament and Mythology', in H.-W. Bartsch, ed., *Kerygma and Myth*, vol. 1 (Eng. tr., SPCK, London, 1953), p. 5.
3. See my survey of such views in *Christian Hope and the Future of Man*, pp. 17–23.
4. Babylonian Talmud, Sanhedrin 97b, 25. See G. R. Beasley-Murray, *Jesus and the Future* (Macmillan, London, 1954), pp. 175f.
5. For this approach, see Jeremias, *New Testament Theology*, vol.1, pp. 122–6.
6. On this issue see Beasley-Murray, *Jesus and the Future*, pp. 172–8.
7. See further Beasley-Murray, *Jesus and the Future*, pp. 183–91; and works cited in my article 'The Value of Apocalyptic', *Tyndale Bulletin* 30, 1979, pp. 72f. A. L. Moore, *The Parousia in the New Testament* (Brill, Leiden, 1966) is a major study concentrating on this topic.
8. See further R. J. Bauckham, 'The Delay of the Parousia', *Tyndale Bulletin* 31, 1980, pp. 28–36.
9. For this understanding of 'began' see I. H. Marshall, *Luke: Historian and Theologian* (Paternoster, Exeter, 1970), p. 87, n. 2.

10. It is quite possible to learn from Conzelmann's insights into Luke's concern with history (as I have tried to do here) without adopting his view that Luke *invented* this approach to Jesus and his significance. I agree with those who argue that Luke is making more explicit what was already present in Jesus's own thinking, e.g., O. Cullmann, *Salvation in History* (Eng. tr., SCM, London, 1967), esp. pp. 186ff.; Marshall, *Luke: Historian and Theologian* pp. 77–88. Luke did not replace an originally eschatological message by a 'salvation-history' approach; both 'salvation-history' and eschatology were present in Jesus's own teaching.

11. See further my discussion of Bultmann in *Christian Hope and the Future of Man*, pp. 65–73.

12. *The Christian Doctrine of the Church, Faith and the Consummation: Dogmatics*, vol. 3 (Eng. tr., Lutterworth, London, 1962), p. 396.

13. *The Nature and Destiny of Man*, vol.2 (Nisbet, London, 1943), p. 302.

14. *Christ the Meaning of History* (Eng. tr., SCM, London, 1966), pp. 28–36.

15. E. W. Ives, *God in History* (Lion, Tring, 1979), p. 79. The whole book is a valuable discussion of this difficult issue of discerning God's activity and purpose in history.

16. Berkhof, *Christ the Meaning of History*, p. 128.

Chapter 4   Mistaken Hopes?

What has been said so far about the coming of Christ will taste like a very restricted diet to some readers. Is there not much more to be said? Does the Bible not speak quite definitely about the return of the Jews to their land? Surely the establishment of the state of Israel in 1948 is a clear sign that we are close to the climax of the present age? And what about the millennium described in Revelation 20, to which so many Old Testament prophecies point?

Many Christians have a very strong sense that the history of the world is racing towards its goal. Catastrophes intensify, pessimism deepens. These must surely herald the triumphant return of Christ to rescue his Church and to set up his thousand-year reign over the earth. And this sense of an imminent end finds support in the doom-laden warnings of the secular prophets, with their analyses of the arms race, the population explosion, the massive crises of food, oil and economics.

But is this a case of secular thought complementing and supporting biblical revelation? Or is biblical interpretation allowing itself to be controlled by secular visions of the future? We must consider with care some crucial questions of interpretation—crucial because our answers will seriously influence our thinking and living. I shall try to show clearly where I believe certain interpretations are wrong. But I shall try also to be charitable, because it grieves me how Christians whose hope is focused on the same Christ can break relationships with each other because of differences over the details of their expectation.

Once when visiting an English city I met a member of an evangelical church, and, noticing that another building labelled 'Evangelical Church' stood a mere two hundred

116

metres down the road, I asked him whether there were good relations between the two churches. 'Oh no,' he replied, surprised that I should even think to ask the question, 'they don't believe in the rapture!' At the time I had not a clue what the rapture was. But I came away wondering how it was that Christians could get on reasonably well with each other despite differing views about baptism or spiritual gifts or politics, and yet 'the rapture' was enough to put a 50,000-volt electric fence between them.

Can we know when Jesus will come?

There have often been people who thought they could calculate the coming of the Messiah. There were Jewish rabbis and apocalyptists who did it, often using a kind of allegorical arithmetic based on juggling with numbers and patterns which they found in the Old Testament and in other Jewish writings. Jesus warned against such an attitude, as we saw in the previous chapter. And one rabbi, reacting against this whole tradition of calculation, went so far as to declare, 'He who announces the messianic times based on calculations forfeits his own share in the future.'[1]

Attempts to predict the time of Christ's coming have been mainly of three kinds. First, there is the method of numerical calculation, like that of the rabbis mentioned above. In the Middle Ages there was Joachim of Fiore, who died about A.D. 1200. He divided world history into three epochs, and predicted (on the basis of the numbers in Daniel 11:3 and 12:6) that the third period would begin in A.D. 1260. Before then, the Roman emperor would remove the papacy, the empire itself would fall to the Saracens, and ten kings from the east would be destroyed by the Tartars. When the new epoch arrived in 1260, it would be an age of universal monastic contemplation, peace and rest. Admittedly, the personal return of Christ does not figure prominently in Joachim's expectation, but he is a famous example of attempts to foretell the future by using biblical numbers.

The second source of date-fixing is prophetic revelation

which is believed to come from God. In the second century the ecstatic prophet Montanus and his two female associates preached the imminent approach of the millennial rule of Christ. Maximilla, the last of the three prophets to die (in A.D. 179), declared, 'After me there is no more prophecy, but only the end of the world.'[2]

Thirdly, estimates of the time of the end are based on passages of Scripture which depict 'signs of the times' (for example, Mark 13) or which prophesy events which can be identified with developments during the lifetime of the interpreter. So, for example, prophecies in Ezekiel 38–9, in Daniel and Revelation, have often been thought to find their fulfilment in events of modern times. Martin Luther was attracted to this approach. In 1530 he worked with frantic haste to finish his translation of the Bible into German, fearing that Christ might come before the work was complete. 'For it is certain', he wrote, 'from the Holy Scriptures that we have no more temporal things to expect. All is done and fulfilled: the Roman Empire is at an end; the Turk has reached his highest point; the pomp of papacy is falling away and the world is cracking on all sides almost as if it would break and fall apart entirely.' (Paradoxically, however, Luther dealt severely in 1533 with Michael Stifel for calculating that the world would end at 8 a.m. on 19th October of that year!)[3] What we see here is an attempt to relate contemporary events to biblical prophecies of things which must take place before the end comes.

A more recent example is Leonard Sale-Harrison (c.1875–1956), an Australian whose speaking and writing were very influential in Britain and North America. In the 1930s he began to match biblical passages with events in the life and times of Mussolini, and to deduce from these that this age would end by the early 1940s. The clay of the statue's feet in Daniel 2 represented the socialists, whilst the iron represented strong men who stood for law and order, such as the Fascists. This latter group would call for a strong ruler (Antichrist) to bring order out of chaos. Mussolini, if not Antichrist himself, would certainly pave the way for him.

Sale-Harrison believed that Mussolini was reviving the old Roman Empire, in fulfilment of Daniel 7–8 and Revelation 13.[4] While he hesitated to set a precise year for Christ's return, his linking of Mussolini with the Antichrist prophecies in effect set the date within his own generation.

Let me cite one more example from the past. On 9th November 1875, the British premillennialist periodical *Signs of Our Times* carried an article by P. B. Morgan which included the following:

> The whole aspect of the world . . . shows that the personal advent of Christ, accompanied with terrible judgments upon every nation, is close at hand, to raise the sleeping saints, to translate the living Christians, to destroy the Popish, Mahomedan, and infidel Anti-Christs, and reign visibly over the earth for 1000 years, as promised in Revelation XX.[5]

Grounds for caution

I have six main problems with such attempts to determine the time of the end. First, the plain fact that many have made such attempts in the past and have been proved wrong by history ought to make us extremely cautious about thinking we can do better. Those who, in their enthusiasm to interpret the signs of the times, ignore the lessons of history, are likely to repeat the mistakes of history. Their writings may be 'more up-to-date than tomorrow's newspaper',[6] and just as quickly out-dated. This continuing pattern of raised expectations followed by disappointed hopes and puzzled readers ought to make us question vigorously the method of using the Bible which leads to such predictions. If we do not do that, we shall find that puzzled Christians increasingly question the whole basis of the Christian's hope.

For questionable interpretation is bound to lead (this is my second point) to pastoral problems. *Christianity Today* in April 1977 reported an interview by Ward Gasque with Hal Lindsey, whose book *The Late Great Planet Earth* sold several million copies in the 1970s. Lindsey argued that the return of Christ would certainly take place before the year 2000. For Matthew 24:34 teaches that Jesus will come within a generation of the predicted 'signs' of that chapter being fulfilled, including appearance of the fig-tree (verse 32)—which Lindsey takes to mean the return of Jews to Palestine. 'But what if you're wrong?' asked Gasque. And Lindsey replied, 'Well, there's just a split second's difference between a hero and a bum. I didn't ask to be a hero, but I guess I have become one in the Christian community. So I accept it. But if I'm wrong about this, I guess I'll become a bum.'[7] And what about the millions who have read his book? If he is wrong, who will guide them to a truer understanding of the biblical hope? Who will pick up the pieces of their disillusion?

It would be wrong for me to dampen hope. Certainly we should not react to Lindsey's predictions by removing the second coming to the mists of the remote future. There is no need to emulate the Book of Common Prayer, which by Act of Parliment in 1752 gives directions for calculating the dates of the church's festivals up to the year 8500 and beyond. Such information does not encourage us to believe that Parliment was living in eager anticipation of Christ's advent! We need to find ways of encouraging expectancy and readiness, without stating dates before which the end must take place. More of that in chapter seven.

Dating by numbers

Thirdly, to calculate dates by means of numbers is to misunderstand their intention in the book of Daniel. Biblical writers seem not to have been very precise about numbers. 1 Kings 6:1 says there were 480 years between the Israelites' exodus from Egypt and the building of Solomon's temple. But in Acts 13:18f. Paul says that the interval between the exodus and the time of Samuel (who of course lived *before* Solomon) was 490 years.[8] This discrepancy is there not because the writers were trying to be chronologically precise and failed, but because the Hebrews frequently used numbers in an approximate way, and were more interested in their symbolic significance.

In Daniel 9:2 we find Daniel musing on Jeremiah's prophecy that the period of the Jews' exile would be seventy years (Jeremiah 25:12; 29:10). As a matter of fact, there is no way of dating the beginning and end of the exile which would make it a period of exactly seventy years. And Ezekiel spoke of a forty-year exile (Ezekiel 4:6). Jeremiah's seventy years represent the ideal length of a man's life, whilst Ezekiel's forty years is the conventional length of a generation. Each in his own way is saying that the generation which experienced the beginning of the exile will not survive to witness the return. Perhaps, also, seventy years was regarded as a fixed term for the completion of God's judgment on his people (cf. Zechariah 1:12; 2 Chronicles 36:21). But in any case the symbolism is what matters; strict chronology is of lesser concern.

There is every reason, then, for *not* seeing in the numbers of Daniel and Revelation a mathematical pattern by which we can discover the dating of future events—if only we can crack the code. The numbers of Daniel 8:14; 9:24–27; 12:11f., are in fact so contradictory and confusing if taken literally that it would require more than a Nobel prize and three Ph.Ds to sort them out. But take them symbolically, and some sense emerges. The number seven, and multiples of it, signified completeness in the ancient world (since there were, for example, seven planets and seven days in the week). The 'seventy weeks of years' in Daniel 9:24, therefore, spoke of the accomplishment of God's purposes for all history without implying that the remainder of history would be literally 490 years. And the differing numbers of days in Daniel 8 and 12 were intended to encourage the faithful to stand firm under persecution because God's day of deliverance would surely come, even if it seemed delayed. 'The timetables were aimed,' says L. Hartman, 'less at the brain than at the heart and hands.'[9]

If Daniel's numbers really had been intended, as many

interpreters have supposed, to give a precise prediction of the date of Jesus's life and death, then it is surely remarkable that neither Jesus nor New Testament writers appeal to this to support their messianic claims. No. To treat apocalyptic numbers as mathematical predictions is to miss the daring, poetic nature of the literature and the pastoral nature of its message.

The fourth point takes us back to what we were saying in chapter three, about Jesus's own condemnation of date-fixing. This should make us extremely cautious in assessing any prediction of dates based on prophetic visions. For one of the principles to be applied in evaluating a prophecy is that it must be consistent with the word of God in Scripture. So if Jesus warned against speculation and declared that the time of his coming is known only to God, it is questionable whether God is going to reveal the timing of his plans to Christian prophets.

Signs of the times

Fifthly, there is the problem of the 'signs' of Mark 13 and similar passages. Are we not encouraged by Jesus himself to look for the fulfilment of these prophecies in order to assess when the end is approaching? I think not, as I have already hinted in chapter three. The difficulty with the attempt to calculate from these 'signs'—earthquakes, famine, persecution, false messiahs, and so on—is that they have been with us right through history. So they cannot tell us when the end is approaching. And it is little use pointing out, as some do, that there have been more famines or more persecutions or more earthquakes in the twentieth century than previously. That may be true, but it gives me no means of knowing for how many more years such things will continue to intensify. Again, we should observe that in the past a period when such phenomena have intensified has been enough to trigger widespread expectation that history could not continue much longer. The famous Lisbon earthquake of 1755, for example, caused many experts all over Europe to imagine that the world was about to come to an end.

Coupled with this, as we have already seen in the cases of Luther and Sale-Harrison, is the guesswork involved in equating some of the signs described by Jesus with events in the interpreter's own day. Why should we assume in our day that we have got the equation right, when so many before us have been wrong?

The signs of Mark 13 are not like the signs which say 'End of Motorway 1 mile'. They are in fact more like the hazard warning lights which warn us of dangers along the way. Jesus spoke of signs, not to satisfy curiosity or to make calculation possible, but to strengthen faith and to warn of dangers that his followers could expect. The signs are signs of the conflict between good and evil, between God's purpose and all that opposes it, which will go on until Christ finally defeats evil and brings in his perfect world at his coming. The keynote of Mark 13 is not in predictions so much as in exhortations—'Keep awake, be on your guard!' (verses 32–37)—and the promises—'the person who holds out to the end will be saved' (verse 13).[10]

Finally, the belief that the end of all things is due in the next few years effectively destroys attempts to remove social evils and to work for the better health of human society. It may stimulate evangelism, but it discourages people from proper planning and working towards a society which is more in harmony with God's will. C. S. Lewis warned against beliefs about the second coming which undermine this concern for the future good of earthly society.

For what comes, [he wrote] is judgment: happy are those whom it finds laboring in their vocations, whether they were merely going out to feed the pigs or laying good plans to deliver humanity a hundred years hence from some great evil. The curtain has indeed now fallen. Those pigs will never in fact be fed, the great campaign against white slavery or governmental tyranny will never in fact proceed to victory. No matter; you were at your post when the inspection came.[11]

The return of Israel

On 17th September 1876, Charles H. Spurgeon said this:

> It is certain that the Jews will return to their own land. They shall build the old waste, they shall raise up the former desolation, they shall repair the waste cities—the desolations of many generations . . . It is certain that the Jews as a people will yet own Jesus of Nazareth, the Son of David, as their King. It is certain that Jesus Christ will come again and that he shall reign among his ancient people gloriously and that there will be a thousand years of peace never known on the earth before.

To say the least, the steady return of Jews to Palestine during this century, and the establishment of the state of Israel in 1948, is a very remarkable event. What Spurgeon looked forward to as the fulfilment of prophecy, we are able to witness as a fact of history. So, not surprisingly, many Christians—and of course many Jews—see modern events in the Middle East as fulfilment of Old Testament prophecy and as the vindication of a literalistic approach to those prophecies. Again, Hal Lindsey is the front-runner. But other popular authors such as Frederick Tatford and Lance Lambert adopt a similar approach.[12]

But is this the right understanding of prophecy? It is easy to be accused of anti-Semitism if one questions the Jews' 'prophetic right' to the land of Palestine. (Incidentally, 'anti-Semitism' is an odd charge, since Arabs are just as Semitic as Jews.) But it is quite possible to believe that the Jewish people have a moral right to territory, and to see God's providence in the development of the State of Israel, without believing that this State fulfils prophecy. That issue must be decided on its merits. So what prophecies are we talking about?

Primarily, there is God's promise to Abraham: 'the whole land of Canaan will belong to your descendants for ever' (Genesis 17:8). And following on from this there are promises in some of the prophets that Jews dispersed from the land will be brought back to it to experience afresh the blessings of God. The implication, therefore, is that even though Israel in her history experienced exile and dispersion from her God-given land, these are to be seen as temporary setbacks. For in the long run God is bound to honour his promise to restore the Jews to the land and bless them there permanently.

Let us look first at the promises that scattered Israel will return to the land. Most of these address the situation of Jews herded away to Babylon after the destruction of Jerusalem in 587 B.C. They promise a return to Palestine after a period of exile. And they *were fulfilled* when in 539 B.C. Cyrus the Persian, recent conqueror of Babylon, issued a decree that captive peoples could return to their own land. The prophecies include passages in Jeremiah, such as the letter which he wrote to leaders of the exiled people in Babylon: 'The Lord says, "When Babylonia's seventy years are over, I will show my concern for you and keep my promise to bring you back home." ' (Jeremiah 29:10). And Ezekiel records his vision of dry bones being restored to life, with its meaning:

> God said to me, 'mortal man, the people of Israel are like these dry bones. They say that they are dried up, without any hope and with no future. So prophesy to my people Israel and tell them that I, the Sovereign Lord, am going to open their graves. I am going to take them out and bring them back to the land of Israel' (Ezekiel 37:11f.).

Such promises were wonderfully fulfilled within a few decades, and there is no point in looking for a future fulfilment. But two objections might be made to the view-point I have expressed. First, It has been argued sometimes that the prophecies I have quoted do refer to the return from exile in 539 B.C., but that there are other prophecies which speak of a return 'from among the nations'. And since Babylon was only one nation, these prophecies must refer to some much later time, when the Jews would again be scattered around the world and would again be restored to Palestine. Thus the fulfilment of such prophecies is found in twentieth-century events. My difficulty with this view is that the prophets themselves frequently fused together references to a return from 'that land' (i.e. Babylonia) and a return 'from among the nations'. To their minds, these were simply variant ways of speaking about the condition of Jews in exile and God's promised restoration. Take Jeremiah, for example. In a single passage God says through him:

> People of Israel, do not be terrified. I will rescue you from that distant land, from the land where you are prisoners. You will come back home and live in peace . . . I will destroy all the nations where I have scattered you, but I will not destroy you! (Jeremiah 30:10f.).

Again, God says, 'I will bring them (Israel) from the north and gather them from the ends of the earth . . . I scattered my people, but I will gather them and guard them as a shepherd guards his flock' (Jeremiah 31:8,11; 46:27f.). So the prophets themselves did not distinguish between two exiles or dispersions of Jews. To argue that they did is to interpret their references to 'that land' and 'all the nations' with a literalism which is foreign to them.

This leads us to the second objection. The way in which Jews returned to Palestine after Cyrus's decree was but a pale reflection of the grandeur of the return envisaged in Ezekiel or Jeremiah or Isaiah 40–55. It turned out to be more like the trickle homewards of the supporters of a third-division football team after defeat in the first round of the Cup than like the thrill of the return of a jubilant Cup-winning team to their home town. To pick up the words of Jeremiah 30:10f., quoted above: did the Jews return to Palestine and live in peace? Were all the surrounding nations destroyed? No, of course not. The Jews went back to a rather precarious existence and were to be threatened again and again by the power of foreign nations. So must we not say that such prophecies remained to be

126

fulfilled long after 539 B.C? And is it not appropriate to see their fulfilment in the events of our own times—the return to the land is well under way, Israel's enemies will soon be destroyed, and Israel will dwell secure in unprecedented peace?

Now of course there is truth in the claim that the prophecies of the return were not completely fulfilled in 539 B.C., and it is appropriate to look for a more complete fulfilment at a later time. But here we must look at what the New Testament does with such prophecies—unless we are content to look at the Old Testament without the light of Christ. And we find that New Testament Christians saw the fulfilment of these prophecies not in some future return of Jews to Palestine, but in the gathering of Gentiles into the church of Christ.

In Acts 15, for example, is a record of the Council of Jerusalem (c. A.D. 49), which debated the question whether Paul and others might welcome Gentiles into the Church without requiring them to be circumcised. James, leader of the Jerusalem church, approved of Paul's attitude and appealed to Amos's prophecy to support it:

> After this I will return, says the Lord, and restore the kingdom of David. I will rebuild its ruins and make it strong again. And so all the rest of mankind will come to me, all the Gentiles whom I have called to be my own (Acts 15:16f.).

Amos was referring to the rebuilding of the Jewish state and the welcoming of Gentiles into it. James said this prophecy was being fulfilled as Gentiles entered the church of Jesus the messiah—and the other apostles present evidently agreed.

Jesus, Israel and prophecy

And this interpretation of Amos is consistent with the New Testament's over-all attitude to God's promises to

Israel. From Jesus's teaching through to the book of Revelation, the promises to Israel are seen as being fulfilled in the Christian church. Consider Jesus's own attitude first.[13]

Jesus believed that Old Testament prophecies about the kingdom of God and the time of salvation were being fulfilled in his own ministry. We saw examples of that in chapter 2. Yet he never applied to himself an Old Testament prophecy about the royal Messiah, the son of David, as the restorer of Jewish political sovereignty. There is nothing in his recorded teaching to suggest that he expected a time when the Jews would have political independence in Palestine. Luke 21:24, which is sometimes quoted as evidence for such an expectation, does say that 'Jerusalem will be trodden down by the Gentiles, until the times of the Gentiles are fulfilled.' But it does *not* say that Jewish sovereignty will be restored after 'the times of the Gentiles are fulfilled'. It leaves that question unanswered. And it would seem more consistent with the general thrust of Jesus's teaching if the only things to follow 'the times of the Gentiles' were the second coming itself and the end of the present age.

Jesus constantly warned Jews of his time that their persistent lack of faith and their failure to respond to God's offers of grace and forgiveness had set them on a collision course. He wept over Jerusalem because it would not come to him. 'Your Temple will be abandoned' (Luke 13:34f.) 'because you did not recognise the time when God came to save you!' (Luke 19:41–44). And little towns in Galilee would fall, to rise no more, because they failed to turn from their sins despite the miracles he worked in their midst (Luke 10:13–15). In predicting Israel's doom, Jesus said nothing of political restoration.

But he said more than this—and here we come to the heart of the matter. Jesus taught that the role of the Jewish nation as the people of God was being transferred to the people who accepted him as Messiah. Recall, for example, the parable of the Tenants in the Vineyard (Matthew 21:33–46), where the tenants' repeated rejection of the owner's representatives comes to its climax in the rejection of his son. And the result? 'He will certainly kill those evil men and let the vineyard out to other tenants . . . And so I tell you the Kingdom of God will be taken away from you and given to a people who will produce the proper fruits' (verses 41,43). This parable is followed by the parable of the Wedding Feast, where the place of the invited guests— who refuse to come to the feast—is taken by all kinds of people brought in off the streets (Matthew 22:1–10).

And who do these 'other tenants' and these people off the streets represent? The answer comes clear in the story about the Roman (Gentile) centurion's expression of faith (Matthew 8:5–13). 'I tell you,' said Jesus, 'I have never found anyone in Israel with faith like this. I assure you that many will come from the east and the west and sit down with Abraham, Isaac and Jacob at the feast in the Kingdom of heaven. But those who should be in the Kingdom will be thrown out' (verses 10–12). The remarkable thing here is that the description of people coming 'from the east and the west' alludes to passages such as Isaiah 43:5f. and Psalm 107:3 which spoke of *Jews* returning from exile. Yet here is Jesus applying it to Gentiles, included among the people of God. The Jews' *exclusive* status as people of God is ended. The privilege of belonging to that people is open to all— Jew and Gentile alike—who have faith in Jesus. For this reason Jesus's vision of the coming of the Son of Man includes the declaration that, after the gospel has been preached to all nations (Mark 13:10), 'he will send the angels to the four corners of the earth to gather God's chosen people from one end of the world to the other' (Mark 13:27).

Jesus saw himself as 'the true Israel', the one who embodied in his own life and work what Israel was meant by God to be. Thus he claimed for himself titles such as 'Son of Man' and 'Servant of God', which in their Old Testament context refer mainly to Israel or to the faithful nucleus in Israel. And he applied to himself Old Testament texts which originally related to the nation Israel. For instance, to combat the devil's temptations, he cited three texts from Deuteronomy 6–8 which speak about the way Israel was supposed to respond to God. Where Israel failed, Jesus would succeed, living out obediently the calling of the nation (Matthew 4:1–11).

And on the basis of his own existence as 'true Israel', Jesus addressed his own followers in terms which show that he saw them as the real people of God, the real inheritors of God's Old Testament promises. As in the Old Testament Israel was God's flock (e.g., Ezekiel 34), so Jesus's followers are his flock (Luke 12:32), and he is the true shepherd (Mark 14:27; John 10:11). As in the Old Testament Israel was God's vine (e.g., Hosea 10:1), so Jesus is 'the real vine', and his followers are its branches (John 15:1–5). As in the Old Testament Israel was the 'community' of God (Greek *ekklesia*), so his followers are the 'church' (Greek *ekklesia*) which he is to build (Matthew 16:18). As in the Old Testament God had a covenant with his people, and promised 'a new covenant with the people of Israel and with the people of Judah' (Jeremiah 31:31), so Jesus enacted this new covenant to his disciples at the last supper, and sealed it with his blood in crucifixion. But it quickly became apparent that this new covenant was not confined to national 'Israel and Judah', for Paul tells us how Gentiles at Corinth shared in the same covenant through their faith in Jesus and their celebration of it in the Lord's supper (1 Corinthians 11:25).

The natural conclusion from all this is that Jesus saw his new covenant community as taking the place of the Jewish people as the people of God. This new community, the church of Jesus, becomes the place where Old Testament promises find their fulfilment. Yet of course there is not a complete break between the Jews and the church. For the followers of Jesus include a remnant, a nucleus of Jews who ensure continuity with the old Israel.

And God has by no means finished with Israel, as we shall see in a moment.

Israel in the New Testament

Jesus, then, foresaw no political future for Israel. He did not re-apply to future political events those prophecies which spoke of a return and renewal of the Jewish people. Instead, he believed that Israel's destiny would be fulfilled in those who follow him, of whatever race. This is why we find New Testament writers constantly applying Old Testament prophecies about Israel to the followers of Jesus. In 1 Peter 2, for example, a host of 'Israel' terms is applied to Peter's congregations in Turkey, which included both Jews and Gentiles. 'Come as living stones, [he writes] and let yourselves be used in building the spiritual temple, where you will serve as holy priests to offer spiritual and acceptable sacrifices to God through Jesus Christ' (verse 5). Ezekiel's vision of a new temple (Ezekiel 40–8) is thus fulfilled not in some future literal temple in Jerusalem (as some believe) but in the church, where God's presence is now focused, and his people offer sacrifices not of blood but of praise and obedient service. And then Peter addresses his readers with the words originally addressed to the Israelites at Sinai: 'You are the chosen race, the King's priests, the holy nation, God's own people.' And he adds applying Hosea 2:23 to the new situation, 'At one time you were not God's people, but now you are his people; at one time you did not know God's mercy, but now you have received his mercy' (verses 9f.).

Paul's approach is similar. He applies to the (mostly Gentile) Christians at Corinth words originally addressed to Jews in exile in Babylon (2 Corinthians 6:2). It is we Christians, he says, who 'have received the true circumcision, for we worship God by means of his Spirit' (Philippians 3:3). 'Abraham is the spiritual father of all who believe in God and are accepted as righteous by him, even though they are not circumcised' (Romans 4:11). Therefore, he says to the Christians in Galatia, 'If you belong to Christ, then you are the descendants of Abraham and will receive what God has promised' (Galatians 3:29). There could hardly be a clearer statement of the fact that the church of Christ is the people of God in continuity with the people of God in the Old Testament. However, it would be wrong to conclude from all this that the Jews no longer have any special place in God's purpose. Although Paul can call Gentile Christians 'descendants of Abraham' who will receive through faith what God originally promised to Abraham, he can also affirm that 'God has not rejected his people, whom he chose from the beginning' (Romans 11:2). In Romans 9–11 he is agonising over the destiny of Jews who have rejected their messiah. And he expresses the conviction that a substantial number of them will respond to Christ: God has not cast off his ancient people for ever. Otherwise his faithfulness would be in question.

How do we reconcile this expression of hope for Israel with Jesus' assertions that the Jews' place as God's people was about to be forfeited? We must see it as a repeat of Israel's experience in the period before Christ.

As in the Old Testament, the word of judgment which sounds like the final word is ever followed by the undeserved word of grace. Indeed, the Israel of any particular generation can be threatened with rejection, can actually be cast off, can be replaced in God's purpose. But God will still keep his commitment to the seed of Jacob as a whole.[14]

But two crucial points must be noted. First, Paul gives no hint here of a political future for Israel, any more than Jesus did. It is the recognition of Jesus's messiahship which concerns him. Secondly, Paul's exposition here does not imply any *distinctive* dealing of God with the Jewish race at a future date—for example *after* the 'rapture' when, according to some theories, Jesus will come to remove Christians to the heavenly world. Paul's whole argument right through Romans, is that 'there is no difference between Jews and Gentiles' (Romans 10:12; cf. 1:16f.; 2:9–11; 3:22f.). There is one Lord, and one gospel for all, one way of salvation—the way of faith. And right through history since the time of Jesus, salvation is offered to Jews as well as to Gentiles: the hope of their response to Jesus is there: 'If the Jews abandon their unbelief, they will be put back in the place where they were; for God is able to do that' (Romans 9:23). When Jews turn to Jesus in large numbers, they will come to him through faith, during the present course of history. And the return of Jews to Palestine—although it happens under the providence of God, and although it could be the prelude to a spiritual turning of Jews to Jesus—is not in itself a specific fulfilment of biblical prophecy.

From this there follows the important point that the conflict over territorial rights in the Middle East cannot be settled by appeal to biblical predictions. A Jew who takes his Bible seriously might see things that way, but a Christian who is sensitive to the New Testament's handling of those promises and knows that Palestinian Arabs also have a historical, legal and moral claim to the land cannot view the situation so straightforwardly.[15] Sadly, many Christians who have enthused at the emergence of the state of Israel and her victories in war since 1948 have shown little understanding for the plight of the Palestinian refugee. And they do untold damage to the work of sharing Jesus Christ with Muslims. In *Crusade*, December 1976, Colin Chapman reported how an advertisement had appeared in the *New York Times* over the name of the American Board of Missions to the Jews. It included sentences such as the following:

> If you want to know where we are in history, look at the Jewish people. They are God's timepiece and the people of prophecy.... He made a covenant with Abraham, promising a large portion of the Middle East as an in-

heritance for him and his descendants. . . The convenant is unconditional. Just like his love . . . And we, knowing him who made the promise, totally support the people and land of Israel in their God-given, God-promised, God-ordained right to exist. Any person or group of nations opposed to this right isn't just fighting Israel. But God and time itself.

Shortly afterwards the advertisement was reproduced with an Arabic translation and editorial comment in a leading newspaper in Amman, Jordan. Imagine the effect of that on Arab readers, and on Arab Christians trying to bear witness to Jesus as the Saviour of all men.

The promise of Abraham fulfilled

But this brings us back to the promise to Abraham: 'The whole land of Canaan will belong to your descendants for ever' (Genesis 17:8). There are clear signs in the New Testament that this, like other prophecies we have looked at, was no longer understood in a literal way. Peter takes the word 'inheritance', which generally in the Old Testament referred to the promised land (e.g., Psalm 105:11), and uses it to refer to the Christian's inheritance in heaven (1 Peter 1:3–5). The writer to the Hebrews speaks about the 'rest' which had been promised to Israel when they settled in the promised land under Joshua, but for him the 'rest' means all that Christians are invited to enjoy in their present experience and in heaven (Hebrews 3–4). And he suggests that even for Abraham the promised land was but a symbol of the 'better country', the heavenly country which is God's ultimate goal for his people (Hebrews 11:8–16). All this suggests that God is fulfilling his promise to Abraham in a way that goes far beyond his orginal promise of a land. Indeed, Paul says as much when he declares that God promised to Abraham and his descendants not 'the land' but 'the world' (Romans 4:13)!

Yet it would be rash to conclude that the land of Palestine plays no more part in God's purpose for Israel.

Whereas the New Testament asserts that in Christ the temple and its sacrificial system have lost their literal significance, it makes no such explicit claim about the land. Perhaps in God's plan for the Jewish people there is a continuing commitment to the land—for identity and security of any people is bound up with their being rooted in a particular area of land.

Hence it seems that, to be biblical, our conclusion must be a paradoxical one. Since the coming of Christ, his followers are the people of God, inheritors of his promises to Abraham. Yet the Jews remain his people, though they fulfil their true destiny only by coming to faith in Jesus. The promise to Abraham of a land where God would work out his plans in history has given way since Christ's coming to the vision of a whole world where Jew and Gentile together may know the blessing of God in Christ. Yet God is not indifferent to the Jews' longing for a land. Whilst the return of Jews to a homeland in Palestine is not a specific fulfilment of Old Testament predictions, it is within God's providential care for his people. Yet this does not mean that Israel's right to the land is absolute and exclusive. For Palestinian Arabs, too, may claim to be descendants of Abraham.

The interpretation of prophecy

In looking at questions about the destiny of the Jews and their land, I have interpreted prophecies in a way which I believe is required by the Bible itself. In order to clarify and defend this approach, I now set out a number of principles by which prophecy should be interpreted.

1. Prophetic language is frequently poetic and therefore symbolic, even extravagant. So when the exiles in Babylon are promised that 'the hills will become a plain, and the rough country will be made smooth' (Isaiah 40:4), they are hearing the language of poetry. And when Jeremiah foresees the destruction of Jerusalem, he does so in extravagant terms which dramatise the horror of what the people of Judah will experience: 'I looked at the earth—it was a

barren waste; at the sky—there was no light. I looked at the mountains—they were shaking, and the hills were rocking to and fro' (Jeremiah 4:23f.). Such language must be understood for what it is, and not be taken with unimaginative literalism.

2. Old Testament prophecy is normally addressed to Israel as God's covenant people. Its concern is not primarily with the nations who strut across the stage of history, but with the goal of God in relation to his people. Prophecy speaks of judgment and hope for them in relation to their obedience and disobedience to the covenant which God has made with them. And if we ask, Who is God's covenant people?, the New Testament's answer is that the church of Jesus Christ shares this role. And, as we have seen, Old Testament passages addressed to Israel are applied in the New Testament to the church.

3. Prophecy is addressed to a particular historical situation. It is meant to challenge or comfort God's people at a particular time. We saw how this was the case with Ezekiel's vision of dry bones (Ezekiel 37). It is true also of the promise in Isaiah 7:14 that 'a young woman who is pregnant will have a son and will name him "Immanuel".' This was originally a promise to Ahaz, the king of Judah in Isaiah's own day, that within a year or two the threat of attack by his northern neighbours would vanish. It came to be applied to Jesus in Matthew 1:23 because the early Christians saw Jesus as fulfilling a pattern of which the Isaiah passage speaks. Jesus fulfils the hopes of Israel, including the longing for security which Isaiah 7 originally referred to. But to see Isaiah 7:14 as *primarily* a prediction of the virgin birth is to do violence to its intention in Isaiah's message.

Because prophecy is tied to a particular historical situation, it uses terms appropriate to those times. Abraham is promised a land. Exiles from a ruined Jerusalem are promised a new Temple (Ezekiel 40–48). But, as we shall see more fully below, a different historical situation at the time of fulfilment may require that the fulfilment should go beyond the literal meaning of the original prophecy. And it is because the prophecies address one particular situation that, once they are fulfilled (for example, in the return from exile), we cannot apply them in detail to another, later historical situation (for example, the Middle East today). At most we can draw general parallels, as the New Testament does, between the situation addressed by the prophet and the situation of today's 'Israel', the church.

4. Biblical prophecy is conditional. That is, it is never simply a matter of saying 'Watch it coming, there is nothing you can do to change it.' When prophets predict the future, they predict so that something can be done about it. Jonah predicted the downfall of Nineveh; his prophecy did not come true, precisely because the people of Nineveh repented at his warning. The biblical view is *not* that the course of history is predetermined like a game of chess programmed by computer. History involves human choices, including their reactions to God. And prophets address situations with words of condemnation and hope, seeking thereby to influence men's actions.

People who insist on the perpetual right of the Jewish people to the land of Palestine often stress that God's promise of the land to Abraham was unconditional. He promised the land saying, 'It is yours, as a gift'—not 'It is yours, as long as you fulfil certain conditions.' But this is to ignore the fact that conditions are often implied in the Bible even when they are not actually stated. For example, Amos predicts the almost total destruction of Samaria: 'As a shepherd recovers only two legs or an ear of a sheep that a lion has eaten, so only a few will survive of Samaria's people, who now recline on luxurious couches' (Amos 3:12).

An unconditional prophecy, it seems. Destruction is bound to happen, and cannot be averted. But elsewhere Amos says to the people of Israel 'Make it your aim to do what is right, not what is evil, so that you may live' (Amos 5:14). Here destruction can be avoided, if only the people will turn to God. So the same condition must be implied in the earlier prophecy of Amos 3:12.

And it is surely only by special pleading that the promise of the land to Abraham can be said to be unconditional. Immediately after the promise of the land in Genesis 17:8, God says to Abraham, 'You also must agree to keep the covenant with me, both you and your descendants in future generations. You and your descendants must all agree to circumcise every male among you' (Genesis 17:9f.).

So there is a condition explicitly stated—circumcision. And it is reasonable to suppose that circumcision is here a specific example of the general response of obedience, which throughout the Bible is the condition for continuing to experience God's blessing. Several times in fact Abraham and his descendants are called to obey God if they are to receive what he has promised (Genesis 18:17–19; 22:18; 26:5). When Jesus predicted the destruction of Jerusalem and declared that the kingdom would be taken away from unfaithful Jews, was he not saying that the promise of the land must now be forfeited by that generation because the condition of obedient response to God had been persistently disregarded?

5. According to the Bible's own testimony, prophecy is not always literally fulfilled. For example, Jeremiah and Isaiah predicted that Babylon would fall to the Medes (Jeremiah 2:11, 28; Isaiah 13:17), and Isaiah described graphically the total destruction of Babylon and the merciless killing of its people (Isaiah 13:14–22). But in fact Babylon fell to the Persians, who had gained control of the Medes before capturing Babylon. And Babylon surrendered without a struggle. The city was not destroyed, and continued to be inhabited. So the prophecy of Babylon's fall was fulfilled substantially, but not literally.

Similarly, Isaiah 10:28–34 prophesied the Assyrian invasion, vividly describing how the Assyrian army would come from north to south, city by city along the hills through Ai, Geba, Gibeah, Anathoth and Nob to Mount Zion itself. In fact, when Sennacherib came with his invading force he followed the sea coast and approached Jerusalem from the west.

One more example. At Pentecost Peter quoted the prophecy of Joel which spoke not only of the outpouring of the Spirit, the seeing of visions and the proclaiming of God's message, but also of blood, fire and smoke, the sun darkened and the moon turning red as blood (Acts 2:16–21). Peter says the prophecy is fulfilled, but we are given no hint that the whole prophecy was fulfilled literally.

Because the form of a prophecy reflects the conditions of the time when it is uttered, we should not be surprised to find it being fulfilled substantially but not literally. A moment's reflection will confirm how inappropriate it is to envisage a literal fulfilment of some prophecies. For instance, there is Isaiah's prophecy of a time when Assyria, Egypt and Israel will live in harmony and be a blessing to the world (Isaiah 19:19–25). Today Assyria does not exist as a nation, and most of the inhabitants of Egypt are racially quite different from the Egyptians of Isaiah's day. Such a prophecy can hardly be fulfilled literally, though it could be a picture of the peace between Jew and Gentile made possible by Christ (cf. Ephesians 2:11–22), or the ideal relations between people of all nations in God's ultimate kingdom.

6. In the goodness of God the fulfilment of a prophecy frequently goes beyond the original prediction. Think of the birth and ministry of Jesus. Who, reading the Old Testament, would have guessed that God's messiah would be exactly like the person Jesus turned out to be? Who foresaw an incarnation, a crucifixion and a resurrection as God's precise way of accomplishing our salvation? Only when the fulfilment came in the life and work of Jesus could people notice how the prophets had foreshadowed the pattern of his living and dying and resurrection. The fulfilment involves an element of surprise, of newness. For God is always moving forward, expanding the scope of his purposes, responding to new situations in unprecedented ways, giving more than he promised because he is the all-loving Father.

It was the literalists of Jesus's day who found it hard to

recognise in him the fulfilment of their expectations. Those who looked for a military and political Messiah, the natural counterpart to David, failed to see that Jesus had more, not less, to offer. Those who accused him at his trial could not get beyond a literal understanding of his prediction that within three days he would rebuild the ruined Temple (Matthew 26:61; cf. John 2:18–22).

This pattern of fulfilment exceeding prediction ought not to disturb us. It arises from the creative character of God. So when a hope is first expressed in the form of prophecy, it is cast in a form appropriate to its time. But God is free to bring that hope to fruition in a bigger way, appropriate to the time of fulfilment. John Macquarrie offers the following parallel. The founding fathers of the United States had a certain vision of what they wanted the nation to become. Now, two hundred years later, the United States both fulfils and yet does not literally fulfil what its founders visualised for it. In some ways it has failed to live up to their hopes. And yet in other ways—and this is the important point for us—it has more than fulfilled their hopes, in the sense that it has gone on to develop new implications of the constitution. These new implications were not in the minds of the founders, and yet may claim to be in continuity with their intentions—and therefore are a genuine fulfilment. It is impossible to say in advance precisely how a hope will be fulfilled, for the very nature of hope—and the creativity of God the source of hope—allows and even encourages new and unsuspected developments in the unfolding of events.[16]

Another illustration might be taken from the family. A little girl looks forward to Christmas and to the present which her parents have promised to give her. A doll that walks is what she has her heart on. Christmas Day arrives, and what is this waiting at the bottom of her bed? A doll that not only walks but talks and weeps and wets her nappy! The little girl did not even know such things had been invented, but she does not dream of complaining that she was not given what she hoped for. Of course not. She is thrilled with the ability of mum and dad to come up with surprises which more than fulfil her expectations.

So in the New Testament we find Old Testament prophecies fulfilled in surprising ways. But there is no doubt that Jesus is 'the "Yes" to all God's promises' (2 Corinthians 1:20), or that his Church is the place where so many of the promises to Israel are fulfilled. Let me cite one more example of this. Ezekiel 40–48 describes the new Temple which God has in store. Those who adopt a literalistic interpretation expect this to be fulfilled in the future on the Temple Mount in Jerusalem, and expect people of all nations to come and share in its worship and sacrifices.[17]

But this is an extraordinary expectation. It is a step backwards, not forwards, because the New Testament declares that all sacrifice has been done away with. Since Christ died to take away our sins, 'an offering to take away sins is no longer needed' (Hebrews 10:18). Recognising this problem, advocates of this view suggest that the purpose of the sacrifices will not be to atone for sin but to aid memory and celebration of Christ's death. But Jesus has given us a way of doing that in the Lord's Supper, and there is no reason to suppose that it will be exchanged for something else. No. The prophecy of the new Temple is already fulfilled in the Christian church. The presence of God which used to be specially focused in the Jerusalem temple is now made real among his people. 'Surely you know that you are God's temple and that God's Spirit lives in you!' (1 Corinthians 3:16). And in 2 Corinthians 6:16 Paul again speaks of the church as God's temple, citing a passage from Ezekiel 37:26f. which promises a new temple for God's people. He could hardly have stated any more clearly that Ezekiel's prophecy is fulfilled in Christ's church!

7. Because of this tendency of prophecy to be fulfilled in ways which could not be precisely foreseen, we must read the Old Testament in the light of the New. Christian prophetic interpretation has no right to use Old Testament prophecies as though the New Testament had never been written and had never put its own stamp on the significance of those prophecies. Time and again we see in the New Testament that the expectations of the prophets reach their

goal not in political, historical events but in the person and work of Jesus and in the life of his church.

8. Even the books of Daniel and Revelation, which offer an apocalyptic type of prophecy with apparently precise descriptions of future events, do not in fact give us a detailed plan for the future. We have already seen the contradictions involved in trying to handle these books in such a way. And I have argued that the course of history is more open than such an interpretation would imply.

The heart of Daniel's message is that, despite appearances in an age of persecution by totalitarian powers, the Lord is king. The kingdoms of this world will give way to a kingdom which comes from God. Because the ultimate outcome is certain, men of faith can remain faithful, even when subjected to a den of lions or a fiery furnace. They know that even death does not have the last word, for beyond it lies the gift of resurrection (Daniel 12:3).

The message of the Revelation to John is not very different, except that the whole of history and Christian experience is now viewed in the light of Jesus, the slaughtered Lamb whose death means victory over evil. The Christian faces his suffering in the assurance that his Lord is 'Jesus Christ, the faithful witness, the first to be raised from death and who is also the ruler of the kings of the world' (Revelation 1:5).

> John is not interpreting the future. John is interpreting the *significance* of the cross and the resurrection *for the future*. John is not looking at a sneak preview of history down through the corridors of time to the end; he is declaring God's revelation of *the meaning* of the cross-resurrection *for time and history until the end*.[18]

There is another important point which tells against the view that Revelation depicts specific events of history leading up to Christ's second coming. The central part of the book describes three sets of visions—the seven seals (6:1–8:5), the seven trumpets (8:6–11:19), the seven bowls (15:1–16:21). These are commonly taken to be a continuous narration of events leading up to the second coming—either a description of significant events right through history since the first century, or a sequence of events in the final years before the end. Hal Lindsey's *There's a New World Coming* expounds this latter view. But the fact that the *visions* follow in sequence is not necessarily a reason for believing that they represent a continuous *historical* sequence. And there are in fact good reasons for believing that the three groups of seven events are *parallel* accounts of the same period.[19] In particular, it is noticeable that the events described in these three visions are very similar to those described by Jesus in his teaching about the 'signs of the end' in Mark 13 (and the parallel passages, Matthew 24 and Luke 21). I have already argued that Mark 13 does not point to specific events which can be identified so as to fix dates, but describes the kind of things which Jesus's followers may expect through history. Exactly the same may be said of these visions in Revelation. The seals, the trumpets and the bowls describe the impact of the battle between God and evil within history. And John has been allowed, for the sake of his readers, to glimpse that history from God's standpoint and to see in it the ultimate victory of the cross.

Will there be a millennium?

In Revelation 20 John describes a vision about a period of a thousand years ('millennium' in Latin), during which Satan is chained up so that he can deceive the nations no more. Meanwhile those who have been martyred for Christ's sake are brought to life again ('the first resurrection') and reign with him for the thousand years. After the thousand years are over, Satan is released to deceive the nations again for a short period, but then meets with final defeat. There follows the description of final judgment and the new heaven and new earth.

Interpreters of this passage have divided into three main schools of thought.[20] *Premillennialists* argue that Christ's second coming will precede the millennium. Jesus will come after the period of turmoil and suffering described in passages such as Mark 13 and 2 Thessalonians 2. He will raise up dead believers and will bring them, together with those Christians who are alive at his coming, to share in his rule on earth over the unbelieving nations for a thousand years. During this thousand-year period Satan will be bound, and so evil will be greatly reduced, though sin and death will still exist. It will be a time of peace, justice and prosperity. At the end of the millennium there will be a brief final rebellion of Satan, which will be put down. There will follow the resurrection and judgment of the unbelieving dead, and the new heaven and new earth. Premillennialism takes its starting-point from the natural assumption that Revelation 20 describes events which follow after what is described in chapter 19—the second coming of Christ. It is a view held by many Christians ever since the book of Revelation was written, and is therefore sometimes called 'historic premillennialism'. It interprets Scripture fairly literally, and sees many Old Testament prophecies of peace and prosperity as being fulfilled in the millennium. It has the strength of showing how Christ's work *on earth* reaches its climax in the demonstration of his victory *on earth*. There is a logic in saying that Christ's rule, which at present is hidden and often denied and resisted on earth, will in the millennium be revealed and asserted on earth.

Postmillennialism is the view that Jesus will come again *after* the millennium. As Christ increasingly extends his rule, the present age will merge into the millennium. This millennium (not necessarily a period of exactly a thousand years) will be marked by peace and justice and the restraint of evil on earth. The gospel will triumph, the world will be truly Christianised, though not every individual will be a Christian, and sin will not be totally eradicated. Christ will then return to a world where his work of salvation has met with marvellous success. Thus postmillennialism, like premillennialism, expects Old Testament promises of a future 'golden age' to be literally fulfilled in the millennium. It has a welcome emphasis on the power of the gospel to win the hearts of men and women and to transform society. This is a welcome corrective to the tendency—common among premillennialists—to think that human society can only go from bad to worse.

Amillennialism is so called because it rejects belief in a literal future earthly millennium (the prefix *a-* in Greek means 'not'). On this view, Revelation 20 is a symbolic description of the present age during which Satan is already bound and the dead in Christ are already reigning with him. In defence of this view, which I favour, the following points may be made:

1. I have already argued that the structure of the book of Revelation involved *parallelism*—visions which follow each other in the book do not describe events in a chronological sequence, but describe the same events in different ways or from different angles. The thousand years of Revelation 20 would thus be a further example of this pattern—the whole of Christian history viewed from the viewpoint of Christ's victory over Satan, beginning with his earthly ministry, death and resurrection.

2. This approach fits in well with the generally symbolic character of John's visions, and it resolves the problem as to why there is no reference to a millennium in the teaching of Jesus, Paul, or other New Testament writers. There seems in fact to be no room for a millennium in Jesus's teaching about the kingdom, or in Paul's expectation. They both contrast 'this age' with 'the age to come' in a way which rules out any long intervening period (e.g., Mark 10:30; Ephesians 1:21).

3. The source of the language about 'binding Satan' (Revelation 20:2) is naturally found in Jesus's image of the binding of the strong man in Mark 3:27. By general agreement, Jesus is there referring to the overcoming of Satan which he began in his ministry and demonstrated in his exorcisms. Thus John's statement that Satan is bound 'So

that he could not deceive the nations any more until the thousand years were over' (Revelation 20:3) would be another way of saying that Jesus's first coming involved decisive victory over Satan's power (cf. Luke 10:17f.; John 12:31; Colossians 2:15) and heralded the preaching of the Gospel to Gentile nations who had previously been deceived by Satan (cf. Matthew 28:18–20). Some may argue that Satan at present seems to enjoy fairly unrestricted power, and that amillennialism therefore fails to do justice to Revelation's assertion that Satan is bound and put out of action. But they must argue their case not only with amillennialists but also with Jesus and Paul and their insistence that in a real sense Satan has been defeated, even though that defeat will not be finalised until Jesus's second coming.

4. Contrary to the assumption of premillennialists, Revelation does not say that the thrones from which Christ and his people rule are on earth. Surely they are in heaven, like all the other thrones in Revelation, apart from those of Satan and 'the beast'. 'The first resurrection' of Christ's faithful people—their coming to life to share in his millennial reign—refers to their sharing in his rule from heaven now, during the period between his first and second comings (Revelation 20:4f.). ('The rest of the dead' who in verse 5 'did not come to life until the thousand years were over' are the unbelieving dead.)

Against premillennialism, we may add:

1. The final judgment, described in Revelation 20:11–15, is elsewhere in the New Testament linked directly with Jesus's second coming (e.g., Revelation 22:12; Matthew 16:27; 25:31f.; 2 Thessalonians 1:7–10). It is difficult, therefore, to insert a long period of time between the coming and the judgment.

2. If Christ were to come and reign with his saints in a millennial world still subject to sin and death, this would be a step backwards from the glory in which they have already begun to share. It would undermine the finality of their experience of glory, and it would cut across the general New Testament teaching that Christ will come 'to usher in,

not an interim period of qualified peace and blessing, but the final state of unqualified perfection'.[21]

3. As we have already seen, there are great difficulties in looking for literal fulfilment of those Old Testament prophecies about Israel's future peace and blessing— promises about the restoration of temple sacrifices, or about peaceful relations with Assyria and Egypt. Rather than look for their fulfilment in a future millennial period, it is more consistent with the New Testament's general handling of Old Testament prophecy to look for their fulfilment in the eternal state, the 'new heaven and new earth' of Revelation 21. Indeed, Revelation 21:3 cites the promise, 'I will be their God, and they will be my people', from Ezekiel 37:27. This passage in Ezekiel is about the new Temple, whose fulfilment many premillennialists would expect in the millennium. But here is John in Revelation promising its fulfilment in the *new* earth, God's eternal destination for his people.

Postmillennialism is in many ways similar to amillennialism, and we need particularly to learn from its vision of what the triumphant Christ *can* achieve in human history. But its weaknesses include its apparent failure to take seriously the ongoing conflict in history between the rule of God and the forces of evil. Nor does it do justice to the biblical theme of the intensification of evil before the end, as found for example in 2 Thessalonians 2. The themes of intensifying evil and of the increasing triumph of Christ must be held together, even if they cannot be tidily harmonised. Finally, there is the difficulty that a postmillennialist must find it hard to 'long for' the coming of Christ or to 'be ready' for it at any moment, since he is expecting the millennium to intervene before Christ's coming.[22]

The trouble with Dispensationalism

There is one more 'ism' to deal with. This is a specific form of premillennialism known as 'dispensational premillennialism' or 'dispensationalism'. Although dispensationalists like to refer to themselves as premillennialists and to give the impression that their viewpoint goes back to the premillennialism of the early church fathers, this impression is quite misleading.[23] Dispensationalism derives mainly from J. N. Darby, one of the early leaders of the Brethren movement towards the middle of the nineteenth century. It received classical expression in the *Scofield Reference Bible*, first published by C. I. Scofield in 1909. Modern dispensational writers include J. D. Pentecost, C. C. Ryrie, J. F. Walvoord, and Hal Lindsey—though Lindsey's writings rarely use the term 'dispensationalism' (as is understandable in popular books) and have hence been widely assumed by less-informed readers to represent the standard evangelical understanding of prophecy. The combination of dispensationalism's extreme interpretation of scripture with its extreme popularity—even among people who have never heard the term 'dispensationalism'—makes it a dangerous force in the church. To try to justify this statement, I will now list the main features of the scheme, adding my criticisms as we go along.

1. Literal interpretation of scripture. Scofield wrote that in the prophetic scriptures 'we reach the ground of absolute literalness. Figures are often found in the prophecies, but the figure invariably has a literal fulfilment. Not one instance exists of a "spiritual" or figurative fulfilment of prophecy . . . Jerusalem is always Jerusalem, Israel is always Israel, Zion is always Zion . . . Prophecies may never be spiritualised, but are always literal.'[24] This principle commits dispensationalists to an unusually strong emphasis on the future—for prophecies which have not yet been literally fulfilled *must* reach their literal fulfilment in the future. It leads them to expect that the boundaries of the land promised to Abraham will literally be restored in the millennium; that Christ will return to sit on a physical throne in Jerusalem to rule a political kingdom with David as regent and a government patterned after existing national governments.[25]

Confusion is multiplied by dispensationalists' tendency to use the word 'literal' in its old-fashioned sense, referring

to the normal and natural usage of words.[26] What they are
really objecting to is the kind of allegorical interpretation
which fails to take seriously what the biblical author intended when he wrote.

But it is over-simplifying to imply that there is a
straight choice between 'literal' and 'allegorical', and that
'non-literal' is therefore equivalent to 'villainous'. I have
given numerous examples in this chapter of how God's
fulfilment of prophecy overflows the bounds apparently
set by the form of the original prophecy, and we shall
see in the following pages what tortuous results
ensue from the attempt to stick to a literal method of
interpretation.

2. A chronological scheme for the future not known
before Darby thought of it. The scheme goes like this:

a) A period of apostasy before Jesus comes;
b) Jesus will come in secret, and will take both dead and
living Christians to be with himself—the so-called 'secret
rapture';
c) A seven-year period known as the tribulation, in which
Antichrist will rule the earth;
d) Then Christ will appear from heaven openly, and will
overthrow Antichrist at Armageddon. This will usher
in Christ's thousand-year reign at Jerusalem, and the
Temple and sacrificial worship will be restored;
e) After the thousand years Satan will be loosed again
and will stir up rebellion against God. His defeat will be
followed by the resurrection and judgment of the wicked,
and then the final, eternal state.

I make no comment at this point on the scheme itself—
derived largely from the book of Revelation. But the newness of the scheme, coupled with the tendency by many of
its advocates to suspect the faithfulness of Christians who
adopt other more traditional positions, ought to make us
cautious about it.

3. A scheme of dispensations which gives the doctrine its

name. Scofield defined a dispensation as 'a period of time during which man is tested in respect of obedience to some specific revelation of the will of God.'[27] The seven dispensations are Innocency, Conscience, Human Government (beginning with Noah), Promise, Law (from Moses to Christ), Grace (the age of the Church) and Kingdom (the Millennium).

This programme of dispensations and the sequence of eight covenants which, according to Scofield, goes along with it, implies that God deals with men and women in quite different ways in different periods. It shatters the unity of scripture and of the purpose of God. It places law in opposition to grace, whereas Paul's argument in Galatians 3 is that the Law serves to further the gospel's ends. It implies that in most dispensations, if not in the dispensations of Promise and Grace, salvation is through works, not faith. But throughout the Bible God's salvation is always a work of his grace, received by faith and followed by the response of obedience.

4. A sharp division between Israel and the church. The promise made to Israel in the Old Testament must be fulfilled literally, and must be fulfilled for literal, racial or national Israel. So all the promises of peace and prosperity for Israel in the Holy Land will be fulfilled during the millennium. Even the promise of a new covenant (Jeremiah 31:31–34) is essentially a promise for Israel, and will therefore not be fulfilled until the millennium. The Christian church is quite distinct from Israel and cannot be the heir of God's Old Testament promises to Israel. The church is in fact a mystery, hidden from the Old Testament prophets. It came about like this:

During his ministry, Jesus offered the kingdom of heaven—an earthly rule over Israel, in literal fulfilment of Old Testament prophecies—to the Jews of his day. The Jews rejected the kingdom, and so it was postponed until a future millennium. In the meantime, Christ introduced the 'mystery form' of the kingdom—the church, where God is at work during the present age. Since the church was not predicted in the Old Testament, it is a kind of detour in the plan of God. It is often said that, when the Jews rejected Christ's offer of the kingdom, the prophetic time-clock was stopped, and will not be re-started until Jesus comes again to gather to church into his presence. The effect of this image, if not the intention, is to make the church age seem like the half-time interval at a football match—a necessary interlude, perhaps, but not a part of the real game. In keeping with this idea of the stopping of the prophetic clock, dispensationalist interpreters of Daniel 9:24–27 make the quite arbitrary claim that Daniel's sixty-nine weeks were completed at Christ's first coming, but that the seventieth week will not begin until the 'rapture', when Christ comes to remove the church from the world.

Other implications follow. Jesus's message about the kingdom—an earthly, political kingdom—is seen as quite distinct from the gospel of grace preached by the church. The millennial kingdom will concern the Jewish people rather than the whole people of God. And because Jesus's teaching in the gospels was addressed to Jews, it cannot be applied directly to the Christian. Words of Jesus which most Christians hold dear—the sermon on the mount, the Lord's prayer, and much more—are 'kingdom truths', which cannot be properly followed until the millennial kingdom comes. The Acts and Epistles, by contrast, are for the church now.

This whole way of distinguishing between Israel and the church will seem extraordinary except to people whose thinking has long been shaped by it. It destroys the Bible's picture of an ongoing plan of God through history. It discounts (as we saw earlier in the chapter) the way in which New Testament writers constantly see Old Testament promises to Israel as coming to fulfilment in the church, the true people of God. It turns the message of Jesus into a legalistic message intended for Jews, instead of a message about God's overwhelming grace to the poor, the outcast, the sinner.

5. The rapture and the tribulation. According to most

dispensationalists, Jesus may come at any time to gather into his presence both dead and living Christians. They will be 'carried away' to meet him in the air (1 Thessalonians 4:15–18; Matthew 24:40). This is the 'secret rapture'. After the church has been removed from earth in this way, Jews and Gentiles left behind will experience the 'tribulation', which represents the Seventieth 'week' of Daniel 9:27, and is described in Matthew 24 and Revelation 6–19. During this seven-year period of unprecedented suffering, a remnant of Israel (the 144,000) will find salvation and 'like 144,000 Jewish Billy Grahams turned loose at once'[28] they will bring countless Gentiles to faith in Jesus (Revelation 7). After seven years, the latter half of which is known as 'the great tribulation', Christ will come to establish his millennial rule, bringing the church to rule with him.

Here again we see dispensationalism's insistence on keeping Israel and the church distinct. The notion of spiriting the church away before the 'tribulation' derives not from any statement of scripture, but from the belief that Israel must go through the tribulation, and *therefore* the church cannot.

There are three other serious problems with this teaching. First, the idea that believers will be off the scene before the worst sufferings in history occur may be very comforting. But it contradicts the New Testament's insistence that Christians are preserved not from suffering but *through* suffering. Nothing in Jesus's teaching in Matthew 24 suggests that tribulation will be restricted to Jews, or to Jews and unbelieving Gentiles. Suffering is one of the distinguishing marks of the Christian's life, as it was of his Lord's.

Secondly, the New Testament does not talk about a *secret* rapture. There is nothing secret about Jesus's coming in Matthew 24: it is 'like lightning', 'with power and great glory', and 'the great trumpet will sound' (Matthew 24:27, 30f.). Thirdly, this scheme involves not one future coming but two: a secret coming *for* his saints (the rapture, 1 Thessalonians 4:15–18) and a public coming *with* his saints (1 Thessalonians 3:13). Once again, a literalistic approach is failing to recognise that New Testament writers are capable of writing about a single event in a variety of ways. In 1 Thessalonians 3:13 the 'holy ones' are probably not Christian people but angels—a quotation from Zechariah 14:5 (cf. the reference to angels in 2 Thessalonians 1:7). It is in fact impossible to sustain the distinction between two comings. The same technical terms—'coming', 'revelation', 'appearing'—are used in the New Testament to describe Jesus's coming to gather his people and his coming for judgment. The Scofield Bible's attempt to distinguish between 'the day of Christ' and 'the day of the Lord' runs aground on the fact that, in the New Testament, these supposedly distinct 'days' serve the same purpose. And passages such as 2 Thessalonians 1:5–10 and Matthew 24:36–44 show clearly enough that judgment and salvation are part of a single event.

6. The millennium. Dispensationalists say the character of the kingdom will be predominantly Jewish, though they vary as to whether the church will share in it. The nations of earth will be subject to Israel. The temple and its sacrifices will be restored. I have already argued that this is inconsistent with the New Testament's description of the church as God's temple, and the gospel message that the death of Jesus was the ultimate sacrifice which ended the need for all other sacrifice.

7. Apostate Christendom. This is a regular theme of dispensationalism, going right back to Darby and his break with the established church. A sharp distinction is made between the true church, which is invisible and heavenly, and the visible church whose end is apostasy. This makes dispensationalists prone to separatism and dissension. The Scofield Bible urges the true believer to 'separate' when apostates are discovered (p. 1279, note 1). But for all his conviction about the dangers in mainstream churches, Scofield is utterly confused in his attempts to provide a biblical basis for this teaching about apostasy. He fails to make meaningful distinctions between apostasy, heresy and error. He offers no grounds for his assumption that

apostasy is incurable. He fails to do justice to the fact that the New Testament writers—insistent as they are about the dangers of false teaching—never tell anyone to withdraw from fellowship with other professing Christians. And it is all very well for some modern dispensationalist writers to tirade against false teaching in the World Council of Churches and see it as a sign that the end is near. But it is time they asked themselves what damage has been caused to the unity of Christ's church by the more dogmatic and exclusivist exponents of their own doctrines.

Conclusion

Dispensationalism's literalist approach to scripture *seems* reverent, and this is no doubt one reason for its popularity. It claims to give a clear meaning to prophetic scriptures which might otherwise appear obscure and remote. When coupled with the vivid style and confident predictions of its more popular advocates, it gives to those scriptures a detailed relevance which makes other interpretations seem vague and unexciting. But this seemingly reverent and relevant use of prophetic passages in fact involves an extreme form of determinism. Dispensationalists who stress the importance of human free will in their evangelistic preaching today insist that, during the tribulation, exactly 144,000 Jews will be converted—because Revelation 7 (understood in a particular way) says they will. It is all so certain, and so different from the more open approach to the future which (I have argued) is characteristic of the prophets. What seems at first sight to be a reverent approach to scripture turns out to be an instance of the 'lust for certitude', the longing to walk by sight in an era when we are called to walk by faith (2 Corinthians 5:7; cf. 1 Corinthians 13:12).

It is indeed extraordinary that such popularity should be attached to a teaching which holds out as the hope of the world the removal of the church from the world, followed by the proclamation of a Jewish gospel by a Jewish remnant during the tribulation. In effect, dispensationalism diminishes the role of the Christian church. It assigns the great commission (Matthew 28:18–20) not to the church but to the Jewish remnant after the rapture to the church. It thus expects the Lord to achieve *after* his coming the work which he has in fact committed to the church *now*, and for which he has promised the Holy Spirit's power.[29]

Notes to chapter 4

1. Rabbi Jose, quoted in D. S. Russell, *The Method and Message of Jewish Apocalyptic* (SCM, London, 1964), p. 187.
2. Quoted in C. E. Armerding and W. W. Gasque (eds.), *Handbook of Biblical Prophecy* (Baker, Grand Rapids, 1977), p. 29. I have found this book useful on several issues discussed in this chapter.
3. T. F. Torrance, *Kingdom and Church* (Oliver & Boyd, Edinburgh and London, 1956) p. 20.
4. See *Handbook of Biblical Prophecy*, pp. 33–6.
5. Quoted in S. N. Gundry, 'Hermeneutics or *Zeitgeist*, as the Determining Factor in the History of Eschatologies?', *Journal of the Evangelical Theological Society* 20, 1977, p. 53.
6. As Hal Lindsey claims in *There's a New World Coming* (Coverdale, London, 1974), p. 7.
7. *Christianity Today* vol. 21, no. 14, p. 40.
8. Scholars differ over what exactly the 40+450 years are meant to cover, but this does not affect my basic point, that biblical numbers often do not correspond precisely to chronological reality.
9. 'The Functions of some so-called Apocalyptic Timetables', *New Testament Studies* 22, 1975, p. 14.
10. For this general approach to Mark 13 and parallel passages, see C. E. B. Cranfield, *St. Mark* (CUP, Cambridge, second edition, 1963), pp. 387ff.
11. 'The Christian Hope', *Eternity* 5 (March, 1954), p. 50, quoted in *Handbook of Biblical Prophecy*, p. 37.
12. E.g., Tatford, *The Climax of the Ages* (Oliphants, London, 1964); *God's Programme of the Ages* (Prophetic Witness, Eastbourne, 1968); *Prophecy's Last Word* (Pickering & Inglis, Glasgow, 1969); Lambert, *Battle for Israel* (Coverdale, Eastbourne, 1976).
13. For what follows I am indebted to R. T. France, 'Old Testament Prophecy and the Future of Israel: a Study of the Teaching of Jesus', *Tyndale Bulletin* 26, 1975, pp. 53–78.
14. J. Goldingay, 'The Christian Church and Israel', *Theological Renewal* no. 23, March 1983, p. 7.
15. But the Christian can and must try to understand sympathetically the feelings which many Jews have about the land of Israel. Abraham Heschel, for example, wrote, 'What should have been our answer to Auschwitz? . . . Is the State of Israel God's

humble answer to Auschwitz? . . . And yet, there is no answer to Auschwitz. To try to answer is to commit a supreme blasphemy. Israel enables us to bear the agony of Auschwitz without radical despair, to sense a ray of God's radiance in the jungles of history'— *Israel: an Echo of Eternity* (Noonday, New York, 1967), pp. 112–15. A Christian can be deeply moved by this, and see God's involvement in it, without affirming that specific prophecies are fulfilled in this way.

16. *Christian Hope* (Mowbrays, Oxford, 1978), pp. 14f. He has a thought-provoking discussion of what this means for the promise to Abraham (pp. 49–55).

17. E.g., Lindsey, *The Late Great Planet Earth*, p. 56.

18. D. Ezell, *Revelations on Revelation* (Word, Waco, 1977), p. 22.

19. See discussion in G. R. Beasley-Murray, *The Book of Revelation* (Oliphants, London, 1974), pp. 28–32, 129f.

20. I shall not deal at length with these various views of the millennium. To do so would only repeat the good discussions in Armerding and Gasque (eds.), *Handbook of Biblical Prophecy*; A. A. Hoekema, *The Bible and the Future* (Paternoster, Exeter, 1979); B. Milne, *The End of the World* (Kingsway, Eastbourne, 1979).

21. Hoekema, *The Bible and the Future*, p. 185.

22. D. G. Bloesch has a helpful discussion of how proper account may be taken of the true insights of the other two positions, within a basically amillennialist position: *Essentials of Evangelical Theology*: vol. 2., *Life, Ministry and Hope* (Harper, San Francisco, 1979), pp. 196–204.

23. Examples of this blurring of distinctions between historic premillennialism and dispensationalism are in J. D. Pentecost, *Things to Come* (Zondervan, Grand Rapids, 1964), chapter 22; and C. C. Ryrie cited in C. B. Bass, *Backgrounds to Dispensationalism* (Eerdmans, Grand Rapids, 1960), p. 13.

24. *Scofield Bible Correspondence Course*, quoted in Bass, p. 150.

25. Not all dispensationalists, however, expect Jesus to rule from a literal earthly throne. Pentecost speaks of him ruling from the heavenly Jerusalem, where the church also will be during the millennium (*Things to Come*, p. 546).

26. E.g., Pentecost, *Things to Come*, pp. 1–15, 39–44, 60.

27. *Scofield Reference Bible* (1917), p. 5, n. 4.

28. Lindsey, *There's a New World Coming*, p. 123.

29. Cf. O. T. Allis, *Prophecy and the Church* (Presbyterian and Reformed, Philadelphia, 1945), pp. 252–62. Readers wanting a fuller critique of dispensationalism than I can give here should consult the books by Allis, Bass and Hoekema; also W. J. Grier *The Momentous Event* (Banner of Truth, Edinburgh, 1970), and J. Barr, *Fundamentalism* (SCM, London, 1977), pp. 190–207.

Chapter 5   Hope Beyond Death

'In the midst of life we are in death,' says the Prayer Book. An approach to life cannot be realistic, let alone Christian, unless it takes account of this fact. The chief purpose of Jesus's coming again, according to the New Testament, is to pass judgment on the lives of all men and to gather his people into God's eternal kingdom. So in this and the next chapter we shall look at how Christian hope responds to these facts of every human life: our death which comes to meet us at some unknown moment, and our responsibility towards God for the way we live our lives.

The hard reality of death

We saw in chapter 1 the anguish of Ecclesiastes' questions. Does death not make life a nonsense? If God is there, why does the same death happen to the good and the bad, to man and animal alike? In Job a similar note is struck:

> There is hope for a tree that has been cut down;
> it can come back to life and sprout . . .
> But a man dies, and that is the end of him;
> he dies, and where is he then?
> Like rivers that stop running,
> and lakes that go dry,
> people die, never to rise (Job 14:7–11).

When David's son died, he said, 'I will some day go to where he is, but he can never come back to me' (2 Samuel 12:23). How often must that cry, mingling despair with resignation, have been echoed by parents bending over the lifeless body of a child.

Human beings alone among God's creatures know that we are going to die. In his *Eclogue for Xmas* Louis Macneice laments this knowledge:

The tin toys of the hawker move on the pavements
    inch by inch
Not knowing they are wound up. It is better to be so
Than to be, like us, wound up and, while running down,
    to know.

But to know we are running down is a responsibility we must learn to bear. Writers of every age have expressed the horror of it. The Greek playwright Aeschylus declared:

When the dust drinks up a man's blood,
Once he has died, there is no resurrection
    (*Eumenides* 647f.).

In the National Museum in Rome there is an ancient mosaic of a man's skeleton, with just a hint of flesh and muscles. The one indication that the man is still living is his over-large index finger, pointing to the inscription KNOW YOURSELF. Does it mean, 'Know yourself—and the most basic thing about yourself is your death'? Or 'You are doomed to die, therefore come to terms with yourself'? Or both, perhaps? In either case, it is a vivid and eerie reminder that death makes no exceptions when looking for his victims.

This was brought home at the funeral sermon for Louis XIV of France, the 'Sun-King' who presided over a court of rare magnificence and extravagance. Masillon, the most famous preacher of the day, looked down at the dead king's coffin and then at the thousands gathered in Notre Dame. 'God alone is great, my brothers,' he began. Yes, God alone is great, and in death every man of the earth is reduced to his proper size.

Dying is feared by many because it is an experience we do not control. By its very nature, it is an act of letting go. And that comes hard to people who have spent a lifetime trying to control events, to do things rather than just let things happen. And it is a lonely experience. A group of theologians or philosophers or undertakers or soldiers can have an interesting discussion about death and dying. But each must die alone. Yet it is not the experience of dying so much as the fact of being dead which we fear most. 'We only die once,' said Molière, 'and for such a long time.' And Shakespeare's Hamlet comes to see that it is not just a matter of 'to be or not to be'. There is also

> the dread of something after death,
> The undiscovered country from whose bourn
> No traveller returns.

Death is unwelcome because it leaves things unfinished, goals not achieved. The poignancy of this is often felt, whether the dying person be young or old. Dylan Thomas urged his dying father to struggle against death rather than face it with resignation:

> Do not go gentle into that good night,
> Old age should burn and rave at close of day;
> Rage, rage against the dying of the light.[1]

This leads us to another point. Fear of one's own death is often easier to bear than grief at the death of another. Arnold Toynbee wrote movingly about his abhorrence at the prospect of surviving the death of someone close to him. 'There are two parties to the suffering that death inflicts; and, in the apportionment of this suffering, the survivor takes the brunt.'[2]

Death has become in the twentieth century a subject of embarrassment, a matter of whispered uncertainties. A main reason for this is that death has ceased to be part of our regular lives. The act of dying has been removed from the home to the hospital, from the neighbourhood to the newspaper and television. Many people reach middle age without ever being close to a dying person. And because death has ceased to be a 'natural' part of life, we have difficulty coping with its reality. Death, we think, is something which only happens to other people.

How much better to adopt the existentialist philosophy of Martin Heidegger, who said that we can only make sense of life if we recognise that the whole of life is a 'being towards death'. Just as a piece of music or a football match would lose its point if it went on for ever, so death brings meaning to life because it sets a boundary. Death enables life to be formed into a finite whole. This approach is certainly preferable to the comparative silence about death which one often finds in humanist philosophers. For example, H. J. Blackham's *Humanism* claims to present the 'human case and the human cause', and to be 'taking and tackling human life in the world'. Yet the book says almost nothing about suffering, pain, evil and death.[3]

Yet there is something in us which cries out for immortality. And Heidegger's stress on the value of coming to terms with death is only one side of the picture. For the unpredictability of the time of our death makes havoc of his notion of living towards death in order to make a satisfying finite whole. What can his philosophy say to the teenager dying of leukemia, or the young mother who dies giving birth to her child?

How then can we assess this longing for immortality, this sense of survival beyond death which has been part of man's thinking for as long as we have any knowledge of him?[4] In the first place, we must stress that there is a world of difference between a sense of survival and a developed belief in personal experience of a full and eternal life beyond death. We can see the development from the one to the other beginning in the Old Testament. From early times the Hebrews, like other ancient peoples, believed in a continued existence after death which was a feeble, shadowy reflection of life on earth. Death was a weak form of life, where no distinction was made between good and bad people. All were together in Sheol, the world of the dead (cf. Job 10:21f.; Psalm 88:11, 15; 115:17). It was a bit like a dump for old cars, where they could rust away, engines silent for ever, just a dim reflection of their former glory and power.

The necessity of life after death

But two factors provoked the Hebrews to discover belief in a life after death which was fuller and better than this life rather than a faint echo of it. These factors remain for us the chief reasons why faith in God requires belief in life after death if it is to make sense.

The first factor is the sense of justice, which surfaces very clearly in Daniel. To people facing extreme persecution there comes the promise: 'Many of those who have already died will live again: some will enjoy eternal life, and some will suffer eternal disgrace' (Daniel 12:2; cf. Isaiah 26:19). Only in this way can there be an answer to the problem why God, if he is just, allows persecutors and evil men to triumph in this life, while the righteous are tormented and done to death. We may broaden the argument from Daniel's particular concern with the persecution of Jewish people. For the problem of suffering and evil in all its facets can be 'solved' only if there is another life beyond this one, where wrongs can be set right and suffering can give way to fullness of life. Wolfhart Pannenberg puts the issue like this: 'In some sense atheism has a point in arguing that the world ought to be different if there were a God who cares for man and even for every individual . . . Only the full manifestation of God's kingdom in the future . . . can finally decide about the reality of God.'[5]

The second factor which gave rise to belief in eternal life was the growing conviction that the deep fellowship with God experienced in this life simply could not stop at death. If God cares for us so much that he enters into relationship with us, and if God is eternal, it is impossible to believe that he would allow death to bring this relationship to an end. The Psalmist wrote: 'You guide me with your instruction and at the end you will receive me with honour. What else

161

have I in heaven but you? Since I have you, what else could I want on earth?' (Psalm 73:23f.). And again.

> . . . I feel completely secure, because you protect me from the power of death, and the one you love you will not abandon to the world of the dead.
> You will show me the path that leads to life; your presence fills me with joy and brings me pleasure for ever (Psalm 16:9–11; cf. 49:15).

These passages do not clearly demonstrate a hope for real relationship with God beyond death, but they show a sense of present relationship with God which is bound to lead to such a hope.

A further reason why life after death is a necessary part of our belief is that it is required for personal fulfilment. For countless millions in this life, potential is cut short by death; growth is stunted by circumstances. If we are made by God for fellowship with him and for the full development of the gifts he has given us, it is hard to see that purpose being realised except in a life beyond death. 'So much to do, so little done,' said Cecil Rhodes on his deathbed. Is this sense of incompleteness not to be answered by God by the possibility of a full and unrestricted life in his presence?

Is life after death conceivable?

Have I given the game away? Do Christians believe in life after death because we *need* to believe it, because we could make no sense of life without it? This is a serious charge, and needs to be dealt with on two levels. In the first place there has been much debate among philosophers as to whether it makes any sense to talk about life after death. Secondly, even if it is logically possible to conceive of life after death, is there in fact any evidence which would point to such a belief?

First, then, we consider whether it makes sense to talk about life after death.[6] The main problem here is whether there is any reason to suppose that any 'part' of us lives on after the death of the body. The old concept of the soul, which used to safeguard the continuity of the person from this life into the next, has been largely abandoned in modern thought. Man's nature is thought of as a unity; he does not consist of two parts, a physical body which dies and a soul which lives on for ever. His 'soul' or 'self' or 'personality' is simply a function of the brain. So when the brain dies, the person dies, and there is nothing left over to enter upon another life. This theory of 'mind-brain identity' is widely accepted among philosophers. And it finds popular expression in Bertrand Russell's words, 'I believe that when I die I rot.'

However, the arguments are not all on one side. H. D. Lewis and other scholars have argued powerfully that the self cannot be reduced to a mere function of the brain.[7] The self uses the brain rather as a broadcasting station makes use of a television receiver to communicate its pictures. But the self is not destroyed when the brain dies, any more than the broadcasting station is destroyed when the television set is smashed to pieces. I will mention here two arguments against the mind-brain identity theory, which regards the mind or self merely as a process within the brain.

First, we all in fact behave as though there were an 'I' who is the *subject* or our bodies' experiences, and not merely a part of those experiences. If there is no such 'I' over and above our bodies, our experience is arbitrary and meaningless. Concepts such as freedom and responsibility make no sense. For if all the cells in my body are different from what they were seven years ago, why do I still feel responsible for what I did then? As a matter of fact, we all sense a continuity of responsibility for our actions. This persistent aspect of human experience cannot be lightly set aside.

The second point is this. Like any determinist system, the mind-brain identity theory is self-refuting, because if it were true it would be impossible to demonstrate the validity of any argument. If our minds are physically determined and are the outcome of processes in the brain, we have no way of deciding whether one theory is true as compared with another. Only if we are free agents, existing in some sense over and above the chemical and electrical processes in our brains, can we check the validity of our own reasoning. A computer—which in effect is what our minds would be if thought were *merely* a function of brain cells—can calculate many things, but cannot check the validity of its own programming. So the mind-brain identity theory can, on its own presuppositions, offer no reason why we should believe it. It makes sense to believe in a mind or self or person which is distinct from the physical body and which could therefore survive the body's death and decay.

A related problem which the philosophers discuss is the problem of *continuity*. If at death the body becomes lifeless and disintegrates, how can we say that at some future time the dead person will be raised to life and will be demonstrably the same person? For there are three factors which we normally appeal to in order to demonstrate that a person is the same person as someone we knew at an earlier date. The three factors are memory (does he remember things which happened to him in former times?), bodily identity (is he physically the same person as before?), and continuity of character or mental characteristics (does he have the same temperament, sense of humour, emotional reactions, etc., by which I recognised him formerly?). Now, when a person dies, bodily identity is clearly lost—unless we are to imagine a resurrection life which strictly reproduces the physical existence which we experience on the earth as it now is. And would there not be a break in memory between death and resurrection? And could our personal character be carried over into a resurrection life? Our three guarantees of continuity all seem to be in question.

However, it is important to observe that we do not normally require all three factors to convince ourselves of a person's identity. If, for example, a person suffers brain damage in an accident, which causes him to lose memory of his former life and to become changed in character, we are still sure that he is the same person because we recognise his physical identity before and after the accident. Similarly, when we think of life after death, we do not need all three factors to safeguard continuity between this life and the next. As long as I have memory of my former life, and retain some of those personal characteristics which are essentially 'me', then there is no reason to doubt that the resurrected person is really me.

Perhaps an illustration will help here. The college where I work began its existence over a hundred years ago. During that period it has moved site several times. It has had different names. None of the people in it now were there at the begin--ning. It has changed and developed in all sorts of ways. And yet no one seriously doubts that it is the same college. There is a certain tradition, a sense of continuity with the past— continuity of personal characteristics, so to speak—which makes it recognisably the college which began life in 1864. In a similar way, it makes sense to conceive of the continuity of a person through physical death into a new life beyond.

But is there any evidence?

So far I have been discussing only whether life after death is conceivable. We must now come to the key issue: even if it is necessary or desirable or conceivable, is there any evidence to suggest that it is *true*?

The first line of evidence to be tried is psychical research. All kinds of psychic phenomena have been investigated by both Christians and non-Christians, to see if they yield evidence for life after death. These phenomena include appearances by recently dead persons, and alleged communication by dead persons through spiritualist mediums.[8] There is certainly a great readiness on the part of many people who do not share Christian assumptions to recognise the strangeness of the universe. There is mysterious evidence to suggest that a purely materialistic account of the nature of things is woefully inadequate. And yet it is notoriously difficult to evaluate the evidence of psychical research. When 'communications from the dead' occur, are

165

they to be explained as actually being caused by the souls of the dead? Or do they arise from the subconscious powers of the medium? Or are they deliberate deceptions by the Evil One? And even if they are genuine communications, what do they demonstrate? Very little of religious value, it appears. They rarely convey any sense of the fullness of life which might be expected from the heavenly world. The images they convey are more like the unexciting Sheol of the Old Testament than the thrilling images of the book of Revelation. And even if they indicate the *survival* of the dead, that is not the same as *eternal* life. They could merely be showing that there is a kind of ghostly echo of the dead for a short period—just as my radio, when it is switched off, goes on emitting sound for a second or two before falling silent. Michael Perry, who has studied these matters thoroughly, concludes 'The most that the evidence of psychical research, even when interpreted at its most favourable, can *prove*, is that a few people continue capable of retaining contact with the earth for a few years after their death.'[9]

In recent years there has been much discussion of so-called 'out-of-the-body' experiences, and their possible importance as evidence for life after death. They come under the general heading of psychic phenomena, but I mention them separately here because of their recent prominence. People who experience cardiac arrest (e.g., during an operation) and are then resuscitated, frequently testify to a sense of looking down on their own bodies during the period of unconsciousness. They are able to recall things which happened in the operating theatre while they were unconscious. Often they see the events of their lives flash before them in rapid succession. They catch glimpses of another world which they describe in terms of light, joy, beauty. In many cases they testify to considerable reluctance to return to this life when resuscitated by the doctor.[10] One example of this kind of experience comes from a friend of mine who told me how he visited the other world whilst critically ill with meningitis. 'I was swimming in a beautiful river,' he said, 'with green fields around, and people clothed in white Grecian garments.'

Many people think that further study of these experiences will strengthen the case for belief in life after death. And yet questions remain. How can it be established that such experiences are 'real experiences' rather than products of the patients' own minds? And why is it that nearly all the reports concern experiences of happiness and heavenly fulfilment, whilst very few offer a glimpse of hell? Is this to be taken as evidence that all people, whatever the character of their lives or their religious convictions, will go to heaven? On this last point, two recent Christian assessments of the issues offer two explanations.

Dr. Maurice Rawlings, a specialist in heart disease, relates a few instances of patients who did have terrifying experiences of going 'to hell and back', but agrees that most people report positive, 'heavenly' experiences. He thinks that the small number of negative experiences is due to patients' suppressing unpleasant memories. And he offers some evidence to show that, if patients can be interviewed immediately after resuscitation, many *can* remember frightening and 'hellish' impressions. John Weldon and Zola Levitt, however, suspect that the 'heavenly' experiences are a ploy by Satan to lull people into a false sense of security. For 'even Satan can disguise himself to look like an angel of light' (2 Corinthians 11:14).[11]

The nature of this evidence and the uncertainty in assessing it prompts me to recall some words of William Temple. Stressing that 'the hope of immortality is strictly dependent on and subordinate to faith in God', he says that, unless love of God comes first in our thinking, the hope of immortality will be selfish and harmful. And it is therefore

. . . positively undesirable that there should be experimental proof of our survival of death—at least of such survival in the case of those who have no spiritual faith on earth. For this would bring the hope of immortality into the area of purely intellectual apprehension. It might or might not encourage the belief that God exists; it would certainly, as I think, make very much harder the essential business of faith, which is the transference of the centre of interest and concern from self to God.[12]

The right kind of evidence

As Temple's words show, the real basis for the Christian's hope is the nature of God as he is revealed to us in Christ. This was the argument used by Jesus himself. When asked a trick question by Sadducees wishing to discredit belief in the resurrection, he accused them of ignorance of the scriptures and of the power of God. He quoted God's words to Moses in the story of the burning bush: 'I am the God of Abraham, the God of Isaac, and the God of Jacob.' And he drew from this the conclusion: 'He is the God of the living, not of the dead. You are completely wrong!' (Mark 12:24–7).

So Jesus was convinced of victory over death because he was aware of God's power, and because he experienced a relationship with God which death could not stop. Long after the deaths of Abraham, Isaac and Jacob, God could speak of himself as their God. And since it is meaningless to speak of dead people having a God, the implication must be that, because God lives, the people whom he loves must also live on after death. I believe that death will be overcome by life because I believe in God—the kind of God whom Jesus shows us, the God to whom we human beings matter. It is impossible to imagine this God scrapping what is precious to him.

This is not proof of life after death as some count proof. We can have no more proof than I can have proof that my wife will give me a birthday present next year, or will look after our daughter while I am away at a conference. And for the same reason. What proof there is lies in our present relationship, with its inbuilt promise of faithfulness. Why should we want more than that?

168

Jesus's resurrection and ours

Yet God in fact offers us more than that. He raised Jesus from death, 'as the guarantee that those who sleep in death will also be raised' (1 Corinthians 15:20).[13] That unprecedented event anticipated God's intention for his people at the end of history. And the New Testament's way of linking our resurrection with Jesus's resurrection makes clear, as nothing else could, that the Christian hope is not for a vague survival in a world of spirits, not for a prolongation or repetition of this life, but for resurrection to a glorious, fulfilled eternal life in relationship with Jesus Christ. The Christian hope is rooted in Jesus—in his vision of the character of God and in his work of dying and rising on our behalf. If we live in relationship with him, we share in his death and resurrection. 'Just as all people die because of their union with Adam, in the same way all will be raised to life because of their union with Christ' (1 Corinthians 15:23). Paul makes the same link in Romans 6:5 and 8:29. And in John 11:25f. we have it even more clearly stated in Jesus's word to Martha: 'I am the resurrection and the life. Whoever believes in me will live, even though he dies; and whoever lives and believes in me will never die. Do you believe this?' (cf. 1 Peter 1:3f.). On Jesus and his resurrection we may with utter confidence stake our future.

Is it all wishful thinking?

We are now in a position to say something about the common criticism that belief in life after death is the supreme example of wishful thinking. Bertrand Russell, for example, used to insist that belief in survival arose 'as an emotional reaction to the fear of death', and that 'we have no right to expect the universe to adapt itself to our emotions.'[14]

The popularity of this charge against Christian belief far exceeds its weight as an argument. As a matter of fact, people believed in survival long before it was clear to them that survival was in any way desirable. We have already seen how for most of the Old Testament period the Hebrews believed in a form of survival, and shuddered at it. And there is the famous example of this attitude in Homer's *Odyssey*, where the Greek hero Odysseus, on a visit to the underworld, meets the dead Achilles. Odysseus acclaims Achilles as 'the most fortunate man that ever was or will be . . . Now, down here, you are a mighty prince among the dead. For you, Achilles, Death should have lost its sting.'

'My lord Odysseus,' he replied, 'spare me your praise of Death. Put me on earth again, and I would rather be a serf in the house of some landless man, than king of all these dead men that have done with life.'[15]

It was not until Jesus came to declare and demonstrate a new quality of life that people wanted it to go on for ever.

The other part of our response to the charge of wishful thinking is this. Our hope of eternal life is not a matter of whistling in the dark, because what we hope for we already experience in part. The Christian longs for the life of heaven not chiefly as compensation for what he lacks now, but as fulfilment of what he already possesses. Paul, for example, sometimes expresses this possession in terms of sharing in Christ's risen life now: 'We know that God, who raised the Lord Jesus to life, will also raise us up with Jesus and take us, together with you, into his presence . . . For this reason we never become discouraged. Even though our physical being is gradually decaying, yet our spiritual being is renewed day after day' (2 Corinthians 4:14, 16).

And sometimes Paul speaks of our present experience of the Holy Spirit as the 'first instalment' or 'guarantee' of eternal life: 'The Spirit is the guarantee that we shall receive what God has promised his people' (Ephesians 1:14; cf. Romans 8:23). The two ideas—the Holy Spirit, and our sharing Christ's risen life—are brought together in Romans 8:11: 'If the Spirit of God, who raised Jesus from death, lives in you, then he who raised Christ from death will also give life to your mortal bodies by the presence of his Spirit in you.'

John's characteristic way of conveying the same message is to speak about the Christian's destiny as 'eternal life'—a quality of life based on relationship with Jesus Christ. But he stresses that this eternal life is experienced *now* by those who belong to Christ: 'Whoever believes in the Son *has* eternal life' (John 3:36). What happens beyond death is a development and fulfilment of present experience.

In a Bible study prepared for the World Council of Churches' conference on 'Salvation Today' in Bangkok in 1973, Paul Minear wrote: 'The deepest cry which the Holy Spirit arouses in man is the yearning cry for heaven, for direct contact with God's throne, for a victory of God over his demonic enemies, for an invitation to the marriage feast of the lamb.' Precisely because we know God at work in us now, we may say with confidence that our expectation of life after death is not wishful thinking, but is a longing put there by God himself—a longing which he himself intends to satisfy.

Resurrection or immortality?

There has been a long debate among Christians about whether it is better to speak about life after death in terms of resurrection or immortality. Both terms have their dangers, and there are in the church some very deep-rooted false ideas based on these dangers. If we speak of immortality, this easily gets confused with sub-Christian ideas, stemming from the Greek philosopher Plato, about the immortality of the soul. Life after death comes to be thought of in terms of the individual's private survival of death. He is imagined as a mere soul (a 'ghost', even), something *less* than the person he is in this earthly life. And immortality tends to be thought of as a natural endowment of man, an inevitable part of his make-up, rather than as a gift of God's grace.

Resurrection, on the other hand, easily comes to be thought of in over-crude physical terms. People get the idea that the actual physical cells of our present body will be put together again for the resurrection life. But that would make the resurrection little more than a restoration to physical, earthly life, like the raising of Lazarus.

Both terms are biblical, and on those grounds it is proper to use both—as long as we safeguard their use against unbiblical misunderstanding. Let us speak of immortality, so long as we recognise that immortality is not inevitable and natural to man, but a *gift* made available through the gospel. God, as an act of his grace, shares his own immortality with those who are open to receive his gift (2 Timothy 1:10; 1 Corinthians 15:50–54).

Resurrection language, however, is much more frequent in the New Testament. Because it offers a richer imagery, and because it links our hope clearly to the resurrection of Jesus, we are right to prefer it to the term 'immortality'. But we must try to get its meaning right. Let us begin with Paul's teaching in 1 Corinthians 15.

Here Paul regards Jesus's resurrection body as a model or pattern for the resurrection of believers. This is clear from the general argument of the chapter, as well as from the specific statement that the risen Christ is the 'firstfruits', the first example and guarantee of other resurrections to follow (verse 20). Now we know from the account in the gospels that, when Jesus appeared to his followers after his resurrection, he was the same Jesus as before—and yet different. He was the same Jesus—even though they did not all recognise him at first, they became convinced that it was he by some characteristic word or action. And yet he was different from before. He was no longer subject to limitations of time and space. There was *something* different about his appearance which sometimes prevented them from recognising him immediately. One thing they never suggested is that he was the old Jesus restored to earthly life. No. He was transformed, living on the new, eternal, glorious level of the age to come. *That* Jesus is the pattern for the resurrection of his people. Not less real but more real. Not so much 'departed this life' as raised up to fullness of life which is God's goal for all his people.

Jesus spoke in these terms in Mark 12:24–27: 'When the dead rise to life,' he said, 'they will be like angels in heaven and will not marry.' In his time angels were not thought of as vague and bodiless, but as beings with glorious bodies suitable for their exalted work of serving God in heaven. In the same way, says Jesus, resurrection for God's people means being raised to a new fullness of life, with bodies fitted for the new situation. And the exclusive sexual aspect of marriage, which is God's gift on earth, will be a thing of the past in God's new world of deeply satisfying relationships among all God's people.

Paul explains the implications further in 1 Corinthians 15:35–58. The resurrection body, he says, may be compared with the full-grown wheat which emerges once the seed has been dropped in the ground. The plant is not the same as the seed, and yet there is a continuity between them. God gives the plant a 'body' as he sees fit. So it is with us. The form we take in the resurrection will be different from the form we have now, and yet it will still be 'us'. Just as for Jesus, so for us there will be discontinuity and continuity.

A further point which Paul makes is that different beings have different types of bodies suited to their different environments. Fish, for example, are different from birds. So the difference between our present bodies and our resurrection bodies is due to the different environment in which we are to live. Mortality will give way to immortality, ugliness and weakness will give way to beauty and strength. The physical body will be superseded by a 'spiritual body'. By this paradoxical phrase Paul is saying that we shall have a body suited to the environment of the age to come, which will be dominated by the Spirit of God.

Finally Paul points out that not all Christians will need to be resurrected, because not all will die. When Jesus comes again the dead will be raised, never to die again, whilst the generation still living will be transformed immediately to enjoy the life of the age to come (cf. Philippians 3:20f.).

When will the resurrection happen?

We have just seen how in 1 Corinthians 15 Paul expects the resurrection of God's people to take place when Jesus comes again. But that immediately poses the problem, what happens when we die, and where do we go between death and the resurrection, if Jesus does not come in our lifetime? There is an apparent contradiction in New Testament teaching. Even within one letter we have Philippians 1:23, where Paul expects 'to be with Christ' if he dies, and 3:20f., where he refers to the resurrection taking place when Jesus comes again.

Various ways of resolving this problem have been suggested.[16] Some think, for example, that, during the interval between death and Christ's coming, the dead are 'with Christ' (Philippians 1:23; Luke 23:43), but in a disembodied form. Only when Jesus comes will they, with all other believers, receive their resurrection bodies. This view looks plausible, but if it is true, why did not the New Testament writers tell us so more clearly? In the passages cited from Philippians 1 and Luke 23 there is no hint that this 'being with Christ' is only an interim stage before the resurrection.

Others, including Jehovah's Witnesses and Seventh-Day Adventists, hold the doctrine of 'soul-sleep'. On this view, there is a time interval for the dead person between his death and the general resurrection, but he spends it 'sleeping', unconscious. The trouble with this approach is that it leans too heavily on the New Testament's occasional use of 'sleep' as a metaphor for death. And it sounds very different from the vivid hope of 'being with Christ' in Philippians 1:23.

Personally, I think it is better to look for a solution which recognises that time is something which belongs to the present world as we know it. It is part of the created order, and is not necessarily experienced by the dead in the same way as we experience it at present. We ought not to assume that when a person dies he remains confined within our

174

space-time system. Thus, when a Christian dies he goes to be with Christ (cf. Philippians 1:23) and receives his resurrection body. From *his* perspective there is no gap between his death and Christ's coming again and the resurrection of all God's people. But from the perspective of those who go on living in earth-bound time, there is an interval between his death and Christ's coming again—hence the passages such as 1 Corinthians 15 and Philippians 3:20f., which speak of a still future general resurrection. What we must *not* do is imagine that the dead person is in some kind of unsatisfactory transit lounge, just because we live on in time after his death. We have no right to assume that the dead would wish to be limited by our own time-bound existence!

Martin Luther has some lively ways of expressing this view. Although he rejected the doctrine of soul-sleep, he did use sleep as an *illustration* of what a person who dies will encounter. 'In a similar way as one does not know how it happens that one falls asleep, and suddenly morning approaches when one awakes, so we will suddenly be resurrected at the Last Day, not knowing how we have come into death and through death.' 'We shall sleep until he comes and knocks at the tomb and says: "Dr. Martin, get up!" Then in one moment I will get up and I will rejoice with him in eternity.'[17]

God's new world

The New Testament does not normally talk about 'going to heaven when we die'. Its focus is on 'new heavens and a new earth' (2 Peter 3:13; Revelation 21:1; Romans 8:21–23). The picture is of a universe transformed, perfected—fit surroundings for God's eternal presence with his resurrected people. We cannot imagine what it will be like, nor need we be too concerned to describe it. Better the evocative language of poetry and the rich biblical imagery than the prosaic attempts of the curious to sort out every detail. Certainly the stress on a new universe is meant to preserve us from supposing that the next life and its surroundings will be less real, less solid than our present world.

But where will it be? And should we be perturbed by the Soviet astronaut's claim that he has been all over the universe and he has seen neither God nor heaven? God's new world will need to be different in many respects from the present world, since we expect all kinds of things to characterise it which are not true of our present world of space and time. But if we must speculate about where the dead are now, whilst our present world continues, we may make use of the idea of 'another space', as developed by some physicists. There is no logical reason why our three-dimensional space is the only kind of space there is. Just as a being confined to a flat two-dimensional world would know nothing of life in three dimensions, so it is conceivable that there is 'another space', undetectable from within our three-dimensional framework. It is, if you like, the world of God, where he is hidden from our sight, but from which he continually interacts with 'our' world.[18]

This new world is the goal of all God's purposes, towards which—as Paul says in Romans 8—the whole creation stretches out. Once on a spring day the poet Goethe found a chrysalis just on the point of being sloughed off. Holding it to his ear he cried in amazement, 'Just listen, will you, how it knocks and strives towards the light! That must be what St. Paul meant, when he speaks of the groaning of creation!'

It is a strange thing that writers have always found it easier to portray hell than to portray paradise. The poet Laurie Lee wrote an essay on 'Paradise' in which he commented how unsatisfying to modern minds most images of paradise have been:

> Too chaste, too disinfected, too much on its best behaviour, it received little more than a dutiful nod from the faithful. Hell, on the other hand, was always a good crowd-raiser, having ninety per cent of the action—high colours, high temperatures, intricate devilries and always the most interesting company available.

In the world of the arts, Milton's *Paradise Regained* was a pale reflection of the power and vigour of *Paradise Lost*. 'Of all the arts, only certain rare passages of music seem ever to have touched the fringes of a credible Paradise.'[19]

The presence of God

Yet we must say what can be said, conscious of the limitations of human language. Here are some of the solid realities of God's new world. (I shall use the word 'heaven' sometimes, not because I think of it as vague and ethereal, but simply because other phrases are rather cumbersome).

First, the overwhelming reality will be God himself—God in his totality as Father, Son and Spirit. 'I heard a loud voice speaking from the throne: "Now God's home is with mankind! He will live with them, and they shall be his people. God himself will be with them and he will be their God"' (Revelation 21:3). And often Jesus in his parables speaks of men's destiny in terms of being in God's presence. It is a wedding feast where God is the host (Matthew 22:1–10), a household where the master graciously rolls up his sleeves and serves his servants (Luke 12:35–38). It is the city of God which Abraham glimpsed from afar (Hebrews 11:10, 16), the city which needs no temple, no sun or moon, because God and the Lamb fill it with the light of their glory (Revelation 21:22f.). There the glimpses of God which we catch in this life will give way to clear vision. As Augustine puts it: 'We shall rest and we shall see; we shall see and we shall love; we shall love and we shall praise; this is what will be at the end without end' (*City of God* 22:30).

Secondly, our entry into God's new world will mark the end of all the things which limit and harm our lives now. There will be an end of *evil*—the evil within me, and the evil which surrounds me. The Devil, the ultimate source of all temptation, will have been thrown to destruction in the lake of fire (Revelation 20:10), and 'nothing that is impure will enter the city' (Revelation 21:27). There will be an end of *suffering* and *death*: God 'will wipe away all tears from their eyes. There will be no more death, no more grief or crying or pain. The old things have disappeared' (Revelation 21:4).

There will be an end of all *insecurity*. Those who live this life exposed to dangers, uncertainties and fears which threaten their well-being will find all those things left behind them. Like Abraham, they will at last have arrived at 'the city with permanent foundations'. They will have received 'a kingdom that cannot be shaken' (Hebrews 11:10; 12:28). We can broaden this out and say that *whatever* it is in this life which contradicts God's purpose, fills us with anxiety, diminishes our full humanity, will be done away with. For a first-century Jew the picture was of the sea disappearing (Revelation 21:1), because the Hebrews of the Bible, who were not good sailors, tended to think of the sea as unpredictable and menacing. For the negro slaves of America, the imagery was naturally different:

> No more sunshine fer to bu'n you;
> no more rain fer to wet you.
> Every day will be Sunday in heaven.

And for us? Whatever it is which each of us battles with, we shall be set free from its menacing jaws.

Heaven is other people

Thirdly, heaven is a place of *community*. Whatever the truth of Sartre's statement at the end of *No Exit* that 'hell is other people', we certainly ought to say that 'heaven is other people'. This is one reason why we shall have bodies. It is through our bodies that we express ourselves and are known by others. The Bible will have nothing to do with the religious individualism vividly denounced by Walter Rauschenbush in 1917:

Our personal eschatology is characterised by an unsocial individualism. In the present life we are bound up with wife and children, with friends and work-mates, in a warm organism of complex life. When we die, we join— what? A throng of souls, an unorganised crowd of saints, who each carry a harp and have not even formed an orchestra.[20]

The New Testament is against such individualism. But it is also against the Eastern mystical idea that after death we lose our individuality and are absorbed into the divine. To have resurrection bodies implies that we shall be distinct persons, with our own identity, able to relate to others and to God. The personal identity makes the relationships possible, but it is the relationships which matter.

To the question, 'Shall we recognise our loved one?', the answer must surely be yes. This is shown by all that has been said about the resurrection body, as well as by Jesus's references to named individuals such as Abraham, Isaac and Jacob in the kingdom of heaven (Matthew 8:11). But even to this we must add what Karl Barth said when asked at a conference of pastors' wives, 'Will we see our loved ones on the other side?' Barth's answer was, 'Yes, but with others too!'

What a marvellous international gathering it will be, crossing the barriers of space and time. I think of some of God's people I have met in countries I have visited, and echo the song sung to Christ by the heavenly creatures:

> You were killed, and by your death
>   you bought for God
> people from every tribe, language,
>   nation and race   (Revelation 5:9).

Fourthly, heaven is a place of *activity*. A new depth of relationship will be possible among God's people. For in that fulfilled kingdom of God the love, peace, righteousness and joy glimpsed by Old Testament prophets and by New Testament writers will become reality. And this gives the lie to the frequently expressed worry that 'heaven would be

179

boring'. I remember a teacher who found it impossible to be interested in heaven after we had sung in school assembly a hymn which referred to the prospect of 'singing ever-lastingly'. Not many of us would relish an infinitely long version of *Hymns Ancient and Modern*. There is a story about F. W. H. Myers, the most famous of psychical researchers. He asked a woman whose daughter had recently died what she supposed had become of her soul. The mother replied, 'Oh well, I suppose she is enjoying eternal bliss, but I wish you wouldn't talk about such unpleasant subjects.'[21]

The worry about boredom arises from two causes. First, there is misunderstanding. A particular biblical image—the image of harps and singing—has dominated popular thought about heaven until it has run out of steam. And the classical descriptions of heaven in the great spiritual writers have often misled us by concentrating on symbols taken from sight rather than from action. And so the idea has built up that God's new world will be a static affair—beautiful, maybe, but more like a sentimental painting of a festival than like the festival itself. The biblical imagery, however, is broader and more varied. Most obvious is the image of the city, conveying ideas of community, relation-ship, vitality, action, creativity. And all the language about love is meaningless unless it involves active self-giving to God and to others in relationship. That is both demanding and fulfilling, but not boring. A lover who is living at a distance from his fiancée and has to make do with letters and telephone calls does not speak of being bored at the prospect of spending unlimited time in her company.

But that brings us to the second cause of worry about boredom. There can be a spiritual cause. A person who is not in love with God *would* be bored at being for ever with him and with others who love him. The world to come is not a kind of Disneyland with endless free rides. It is the New Jerusalem, where God is loved and his will is done. Those who are not very interested in doing his will now may be bored at the prospect of doing it then. We may be confident that there will be things for God's people to do, even though we can barely imagine what form they will take. And if it is the prospect of loving and serving God *for ever*, rather than for a mere lifetime, that perplexes us, then we must trust the God who leads us there. He who promises to answer our deepest needs and to make us perfect must have his own answer to that problem. 'What we see now is like a dim image in a mirror; then we shall see face to face. What I know now is only partial; then it will be complete—as complete as God's knowledge of me' (1 Corinthians 13:12).

This world's treasures in the next world

The fifth point about the world to come is that it will involve some *continuity* with this world's culture. We have already seen how the Bible speaks of the transformation of this world rather than of its destruction, and how Paul speaks in 1 Corinthians 15 of the continuity of our personalities through death into resurrection. There is a parallel continuity of what we may loosely term 'culture'. Revelation 21:26f. says 'The greatness and the wealth of the nations will be brought into the city. But nothing that is impure will enter the city.' This suggests that, because God is a creative God who affirms the goodness of the world he has made, he will not simply write it off with all its wealth of art and beauty and human inventiveness. In God's economy nothing is wasted. All the creative work of men and women which reflects the abundant creativity of God will be carried over into the transformed world. We can only guess at how this may be. But it tells us something of how God values the creative work of men and women—much of it produced out of suffering and at great personal cost. And it is another sign that the world to come is not a colourless, shadowy existence, but a totally fulfilling world, worthy of its Creator.

Finally, *worship* will be a central activity of God's people. Not worship as a dull ritual which has to be got through, but worship which expresses the depths of our love towards

God. The hymns in the book of Revelation give a glimpse of what such worship might be like. Or we may let our imaginations range over C. S. Lewis's description of the 'eternal dance', which is one way in which that worship may be expressed:

All pains and pleasures we have known on earth are early initiations in the movement of that dance: but the dance itself is strictly incomparable with the sufferings of this present time. As we draw near to its uncreated rhythm, pain and pleasure sink almost out of sight. There is joy in the dance, but it does not exist for the sake of joy. It does not even exist for the sake of good, or of love. It is Love Himself, and Good Himself, and therefore happy. It does not exist for us, but we for it.[22]

Notes to chapter 5

1. *Dylan Thomas: The Poems*, ed. D. Jones (Dent, London, 1971), p. 207.
2. *Man's Concern with Death* (Hodder, London, 1968), p. 271.
3. *Humanism* (Penguin, Harmondsworth, 1968)—quotations from p. ix.
4. For a possible example of this from 60,000 years ago see A. Toynbee *et al.*, *Life after Death* (Weidenfeld and Nicholson, London, 1976), pp. 175f.
5. 'Can Christianity do without an Eschatology?' in G. B. Caird *et al.*, *The Christian Hope* (SPCK, London, 1970), p. 31.
6. I have discussed this issue more fully in *Christian Hope and the Future of Man*, particularly pp. 98–108, 115–17.
7. Lewis, *The Elusive Mind* (Allen & Unwin, London, 1969); R. Aldwinckle, *Death in the Secular City*, ch.5; P. Badham, *Christian Beliefs about Life after Death* (Macmillan, London, 1976), chs. 6–8.
8. See, e.g., several essays in *Man's Concern with Death* and *Life after Death* (notes 2 and 4 above); and M. Perry, *The Resurrection of Man* (Mowbray, Oxford, 1975), ch. 3.
9. *The Resurrection of Man*, p. 39.
10. The standard texts are R. Moody, *Life after Life* (Corgi, London, 1977) and E. Kübler-Ross, *On Death and Dying* (Tavistock, London, 1973).

11. Rawlings, *Beyond Death's Door* (Sheldon, London, 1979); Weldon and Levitt, *Is there Life after Death?* (Kingsway, Eastbourne, 1977).

12. 'The Idea of Immortality in Relation to Religion and Ethics', in C. S. Duthie (ed.), *Resurrection and Immortality* (Bagster, London, 1979), pp. 5f.

13. On the evidence for and nature of Jesus's resurrection, see G. E. Ladd, *I Believe in the Resurrection of Jesus* (Hodder, London, 1975).

14. *The Great Mystery of Life Hereafter* (essays by Russell and others) (Hodder, London, 1957), pp. 25, 27.

15. *Odyssey*, book 11, E. V. Rieu's Penguin translation (Harmondsworth, 1946), p. 184.

16. See my discussion in *Christian Hope and the Future of Man*, pp. 110–12.

17. Quoted in H. Schwarz, *On the Way to the Future* (Augsburg, Minneapolis, 2nd edition 1979), pp. 231f.; cf. pp. 226ff. I stress that Luther is using the image of sleep only as an illustration; from the viewpoint of the person who sleeps, nothing happens between his going to sleep and his waking up. The fact that others may be awake, watching time tick by on the clock, is irrelevant to the point being illustrated.

18. On this concept see K. Heim, *Christian Faith and Natural Science* (Eng. tr., SCM, London, 1953), pp. 126ff.; and *The World: its Creation and Consummation* (Eng. tr., Oliver and Boyd, Edinburgh, 1962), pp. 137–49.

19. *I Can't Stay Long* (Penguin, Harmondsworth, 1977), pp. 72f.

20. *A Theology for the Social Gospel* (Macmillan, New York, 1917), p. 235.

21. Bertrand Russell, *Unpopular Essays* (Allen & Unwin, London, 1950), p. 141.

22. *The Problem of Pain* (Centenary Press, London, 1940), p. 141.

Chapter 6   The Dark Side of Hope

God has made us to live joyfully for ever in his presence. That is the destiny which he has made possible for us in Christ. And yet we kid ourselves if we ignore the persistent biblical note of judgment. As the Creed summarises it: 'He will come again to judge the living and the dead.' It is the conviction of all New Testament writers that two possible destinies lie before men and women. Paul, for example, speaks of 'those who are being saved and those who are being lost' (2 Corinthians 2:15). And his explanation of the Christian gospel in his letter to the Romans describes man's situation as being under God's 'anger', destined for 'punishment' and 'judgment' (Romans 1–3), before going on to show how deliverance from this destiny is possible through trust in Christ and his work (Romans 3–8). If 'life' and 'glory' and 'salvation' are God's possibilities for men and women, there remains the possibility of 'death', 'destruction', 'condemnation'.

Nor is this some harsh doctrine cooked up by a half-enlightened follower of Jesus. For no one spoke more vigorously of God's judgment than Jesus himself.[1] He spoke parables about God's judgment (e.g., Matthew 18:23–35; 25:31–46). He used the image of fire and its power to destroy. He warned of a sin which is not capable of being forgiven (Mark 3:28–30).

So what are we to make of this discordant note in the Christian message? To begin with, we must acknowledge that it has often been preached in ways which ought now to make us shudder, not with fear but with embarrassment. Augustine, for example, envisaged a literal fire in which 'people are kept burning without being consumed, and in pain without dying, by the miraculous power of God'.

Or consider this extract from Jonathan Edwards' famous sermon, 'Sinners in the Hands of an Angry God', preached in 1741:

> The God that holds you over the pit of hell, much as one holds a spider, or some loathesome insect, over the fire, abhors you, and is dreadfully provoked; his wrath towards you burns like fire; he looks upon you as worthy of nothing else but to be cast into the fire. . . . O sinner, . . . you hang by a slender thread, with the flames of divine wrath flashing about it, and ready every moment to singe it, and burn it asunder.[2]

The trouble with this approach is that it plays on fear in such a way that any response it evokes is more likely to be based on fear of the consequences of not responding than on any genuine love for God in response to his love.

Yet still, I believe, it is essential that the message of God's judgment on human lives be given space in our thinking and teaching. The need for judgment follows from our belief in God's love. Many people carry around the idea that, according to Christian belief, God has arranged life as a great obstacle race for which the booby prize is to be thrown on the bonfire by God, the cosmic sadist. That is the kind of caricature which results when belief in judgment is separated from belief in God's love. From the fundamental truth that God is love, it follows that he pays us the compliment of treating all our actions as significant. The notion that all shall 'give account' to God—that we shall be judged by him—safeguards this truth. If God did not hold us responsible for our actions, our attitudes and decisions, that would mean that ultimately nothing we do is significant. Our humanity would be diminished. An initially attractive idea—that we can do what we like and 'get away with it'—would turn out to be the death-knell of any truly human life.

Our age has witnessed an increasing reluctance to speak of human behaviour in terms of sin and responsibility.

There are many things in society which we are inclined to call 'evil', 'corrupt' or 'harmful'. But we are reluctant to call anything 'sinful'. For 'sinful' implies that someone is guilty, responsible and accountable—and these are concepts which we prefer to avoid. But it is hardly an accident that a generation which shrinks from thinking in terms of sin and responsibility is also experiencing a sense of dehumanisation, a feeling that individuals matter less and less. A renewed stress that people have real choices to make, and a real responsibility towards other people and towards God, would be a significant contribution towards the health of society.

I do not, of course, mean that a court of law should never make allowances for an offender's background and circumstances when it passes sentence. Nor am I denying that when God judges us he takes into account what opportunities we have had to respond to his love. But if you deny entirely that people are responsible to God, you take away one of the most significant things about our humanity.

A further consequence of belief in God's love is an emphasis on human freedom. Love never forces itself on its object. If it did so it would cease to be love. The loving parent—like the father in the story of the prodigal son—may plead with his son not to go away and make a mess of his life. But if he is to be truly loving he must in the end respect the son's freedom to choose how he is to spend his life. God pays us the compliment of allowing us to choose whether we will have him as our God. Precisely because he loves us, we are free to reject him—and to reject him, if we will, for ever. It is God's respect for human freedom which makes hell possible. As C. S. Lewis put it, Christianity presents us with 'a God so full of mercy that he becomes man and dies by torture to avert that final ruin from his creatures, and who yet, where that heroic remedy fails, seems unwilling, or even unable, to arrest the ruin by an act of mere power. . . . And here is the real problem: so much mercy, yet still there is Hell.'[3]

Judgment: a present reality

We turn then, to New Testament teaching about God's judgment. The first thing to note is that judgment is not reserved for an occasion after our death or at Jesus's second coming. In a real sense, judgment is taking place now and all the time. In Jesus, God has already spoken his final word and has acted decisively to deliver men and women from the power of evil. Ever since, whenever people have been confronted by Christ and his gospel, they have responded to him or turned from him. Our response to Jesus *is* our response to God, and in making up our minds about him we bring judgment or salvation on ourselves. This is expressed with stark clarity in John's Gospel. 'God did not send his Son into the world to be its judge, but to be its saviour' (John 3:17). Yet if people refuse to be saved, they are expressing their opposition to God, and anticipating a verdict of condemnation at the final judgment. By the choices we make, we sentence ourselves:

> Whoever believes in the Son is not judged; but whoever does not believe has already been judged, because he has not believed in God's only Son. This is how the judgment works: the light has come into the world, but people love the darkness rather than the light, because their deeds are evil. Anyone who does evil things hates the light and will not come to the light, because he does not want his evil deeds to be shown up (John 3:18–20).

This understanding of judgment is not peculiar to John. We find it in Paul. Read Romans 1:18–32 in a modern translation, and you have a vivid description of the process of judgment. 'God's anger is revealed from heaven against all the sin and evil of the people whose evil ways prevent the truth from being known,' he begins (Romans 1:18). Three times he says, 'God has given them over' to the consequences of the choices they have made (verses 24, 26, 28). In other words, Paul is saying, 'Look at the society in which you live, with its injustice and immorality and ungodliness. What you are seeing *is* the wrath of God. God's wrath is happening now! When people turn their backs on God, his grace is withdrawn and he allows them to experience the consequences of their choice. The wrath of God does not mean some cataclysmic act of destruction. Rather it is God's withdrawal of his blessings and his presence from those who have refused to receive them.' To quote Karl Barth's famous comment on Romans 1:24, 'The enterprise of setting up the "No-God" is avenged by its success. . . . Our conduct becomes governed precisely by what we desire.' He adds, 'when God has been deprived of his glory, men are also deprived of theirs.'[4] Once Nietzsche had said, 'God is dead', it was only a matter of time before Sartre would say, 'Man is dead'.

When he was general secretary of the Church Missionary Society, John Taylor reported on a conference where groups were asked to discuss the question: Where do you see the hand of God at work in Northern Ireland? Some, he said, mentioned incidents of peace-making or co-operation between Catholics and Protestants, or the patience of the soldiers, or the increasing numbers of Christians at prayer-meetings. But 'no one saw the hand of God over Northern Ireland as Amos saw it over Northern Israel. No one heard his voice in the explosions at Derry as Jeremiah heard it in the fall of Jerusalem.'[5] No one saw the tragedies of Ulster as the outworking of people's refusal to let God be God and stamp his will on the situation. No one saw judgment in terms of Romans 1—and that is part of our blindness to the full biblical picture of how God works amongst men and women. Walter Hollenweger urges Christians to recognise in today's films and literature, newspapers and television, the images and reflections of life which are 'an open invitation for interpretation' by those who have learnt how the New Testament sheds light on these situations.

He is a true evangelist who is able to put over against Sartre's vision of hell an evangelical view of hell, over against Bergman's 'silence' a redeeming word which breaks through silence, over against Fellini's 'street' without an end the final goal of the evangelical way.[6]

Jesus himself used images of darkness (Matthew 8:12), deadness (Luke 15:24), lostness (Luke 15), which are often strangely similar to descriptions of modern man in films, songs and novels. The central figure in Camus's *The Stranger* is a 'nothing man', with no purpose, no ideals, no love, no hope, who finally finds some sense of fulfilment in the thought that at his execution men will hurl abuse at his jerking body. Ordinary people organise their lives without reference to God, and wonder why things do not hold together. It is as if I were to walk into a hi-fi shop and complain that my tape-recorder would not work under water. It was not designed for that purpose. And man is not designed to live in God's world without reference to God. The sense of alienation, loss of identity, lack of purpose, which characterise so much human life today, are symptoms of the absence of God.

However, there is another element in Jesus's teaching on the present judgment of God. It is not final. Men experience this godlessness only so long as they refuse to enter the kingdom of God. While earthly life continues they can change sides. The labourers can leave the market-place and enter the vineyard. The wedding invitation remains open. The prodigal son can repent and return to his father's home. Only at the last judgment does the verdict become final. Meanwhile the gospel message warns and challenges: 'This is the hour to receive God's favour; today is the day to be saved!' (2 Corinthians 6:2).

The final judgment

No one escapes death. And no one escapes judgment, either. God will judge 'the living and the dead' (Acts 10:42; 2 Timothy 4:1; 1 Peter 4:5). The traditional picture of the 'great assize', with God and Christ sitting on the judgment-throne with all nations gathered before them (as in Matthew 25:31–46), is a way of emphasising this.

God will judge all people. And he will judge us 'according to works' (Matthew 16:27; Romans 2:6; 2 Corinthians 5:10; Revelation 22:12). This emphasis in the New Testament may seem to be in conflict with the message of justification through faith. If God brings us into relationship with himself and gives us eternal life through *faith*, how can he judge us according to our *deeds*? The contradiction is more apparent than real. For in Paul's teaching, deeds are viewed as the evidence of the reality of faith. The only kind of faith which Paul will recognise as real, saving faith is faith which shows its reality by the works it produces—'faith that works through love' (Galatians 5:6). We receive salvation through faith in Jesus, opening our lives to his work within us. It is a gift of his grace. But that gift requires our response of gratitude and obedience, which alone can show that our faith is genuine. In other words, we may say that our lives are a collection of responses, attitudes, actions, which God alone sees as a whole. When he judges us, he, who alone knows us as we really are, will judge us as whole persons. The truth about us, the real direction of our lives—whether it is for him or against him, towards him or away from him—will be exposed. 'God through Jesus Christ will judge the secret thought of all' (Romans 2:16).

The grounds of judgment

We can see from Jesus's teaching what kinds of actions and attitudes are in particular danger of meeting with God's condemnation. He warned against the accumulation of wealth which hinders a man from putting God first and following Jesus in costly discipleship. We see this in his response to the rich young ruler (Mark 10:17–31), and in the parable of the rich fool who knew how to store up earthly wealth but was poverty-stricken in relation to God (Luke 12:13–21). He warned of the folly of putting the kingdom of God second or third in one's order of priorities:

Be concerned above everything else with the Kingdom of God and with what he requires of you.

If your hand or your foot makes you lose your faith, cut it off and throw it away! It is better for you to enter life without a hand or a foot than to keep both hands and both feet and be thrown into the eternal fire (Matthew 6:33; 18:8).

Lack of care for the poor was, according to Jesus, yet another sure way of incurring God's condemnation. The message is there in the parables of the rich man and Lazarus (Luke 16:19–31), and the sheep and the goats (Matthew 25:31–46). One striking thing in this latter passage is the way in which neither the 'sheep' nor the 'goats' have consciously realised that, in caring or not caring for the poor, they have in fact been responding to Christ. 'When, Lord,' the righteous ask, 'did we ever see you hungry and feed you, or thirsty and give you a drink?' Nothing could express more sharply than that how the deeds which God approves flow naturally out of a right relationship with God. It is what a person does when he is not seeking approval that shows his true character.

Rather than expound Matthew 25:31–46 in standard fashion, I offer three 'comments' on it which challenge our thinking and action about meeting Christ in other people and caring for him by caring for them. First, Martin Luther's words from Christmas, 1534:

There are many who think: 'If only I had been there. How quick I would have been to help the Baby. I would have washed his linen. How happy I would have been to go with the shepherds to see the Lord lying in the manger.'

Yes, you would. You say that because you know how great Christ is, but if you had been there at that time you would have done no better than the people of Bethlehem. Childish and silly thoughts are these. Why don't you do it now? You have Christ in your neighbour.

191

Then a poem:

> Under our noses, before our eyes,
> Not in the clouds, not in the sky,
> He passes. And we pass him by.
> Humanity is his disguise.
> (It works too well).[7]

Finally, a story from C. S. Lewis: 'I once talked to a Continental pastor who had seen Hitler, and had, by all human standards, good cause to hate him. "What did he look like?" I asked. "Like all men," he replied, "that is, like Christ." '[8]

Again, Jesus warned that the person who is unwilling to forgive will find himself beyond reach of God's forgiveness. He told of a servant who was let off a great debt, but refused to write off a trivial sum which was owed to him by another servant. On hearing this, the king who had let him off the great debt had him sent to jail 'until he should pay back the whole amount'—which of course would mean for life, because he had no hope of paying. And Jesus concluded, 'That is how my Father in heaven will treat every one of you unless you forgive your brother from your heart' (Matthew 18:21–35).

General Oglethorpe, to whom the young John Welsey was chaplain in the colony of Georgia in America, once said to Wesley with great pride, 'I never forgive.' Wesley replied, 'Then I hope, sir, you never sin.'

A further target for Jesus's condemnation was the causing of little ones to stumble: 'If anyone should cause one of these little ones to lose his faith in me, it would be better for that person to have a large millstone tied round his neck and be drowned in the deep sea' (Matthew 18:6). How dimly we glimpse the sense of horror with which Jesus viewed the sin of those who lead vulnerable people away from God. We do well to consider what forms this takes in our own society, and to reflect on the responsibility borne by leaders of people and shapers of public opinion.

The final target of Jesus's warning which we may notice is

self-righteousness. This is typified by the Pharisee in Luke 18:9–14, who—in contrast to the tax-collector—is full of his own moral and religious achievement. He is the shining example of the respected religious leader, the good man whom all should wish to emulate. But it was the tax-collector and not the Pharisee who went home in the right with God. Scandalous! Yet it brings us to the heart of the gospel. For when God judges us 'according to works' he will not look to see how pleased we are with our achievements. He will look to see how our actions and attitudes reveal us to be people who, with no illusions about our own goodness, trust in his grace for all that we strive to become.

This makes clear, as perhaps nothing else could, that the religious person is not exempt from judgment by virtue of his being religious. Jesus warned his Jewish contemporaries that it was possible to be associated with God's people and yet to reject God's Messiah (Mark 12:1–9). It is possible to perform religious acts and still be a stranger to Christ: 'When Judgment Day comes, many will say to me, "Lord, Lord! In your name we spoke God's message, by your name we drove out many demons and performed many miracles!" Then I will say to them. "I never knew you. Get away from me, you wicked people!" ' (Matthews 7:22f.).

The message of judgment in the gospels is directed less to people outside the church than to the complacent ecclesiastical people whose confidence is based on the fact that they are well within it. This doctrine is meant, not to undermine Christian assurance, but to remove complacency, that besetting sin of religious man. The purpose of the judgment will be to reveal which side of God's dividing-line we are really on.

The outcome of the judgment

In the last few pages I have illustrated the standards by which, according to Jesus's teaching, men and women will be judged. The actions and attitudes which we show now will indicate the true nature of our relationship towards God.

The outcome of the judgment must also be understood in

CHRIST WILL COME AGAIN

terms of relationship towards God. We saw earlier how Jesus described the coming kingdom of God in terms of God's presence and his people being in relationship to him. Rejection at the judgment, on the other hand, means to be excluded from God's presence. It means to arrive too late and find the door shut (Luke 13:25–29). It means to be excluded 'outside in the dark' (Matthew 22:13). The same message is expressed in a different way in Mark 8:38, where Jesus warns that 'if a person is ashamed of me and of my teaching in this godless and wicked day, then the Son of Man will be ashamed of him when he comes in the glory of his Father with the holy angels.' The word 'ashamed' here conveys the idea of a decisive rejection of another person. And in the three parables of Matthew 25 we find the foolish virgins shut out in the night, the unproductive servant thrown into the darkness outside, and the goats commanded to depart into eternal punishment. The emphasis in all these passages is not so much on a place into which the unrepentant are put, as on that from which they are excluded, the community of God's people in his final kingdom. 'Hell' is not so much a place as 'a "nothing realm", a kind of terrible negative'.[9]

Paul too thinks of the outcome of the judgment in terms of relationship of God. Heaven means 'to be at home with the Lord' (2 Corinthians 5:8; cf. 1 Thessalonians 4:17). And condemnation for 'those who reject God and who do not obey the Good News about our Lord Jesus' will mean 'eternal destruction, separated from the presence of the Lord and from his glorious night' (2 Thessalonians 1:8f.). The final judgment, then, means God's underlining and ratification of the relationship towards him which we have chosen in this life. If we have fellowship with God now, through repentance and trust in his grace, we shall enter into a fuller experience of his presence then. If we do not know him now, we shall not know him then.

The choice is yours

By our response to Christ, then, we choose our destiny. In another of Paul's images, we reap what we sow:

No one makes a fool of God. A person will reap exactly what he sows. If he sows in the field of his natural [i.e. sinful] desires, from it he will gather the harvest of death; if he sows in the field of the Spirit, from the Spirit he will gather the harvest of eternal life (Galatians 6:7f.).

That our destinies are self-chosen is stressed in other ways, too, in the New Testament. We have already looked at John 3:17–21, with its message that God's purpose in Jesus is to save, not to condemn, and yet some people choose darkness rather than light. It is not God's *desire* to condemn, any more than it is the *purpose* of light to cast shadows. But shadows are inevitably cast when someone stands in the way of the light. Notice also how, in the parable of the sheep and the goats, the righteous are told, 'Come and possess the kingdom which has been prepared for you ever since the creation of the world.' But to the other group the king says, 'Away to the eternal fire which has been prepared for the Devil and his angels' (Matthew 25:34, 41). The first destiny is God's plan and desire for human beings. The second was never meant for men at all, and if they go there, their going brings grief and not pleasure to God.

Someone, however, may object to my stress on our free will and ability to bring judgment on ourselves, on the grounds that it undermines the doctrine of predestination. My reply would be that one *ought* to undermine the kind of teaching which says that God rigidly predetermines that certain people should be saved, and certain others should be damned. There is of course in the New Testament a doctrine of predestination or election (see, e.g., Romans 8:29f.; Ephesians 1:4f.). But this is a way of stressing that salvation is an act of God's gracious initiative, and Christians have always felt that salvation comes to them not so much because they chose it as because God out of sheer grace came and lovingly laid hold of them. But the New Testament does not teach the parallel idea that other men are predestined by God to eternal damnation. It says, in effect, 'If God wills to save you who are a sinner, that is his pure grace. If you refuse God's offer, you run the risk of bringing damnation on yourself.'

When Jesus himself spoke about human destiny, he always did so in a way which was designed to provoke choice and decision. He spoke about 'Gehenna' (which we normally translate as 'hell'), but never in a speculative way. He said little about the nature of Gehenna, and refused to discuss how well populated it might be. Every time, his words of judgment were directed to the people standing in front of him, urging *them* to take steps to avoid it. And when someone asked, 'Sir, will just a few people be saved?', he replied, 'Do your best to go in through the narrow door; because many people will surely try to go in but will not be able' (Luke 13:23f.). Not theoretical discussion about some other persons, but personal challenge to the hearers. The doctrine of hell is not about Judas or Hitler or Stalin. It is about you and me.

This so-called existential nature of Jesus's teaching—its personal and challenging, rather than theoretical, form—has led some scholars to suggest that hell is not a 'real destiny'. The language about judgment and hell is a way of provoking decision and of urging upon people the seriousness of deciding for God. But in the end no one actually finds himself in hell. I fail to see how this approach—even in its more sophisticated forms, as presented by John Robinson and John Hick[10]—does justice to the message of Jesus. What is the use or the morality of a threat which turns out to have no corresponding reality?

The nature of final destiny

If it is true that some people are excluded from God's final kingdom, what form does their destiny take?[11] The traditional view, which we have already noted in Augustine, is the doctrine of eternal punishment—an unending conscious experience of torment and anguish. In the last hundred years considerable ground has been gained by an alternative view, known as 'conditional immortality' or 'annihilationalism'. This is the view that after death, or after the judgment, those who have rejected Christ cease to exist. In my view the New Testament does not express itself clearly for one or other of these options. But the following observations are important.

First, we have already seen that Jesus had much more to say about how to avoid exclusion from God's presence than about what form such exclusion might take. His restraint on this matter is very striking when it is set against the full and lurid descriptions in some of the Jewish apocalyptic books (such as 1 Enoch) which were in circulation in Jesus's time. Even when he used a specific term such as 'Gehenna' (e.g., Matthew 10:28; Mark 9:43, 45, 47) he gave no descriptive content to it. Gehenna (the Valley of Hinnom) was in fact the valley to the south-west and south of Jerusalem which had become a byword for all that is abhorrent to God ever since it had been a place of child sacrifice in Jeremiah's day (see Jeremiah 7:31f.). There is, incidentally, as far as I know, no evidence earlier than the twelfth century A.D. for the popular view that the Valley of Hinnom was Jerusalem's rubbish dump in biblical times.

Jesus's language about the destiny of unbelievers is allusive rather than descriptive. Even the parable of the rich man and Lazarus, which might seem to offer a fuller description of conditions in the next world, cannot be used for this purpose. For Jesus is here making use of a popular Jewish tale, and so we would be rash to press the details of the story (Luke 16:19–31). And other New Testament terms, such as Paul's use of 'death', 'destruction', 'corruption', take us no further towards an actual description of hell. Only in the apocalyptic picture-language of Revelation, and one or two places such as Jude 6 and 13, do we find any fuller description. And it *is* picture-language.

There is good reason for all this restraint. Jesus and his apostles were concerned that people should decide for God and against hell, not out of desire for the comforts of heaven nor out of fear of the discomforts of hell. They wanted people to choose on the only proper grounds—desire for God himself and for the doing of his will. This is why Jesus spent time telling people how to avoid condemnation rather than describing what the existence of the condemned would be like.

There is a second important point. As we have seen, the New Testament understands salvation and condemnation in terms of relationship or lack of relationship towards God. Now, once this idea of relationship is seen to be fundamental, questions about the details of the after-life become ultimately irrelevant. If we know that heaven means to be with Christ, we do not need to know much else about it. And if hell means being without Christ, that is an enormous tragedy, and the New Testament writers see little point in asking whether the lost continue to be conscious or are annihilated. It is, perhaps, because we have been more concerned about happiness and misery than about godliness and sin that we have kept asking such questions.

Nevertheless, we must say something about the debate between 'eternal punishment' and 'conditional immortality'. If pressed, I must myself opt for the latter. The case for eternal punishment rests primarily on belief in the immortality of the soul, the requirement of divine justice that the sins of this life should be appropriately punished in the next, and the apparently explicit teaching of biblical passages such as Matthew 25:34,41,46; Mark 9:42f.; 2 Thessalonians 1:9; Revelation 14:11; 19:3; 20:10.

Supporters of 'conditional immortality', on the other hand, argue as follows. First, immortality of the soul is a non-biblical doctrine derived from Greek philosophy. In biblical teaching man is 'conditionally immortal'—that is, he has the possibility of becoming immortal if he receives resurrection or immortality as a *gift* from God. This would imply that God grants resurrection to those who love him, but those who resist him go out of existence.

Secondly, biblical images such as 'fire' and 'destruction' suggest annihilation rather than continuing conscious existence.

Thirdly, New Testament references to 'eternal punishment' (Matthew 25:46; cf. 2 Thessalonians 1:9; Hebrews 6:2) do not automatically mean what they have traditionally been assumed to mean. 'Eternal' may signify the permanence of the *result* of judgment rather than the continuation of the act of punishment itself. So 'eternal punishment' means an act of judgment where results cannot be reversed, rather than an experience of being punished for ever.

Fourthly, we must recognise that such New Testament language is picture-language. The fact that Jesus can speak of hell in terms of both 'darkness' and 'fire' surely makes it clear that such language must not be taken too literally. This of course does not remove our responsibility to take it very seriously, but it indicates that we should be very cautious about pressing such language into service in defence of eternal punishment.

Fifthly, eternal torment serves no useful purpose, and therefore exhibits a vindictiveness incompatible with the love of God in Christ.

Finally, eternal punishment requires that we believe in heaven and hell existing for ever 'alongside' each other. It seems impossible to reconcile this with the conviction that God will be 'all in all' (1 Corinthians 15:28). As we saw earlier, in Jesus's teaching the emphasis is not on hell as a place *into* which the unrepentant are thrown, but rather on the kingdom of God as a realm *from* which the unrepentant are excluded. So we are back again to the concept of relationship or non-relationship to God. That is what matters.

Will God not save all people?

During the twentieth century there has been a great increase in popularity of the doctrine known as universalism. This is the belief that ultimately God will bring all human beings to salvation and eternal life in his presence, so that no one in fact suffers condemnation to hell or annihilation.[12] Let us first survey motives which have led people towards this view.

First, there is a pastoral motive. How can it be right, many will say, to preach the doctrine of judgment outlined above to a congregation which includes people who have lost loved ones who did not seem to be Christians?

Second, there is the conviction that if anyone were to be excluded from God's kingdom for ever, then this would mean defeat for God's loving purpose. Only the salvation of all men can demonstrate that God's purpose is totally loving and that he has the power to carry it out.

Thirdly, there is the feeling that to fix a person's eternal destiny at the moment of death seems arbitrary. Why should we not imagine that there will be further opportunities beyond death when a man may recognise God's love and respond to it? And will not a God of love go on giving such opportunities, however many may be required, until his love meets with a response of love?

The fourth motive is the awareness that many millions of people do not or cannot respond to Christ because they belong to one of the non-Christian faiths, or because they have never heard the Christian message. Do the 700 million Hindus of India, for example, or its 100 million Muslims, have no place in God's saving purpose? And how can we believe that God would simply write off the 3,000 million people in today's world who, it is estimated, have never heard the gospel? The issue is put starkly in this story about the Indian Christian evangelist Sadhu Sundar Singh. Once when he was in England someone suggested that his mother, a saintly Sikh, was in hell because she had not been a Christian. The Sadhu's eyes flashed with indignation. 'If I cannot find my mother in heaven,' he said, 'I will ask God to send me down to hell so that I may be with her there.' And similar concerns are expressed about the status of those, such as children and the mentally ill, who have no possibility of understanding or responding to the Christian message.

Against such a background we can understand the attractiveness of universalism as expounded, for example, by John Robinson and John Hick.[13] Both argue that New

Testament language about judgment and condemnation is not a description of an ultimate destiny which some people will actually experience, but is 'mythical' language designed to provoke response to God. Both claim that God's love will in the end draw from all men the free response of love. In order for this to happen, Robinson implies, and Hick expounds in detail, a process of divine invitation and human response which is to take place after death. This is a drastically revised form of the old doctrine of purgatory. Whereas in the Roman Catholic doctrine the inhabitants of purgatory are the souls of the faithful departed being made fit for heaven, in this new doctrine they are joined by a new group of inhabitants—the *un*faithful departed. In this way Robinson and Hick are able to take care of those who in the present life have not heard or have not responded to the Christian message. Beyond death God will continue to draw them to himself until all respond freely to his love, and so rejoice in his presence.

Universalism assessed

It would be a strange Christian who did not feel the pull of universalism. Anyone who has deeply sensed the love of God must surely long that somehow God would bring every man and woman to experience that love. Universalism has a fine emphasis on God's love and his sovereignty in achieving his purpose. It offers hope and comfort to the bereaved. And yet these advantages are dearly bought, for the doctrine is a serious distortion of biblical teaching.

Let us come first to this question of what the New Testament teaches. I have already said enough about sayings of Jesus and other passages which warn of judgment to come, and which speak of two distinct possible destinies for human beings. And I have criticised the view that warnings of judgment are 'mythical' language, words of challenge, which turn out to be (in the strict sense) empty threats. But there are other New Testament passages which do seem to offer hope of universal salvation. Here are three of them:

> . . . God our Saviour, who wants everyone to be saved and to come to know the truth (1 Timothy 2:4; cf. 4:10).
>
> God has made all people prisoners of disobedience, so that he might show mercy on them all (Romans 11:32; cf. v. 26).
>
> This plan, which God will complete when the time is right, is to bring all creation together, everything in heaven and on earth, with Christ as head (Ephesians 1:10).

Other examples are John 12:32; Romans 5:12–21; 1 Corinthians 15:22; Colossians 1:20.

Some of these passages—notably 1 Timothy 2:4 and Ephesians 1:10— make it quite clear that God's expressed *desire* is that all people should be saved. But they cannot bear the weight which some universalists have wished to put on them. The wider context of these verses makes a universalist interpretation impossible to sustain. 1 Timothy contains a doctrine of final judgment irreconcilable with universalism (e.g., 4:18; 5:24; 6:9f.). And so does the letter to the Romans. How can anyone sensibly maintain that Romans 5 and 11 teach universalism, when Paul's closely-knit argument has already declared that all men are liable to God's judgment, and that salvation may be received only through faith (Romans 1–4)? When these passages in Romans about 'salvation for all' are understood in context, it is clear that they mean, not 'all human individuals, without exception, will be saved', but 'salvation is available to Jews and Gentiles alike'.

We must also observe that nearly all such 'universalist' statements occur alongside other statements about the need for faith in order to experience salvation. For example, in Colossians 1:19–23, God's plan 'to bring the whole universe back to himself' is said to include the Christians at Colossae *provided that* you continue in the faith'. So we can hardly take these 'universalist' statements as declarations of what *will* happen. Rather, they declare that God's saving purpose, focused in Jesus, has universal scope, even though some people may refuse to enter into that purpose.

If that, in essence, is the biblical case against universalism, what may we say about the motives which, as we saw, draw Christians towards the universalist viewpoint? We certainly cannot dismiss them as misguided or unworthy of serious attention. Let us take them one by one.

First, the pastoral motive. Whilst in the short term it may sometimes seem wisest to soft-pedal an unpleasant truth, this only leads to confusion in the long run. Truth itself is more important than pastoral expediency. A major reason why many people are in doubt about their relationship to God is that for many years they have not been taught clearly the message of judgment and salvation from judgment. But of course when confronted by the case of a particular individual, if there is doubt about whether he 'died in faith', we must 'err on the side of charity'. It is God's job, and not anyone else's, to judge how people stand in relation to him. Despite speaking so clearly about the choice which confronts people, Jesus and the New Testament writers refused to dogmatise about the eternal destiny of particular persons.

As for the argument that God's love must win all men in the end, I have already stressed that the nature of love itself prevents us from making such a dogmatic claim. Because love by definition must allow its object freedom to choose whether to respond or not, we *cannot* say that God's love will be successful in winning all men. Hick pictures God as a divine psychiatrist guiding people to their true goal. But what of the man who refuses to go to the psychiatrist? Hick does not take that problem seriously enough. If we are free to reject God, we must be free to reject him for ever.

Does that mean that God is defeated? Listen to C. S. Lewis: 'What you call defeat, I call miracle: for to make things which are not Itself, and thus to become, in a sense, capable of being resisted by its own handiwork, is the most astounding and unimaginable of all the feats we attribute to the Deity.' And he adds that if the gates of hell are locked, they are locked from the inside.[14]

The third motive was the feeling that opportunities for changing one's ways and responding to God ought to be available after death. Now there is no biblical teaching to support the idea of further chances after death. If anything about the nature of the next world can be drawn from Jesus's parable of the rich man and Lazarus (Luke 16:19–31), it is surely that our destinies are firmly fixed at death. And Hebrews 9:27 makes explicit what is implicit throughout the New Testament: 'Everyone must die once, and after that be judged by God.'[15] We live in a real world where real choices have to be made. It is folly to suppose that we shall have the opportunity or the will at some future time to make decisions which we refuse to make now.

Also, the idea of further chances after death involves belief in some kind of purgatory, and is open to the usual objections against any doctrine of purgatory.[16] Hick's scheme involves a long and tortuous progress from death until final salvation, which is quite different from Jesus's message of present salvation to be received or lost in immediate response to his preaching.

The challenge of other religions and the question of those who have had no real opportunity to respond to the message of Christ is the most weighty argument against the traditional Christian view of judgment and salvation. But it *is* possible to affirm the possibility of salvation for such people, *without* surrendering the belief that Jesus is God's unique means of salvation. People who lived before Christ or after him in non-Christian cultures may find salvation through Christ, even though they do not know his name, by casting themselves on the mercy of God. If a Hindu finds salvation, it is not by virtue of being a good Hindu, any more than a Christian is saved by being a good Christian. Whatever a person's religious background, 'saving faith' involves coming to an end of one's own 'religion' and abandoning oneself to the grace of God.

We cannot say how many people might be saved in this

way. But we can say that the God who reveals his love in Jesus is to be trusted to deal with all his creatures in the light of his love and his full knowledge of our lives. All our questions about the destiny of any person must be left with him, in even greater confidence than Abraham expressed when he exclaimed, 'Shall not the Judge of all the earth do right?' (Genesis 18:25). And we can say that there is a biblical hint that such an approach to non-Christian religions is right in the story of Cornelius (Acts 10). When Peter met this god-fearing Roman centurion he said, 'I now realise that it is true that God treats all men alike. Whoever fears him and does what is right is acceptable to him, no matter what race he belongs to' (Acts 10:34f.). Peter thus acknowledges that someone humbly seeking to serve God and depending on his grace (however hesitantly) may find favour with God. And yet of course he goes on to tell Cornelius the good news about Jesus and to baptize him and his family. From this we may be sure that any approach which says, 'A person may find salvation without explicitly putting faith in Jesus, and therefore it is wrong to evangelise people of other faiths', is out of step with the spirit of the New Testament.

Universalism, then, is both attractive and inadequate. God's loving desire for all people is that they should come to a knowledge of him. But a proper understanding of God's love and human freedom rules out the dogmatic assertion that God will certainly save all people eventually. We can never preach the love of God too much. But we can preach it too exclusively. That best known of all statements of God's love underlines the danger of failing to trust in the God of love: 'God loved the world so much that he gave his only Son, so that everyone who believes in him may not die but have eternal life' (John 3:16).

Living in face of death

The theme of judgment, then, is a theme in a minor key which highlights the glory of the main theme—the message that, for all who believe, Jesus Christ promises victory over death, and life in his presence. The fact of death we must take seriously. The New Testament does not encourage us to think of death as a friend. Death is an enemy to be conquered in the power of Christ. And we cannot live a full life unless we have come to grips with the prospect of death. Part of the unreality of our age is our sense that death—especially early death—is something which happens to other people. The composer Mozart expressed a healthier view in a letter to his father:

> . . . death is the key which unlocks the door to our true happiness. I never lie down at night without reflecting that—young as I am—I may not live to see another day. Yet no one of all my acquaintances could say that in company I am morose or disgruntled.
>
> For this blessing I daily thank my Creator and wish with all my heart that each of my fellow creatures could enjoy it.[17]

If we have faced the prospect of death, and have been released from the fear of death which saps our energy and misdirects our lives, we can face life with a new sense of commitment and a new sense that each day is God's gift. Geoffrey Lampe was Regius Professor of Divinity at Cambridge in the 1970s. One of the last things he wrote before his death in August 1980, was a sermon which ended like this:

> It seems, then, that to prepare against the fear of death we need to make the most of life: to enjoy life ourselves and to be thankful for it; to do our best to make it possible for other people to enjoy it more; to move through the enjoyment of life into enjoyment of God the source and giver of life, and to begin to experience that renewal of ourselves through his love which gives us the promise of fuller life to come.[18]

It is in clinging to Christ and serving him—who was crucified and raised victorious over death—that we are able to face our own death. For, as the writer to the Hebrews puts it, 'on our behalf Jesus has gone into heaven before us' (Hebrews 6:20). He is our fore-runner, our trail-blazer. And where he has opened the way, however dark it may seem, we can follow with confidence. If heaven means being welcomed into the presence of God, if it means the fulfilment of all our highest hopes and the transformation of our frail bodies, then in that we can rejoice.

We began the previous chapter with those words from the Prayer Book, 'In the midst of life we are in death.' But there is a deeper truth in Luther's triumphant cry: 'In the midst of death we are surrounded by life.' [19]

Notes to chapter 6

1. Even though some scholars have argued that some of Jesus's sayings in the gospels may not have been originally spoken by him, they have persuaded no one that *all* such sayings can be eliminated in this way. See the careful discussion in W. Strawson, *Jesus and the Future Life* (Epworth, London, second edition 1970), esp. chs 4,8.

2. *Select Works of Jonathan Edwards*, vol. 2 (Banner of Truth, London, 1959), pp. 191f.

3. *The Problem of Pain*, pp. 107f. I have offered a detailed exposition of the theme of judgment in the Bible in *Christ and the Judgment of God* (Marshall Pickering, Basingstoke, 1986).

4. *The Epistle to the Romans* (Eng. tr., Oxford University Press, London, 1933), p. 51.

5. *CMS News-letter* no. 367, January 1973, p. 2. Helmut Thielicke urged a similar understanding of events on Germans in the 1940s: see *The Prayer that Spans the World* (Eng. tr., James Clarke, London, 1965), pp. 57f.

6. *Evangelism Today* (Christian Journals, Belfast, 1976), p. 75.

7. Quoted in Action, WACC newsletter October 1977, p. 8, from *Good News* (Sunday Publications, Lake Worth, Florida).

8. *Letters to Malcolm* (Bles, London, 1964), p. 99.

9. J. A. Baird, *The Justice of God in the Teaching of Jesus* (SCM, London, 1963), p. 217.

10. Robinson, *In the End God* (Collins, London 1968); Hick, *Death and Eternal Life* (Collins, London, 1976).

11. I have said more than there is space for here in *Christian Hope and the Future of Man*, pp. 133–6.
12. Recent surveys of the development of this belief are by R. J. Bauckham, 'Universalism: a historical survey', *Themelios* 4.2, January 1979, pp. 48–54; and A. M. Fairhurst, 'Death and Destiny', *Churchman 95, 1981 pp. 313–325.*
13. See note 10 above. I have discussed their views more fully in *Christian Hope and the Future of Man*, pp. 125–33.
14. *The Problem of Pain*, p. 115.
15. The old idea that 1 Peter 3:19f. refers to Christ's preaching to people after death has now been abandoned by most commentators. It refers to Christ's proclaiming his victory to supernatural powers. And 1 Peter 4:6 is probably about people who were *now* dead (at the time of writing of 1 Peter) but to whom the gospel had been preached during their lifetime.
16. See *Christian Hope and the Future of Man*, pp. 119, 130f; and N. T. Wright, 'Universalism and the World-Wide Community', *Churchman* 89, 1975, pp. 204f.
17. *The Letters of Mozart and his Family*. transl. E. Anderson (Macmillan, London, 1938), vol. 3, p. 1351.
18. 'Life after Death', *Epworth Review* vol 7, no. 3, 1980, p. 49.
19. *Works* (Weimar edition), 11.141.22.

Chapter 7   Living in Hope

To live in hope means to live by the truths which we have studied in previous chapters. For hope has two basic senses. It means, first, the *object* on which we set our expectations— for example, the second coming of Jesus and all that we associate with that event. Secondly, it means the *attitude* and style of life we adopt in the light of that expectation. Hope in the second sense without any objective basis is delusion. To claim to have a hope in the first sense without a corresponding effect in attitudes and lifestyle is sheer hypocrisy.

The need for hope is everywhere to be seen. Watch the junior school child, his eyes bright with hope and with wonder at the world. Then see this turn to the cynical frustration of the teenager, and the resigned routine of the adult who has discovered that life has to be lived but it is unwise to expect much of it. The only difference between the teenager and the adult is that the adult prefers to conceal even from himself his aimlessness, whereas the teenager publicises it and makes it his rule of life. Don McLean's lines catch the mood:

> If I knew the future
> you'd be the first to know,
> but I know nothing of what life's about—
> as long as you live you never find out.

Then comes, very often, the depression of the parents whose children have grown up and left home, and who are left with no goals to work for. And the narrow street of old age, with its sign, 'No Through Road'. J. B. Priestley writes with great honesty about what it feels like to be old in his autobiography, *Instead of the Trees*: 'I detest being old . . . In old age we are compelled to play a bad character part, not belonging to our essential and enduring self. . . . We have no longer anything important to contribute.' He speaks of the effort of daily routine, and the 'hideous loss' of friends. 'Just over 50 years ago, a large group of us, including some famous literary figures, used to meet in a Fleet Street pub to drink and air our wit. Only two of us are left.'[1] Equally eloquent was the suicide note left by an old person: 'So tired of buttoning and unbuttoning'.

The loss of hope is not put right by trivial answers. And it is not only a matter of the personal attitude of the person who has lost hope. The young person is deeply influenced by the moral confusion, the low prospects of employment, the unattractiveness of work in the society which he enters. The despair of the old person may be caused more by other people's thoughtlessness and lack of love than by his own attitudes. And yet the Christian must declare that for people of all ages and situations hope can be found again—not necessarily to remove the pain, but to face it. Here are three ways in which hope is pictured in the Bible.

Pictures of hope

First, hope is a *door*. In Hosea 2:15 God promises to Israel, 'I will make Trouble Valley a door of hope.' Trouble Valley was the burial-place of Achan, who at the time of Joshua's conquest of Jericho had stolen part of the spoil from that city. When his disobedience was discovered he and his family were put to death (Joshua 7). Now, says Hosea, the very place of disobedience and destruction can become a door of hope. Why? Because God cannot give up his constant love for Israel and will turn her to repentance. Because there is God, there is hope. We can go back to the point where we ceased to trust God, even if it was a point of great disobedience, and find ourselves offered a new beginning, a new future. Even in the midst of trouble, the God of hope comes near to us.

Hope is also a *helmet*. 'We must wear our hope of salvation as a helmet' (1 Thessalonians 5:8). Like a soldier equipped and alert to resist attack, we can resist fear, anxiety and fatalism because we are secure in the knowledge that our future is in God's hands. 'God did not choose us to suffer his anger, but to possess salvation through our Lord Jesus Christ, who died for us in order that we might live together with him, whether we are alive or dead when he comes' (1 Thessalonians 5:9f.).

Thirdly, hope is an *anchor*. 'We who have found safety wth God are greatly encouraged to hold firmly to the hope placed before us. We have this hope as an anchor for our lives' (Hebrews 6:18f.). The writer to the Hebrew Christians was faced with a group of readers tempted to abandon faith in Jesus. They felt the pressures of persecution and the uncertainty involved in being a young church on an uncharted voyage away from the familiar landmarks of Judaism. But the writer tells them that, whatever storms they may face, they are moored to an immovable object. Hope is 'safe and sure' because it is grounded in the risen Jesus, who has entered heaven as our fore-runner and who guarantees that we shall follow him there (verse 19). This promise of life in Jesus beyond death is not the only part of Christian hope—'pie in the sky when we die' is a lop-sided view of the Christian message. But if we can know security in face of the ultimate issues of life and death, how much more can we face with hope the other challenges of life?

Resources for hope

A distinctive feature of Christian belief, as we saw in chapter 3, is that our hope arises from what God has done already in Christ. We look forward to God's final kingdom not out of a desperate desire for compensation for what we lack now, but out of a present experience of God which encourages us to ask for more. Our hoping is based on four facts of present experience.

First, we live by *the promises of God*. 'Promises, promises!' has in our day become the cynical retort of people weary with the tricks of advertisers and politicians. Yet the whole history of God's people from Abraham onwards is the story of a people sustained and led forward by a God who does not break his word. The ability to keep promises depends on the faithfulness and power of the one who promises. And God's people have found him to be one who keeps his promises. 'Let us hold on firmly to the hope we profess, because we can trust God to keep his promise' (Hebrews 10:23; cf. 11:11). That is what enabled people such as Abraham and Moses to take the risks of faith which they took. They lived not by their feelings, not even by evidence. They were able to keep going on little evidence, because they sensed that God would always do what he had promised—even if his methods and his timing were sometimes surprising. The church today needs leaders and people who, when clear evidence of God's activity is sparse, can survive because they are nourished by God's promises.

Secondly, we live in *a new era*. The letters of Paul, for example, exude this sense of newness. Because Jesus has come, has died and has risen, he has brought the life of God's longed-for kingdom into present experience. Through union with Christ we already, in a real sense, experience the blessings of the heavenly world (Ephesians 1:3). We are part of a 'new creation' (2 Corinthians 5:17). We have put on the 'new self', 'the new being which God, its Creator, is constantly renewing in his own image' (Colossians 3:10). We are the people of a 'new covenant' (1 Corinthians 11:25). This sense of decisive fulfilment, the sense that God's purposes have entered a new stage and he is closer to men and women than ever before, is a powerful incentive to hope.

Another way of expressing this is to say that we are *risen with Christ*. Not only does his resurrection imply our future resurrection from death. But if we are united with him we already share in the newness of his risen life. We can already experience something of the godly and eternal quality which characterises that life. 'By our baptism, then, we were buried with him and shared his death, in order that, just as Christ was raised from death by the glorious power of the Father, so also we might live a new life' (Romans 6:4; cf. Colossians 3:1–4). Because he is risen and shares the power of his life with his people, we too may rise again. Whoever and whatever we are—self-seeking or self-pitying, insensitive or broken-hearted, enslaved by habits or by meaningless routine—we dare never say that the God who raised Jesus from the dead can do nothing with us. Risen with him, we share his destiny.

The fourth resource for hope is *the Holy Spirit*, whom the New Testament describes as the 'first fruits' and the 'guarantee' of the life of heaven (Romans 8:23; 2 Corinthians 1:22; Ephesians 1:14—once again, it is Paul especially who brings us this perspective). In other words, the Spirit gives us now a foretaste of the full blessings of the coming kingdom. Only a foretaste—there is more to come—yet a real taste. He makes us aware of our relationship to God as children to a father, and enables us to call God 'Abba', thus echoing that term of intimate obedience used by Jesus himself (Romans 8:15f.; Galatians 4:6). The full experience of 'sonship' must wait until the final revealing of God's kingdom (Romans 8:23).

Not only does the Spirit make us children of God, he also pours into our hearts that supreme characteristic of heaven, love (Romans 5:5). And he enables us to glimpse now the dazzling glory of his presence (2 Corinthians 3). The Holy Spirit is *the* distinctive sign of the present era in God's purposes, the guarantee that our 'hope does not disappoint us' (Romans 5:5).

The direction of hope

You can never go back to God. He is always in front, leading his people forward. In one of my occasional nightmares, I am playing in an orchestra, and the composition we are playing gets increasingly complex and difficult as the piece progresses. I reach a point where I feel defeated by the difficulty and decide to go back to the beginning. And then I wake up. . . . The fact is, the orchestral player cannot go back. The music is going on around him. He must stay with it, trusting the conductor to guide him through the cross-rhythms till the climax is reached and he is enveloped in relief and applause. As Hebrews 11 shows so vividly, those Old Testament men of faith followed God's leading, despite hesitations about their own ability to stand the pace. They clung to his promise, 'I will never leave you; I will never abandon you' (Hebrews 13:5).

The most basic term we use for the Christian life is a term of movement. We talk about 'following Jesus'. And that implies a refusal to stand still. We stick with him, we follow him, even when he does not tell us exactly where he is taking us or how we are going to get there. Living in hope is a life of adventure, of openness to the future with all its hidden possibilities. I do not think the subject of God's guidance for our lives is an easy one to handle. There do not seem to be any clear-cut rules by which to work things out. But if there are rules, one of the most basic ones is that we should be ready for surprises! God does not get himself stuck in ruts, and we may confidently expect that at some stage he will jolt our routine and provoke us to some quite radical change in our lives. A man in Germany got a divorce after ten years of marriage on the grounds that his wife gave him a tie and a pair of socks every Christmas. This was accepted as evidence that the marriage had 'gone dead'. A Christian life which is as predictable as that and has lost all sense of surprise and adventure has gone dead, too.

Not only adventure, but purpose also is implied by God's leading us forward. A Frenchman chose these words for his epitaph: Here lies a man who went out of the world without knowing why he came into it.

The hope of Christ's return, by contrast, fills our lives with purpose because it lays bare the ultimate issues of life.

It tells us God's purpose for us—life in a kingdom of righteousness and love—and thus directs us to goals in this life which demand all our energy and which are deeply satisfying. They are satisfying precisely because they are what we are made *for*, in contrast to the false ideals, the escapism, the aimlessness which characterise so many people's lives. 'You have been set free', wrote Peter, 'from the worthless manner of life handed down by your ancestors . . . Through Christ you believe in God, who raised him from death and gave him glory; and so your faith and hope are fixed on God' (1 Peter 1:18, 21).

Jesus spoke of the purpose of life like this, 'Whoever wants to save his own life will lose it; but whoever loses his life for me and for the gospel will save it' (Mark 8:35). We discover the purpose of life not by looking first to our own needs, not by trying to satisfy our own lust for self-expression and personal success, but by self-giving in love for God and neighbour. There is no point in climbing the ladder of success only to find that it is leaning against the wrong wall.

A life of Christ-likeness

When Jesus comes again we shall be like him. We shall be perfect, free from sin, and full of love. And our whole Christian life now is a movement towards that goal. This is the argument of John:

> My dear friends, we are now God's children, but it is not yet clear what we shall become. But we know that when Christ appears, we shall be like him, because we shall see him as he really is. Everyone who has this hope in Christ keeps himself pure, just as Christ is pure (1 John 3:2f.).

Just as a mirror reflects the image of the person who stands before it, so we shall reflect the character of Christ when we stand before him. And we are called now—by the power of

God's Spirit within us—to live in anticipation of that perfect Christ-likeness.

It used to be called 'holiness', and that is not a popular concept these days. But if we have thrown out the conviction that God sets before us the demanding goal of becoming increasingly Christlike in character, then we have thrown out something indispensable to true Christian living. Stephen Neill puts it graphically when he writes:

> Whenever any ideal is presented to the Christian other than that of complete transformation after the likeness of Christ, the indolence of man naturally sinks down to a placid contentment with mediocrity, and supposes that God has nothing better to do than to ferry unchanged men over the troubled waters of this world to a peaceful habitation in heaven.[2]

It is true that we shall not attain sinless perfection in this life. But to use that as an excuse for refusing to strive towards the goal is a refusal to take seriously the Holy Spirit whose work it is to produce within us the life of heaven now.

John Wesley put it like this: 'Repentance is the porch of religion, faith is the door of religion, holiness is religion itself. . . . None shall live with God but he that now *lives to* God; none shall enjoy the glory of God in heaven but he that bears the image of God on earth.'[3] Wesley defined holiness primarily in terms of Christian love, and in doing so he was certainly in tune with the emphasis of the New Testament. Paul argues in 1 Corinthians 13 that, because love endures through eternity, it is to be the chief mark of our lives now. Self-giving, Christlike love is never wasted: its effects continue for ever.

A life of tension

In a real sense, as we have seen, the kingdom of God has already come, and its blessings are part of our present

216

experience. But the kingdom has not yet fully come. The present age, with its imperfect conditions and imperfect people, continues. We live 'between the times', and this involves conflict and tension. Any account of the Christian life which ignores this tension is unbalanced fantasy. Let me illustrate how the tension works out.

There is a tension in our *spiritual life*, because of the conflict between the Holy Spirit and what Paul calls 'the flesh'—that is, our sinful nature. Paul describes this conflict in Galatians 5:16–26 and in Romans 7. It is a conflict which stays with us as long as we live this earthly life. Always there is the possibility of surrendering to the desires of our sinful nature. But always there is the possibility of living by the power of the Spirit, the possibility of being Christlike. So we must seek always to be open to the help of God's Spirit, we must see ourselves as *new* people, confident in the Spirit's ability to make us live like new people. But when we fail, we should not imagine that God has abandoned us. The Spirit is absent when we give up fighting the war, not when we lose a particular battle. But neither must we imagine that we are ever immune from temptation. Paul dealt sternly in his Corinthian correspondence with people who thought that they had somehow passed beyond the level of this conflict between Spirit and flesh. 'Do you already have everything you need? Are you already rich? Have you become kings, even though we are not? Well, I wish you really were kings, so that we could be kings together with you' (1 Corinthians 4:8). You are fools, he is saying, if you imagine that you are already experiencing the perfect life of God's final kingdom. If your ecstatic spiritual state has led you to think that you have left behind this world of suffering and temptation, then it is not a genuinely Christian experience. For the pattern of genuine experience is always the pattern of both dying and rising, both suffering and hope, both temptation and victory—which is the pattern of our crucified and risen Lord (see 1 Corinthians 4:8–13; 2 Corinthians 13:4; Philippians 3:12–16).

Secondly, there is tension in our *use of time*. In one sense, the Christian has 'all the time in the world'. We need not panic, as though this life were all there is. We can relax in the knowledge that God controls all time and sees time from the perspective of eternity—there is no difference in his sight between one day and a thousand years (2 Peter 3:8). We can entrust our time to God because God alone knows how much time remains before the coming of Jesus or our own death.

Yet in another sense time is short, and there is a lot to be done. This sense is heightened when the reality of death is close. Janani Luwum, Archbishop of Uganda, died on the night of 16th February 1977, the victim of Idi Amin's tyranny. Two months earlier he had said

> I do not know for how long I shall be occupying this chair. I live as though there will be no tomorrow. I face daily being picked up by the soldiers. While the opportunity is there, I preach the gospel with all my might, and my conscience is clear before God that I have not sided with the present government, which is utterly self-seeking. I have been threatened many times. Whenever I have the opportunity I have told the President the things the churches disapprove of. God is my witness. [His final words to his fellow-bishops, as he was led away to meet Amin and death, were] I can see the hand of the Lord in this.[4]

It is a cliché, but nevertheless true, that people who have survived a close brush with death have a vivid sense of the need to treat every moment as a gift, and to give priority in life to things which have some ultimate value. Flute-player James Galway describes how an almost fatal road accident affected him:

> I decided that henceforward I would play every concert, cut every record, give every TV programme as though it were my last. I have come to understand that it is never

possible to guess what might happen next; that the roof might fall in any time and that the important thing is to make sure that every time I play the flute my performance will be as near perfection and full of true music as God intended and that I shall not be remembered for a shoddy performance.[5]

John Wesley said: Never be triflingly employed.' For him that meant 'Never relax', which overplays one side of the tension which I am trying to describe. For us, perhaps, it means, 'Always live responsibly before God, learn to distinguish the things that matter from the things that matter less, and whether you are working or relaxing do it with a sense that your time is God's gift.' It is quality, not quantity, which matters in life as in most things.

This tension in our thinking about time also suggests how we should think about planning for the future in the light of Christ's second coming. As individuals and as churches we must plan wisely for the future, since we do not know when Christ will come. Without planning, we simply go round in unproductive circles, and that brings no honour to God. It is as silly for a church not to plan its goals strategically for the next year or the next five years, as it would be for me to go shopping for only one day's food at a time on the grounds that Christ might come before next week. But because we do not know when he will come, there must be an urgency, a sense that what we do *now* matters. At a meeting of the Connecticut Assembly in 1780 there was a sense of approaching judgment, of the world coming to an end. Outside, there was a threatening roll of thunder. The Speaker said, 'Either this is the end of the world or it is not. If it is not, we should proceed with the business. If it is, I prefer to be found doing my duty.'

The Christian and this world

The third tension is in our *use of this world's wealth*. On the one hand, we recognise this world as God's world and we rejoice in its rich variety of people and resources. 'Everything that God has created is good: nothing is to be rejected, but everything is to be received with a prayer of thanks. [God] generously gives us everything for our enjoyment' (1 Timothy 4:4; 6:17). The Bible does not idealise poverty. It does not say everyone ought to be poor. The implication of God's instructions to man in Genesis 1, of many Psalms such as Psalm 104, of the theme of harvest and man's stewardship over the created world, is that God generously gives what is needed for a richly satisfying human life. And the Bible's pictures of God's final kingdom make clear that God intends people to 'lack no good thing'. The miracle of the feeding of the five thousand was a sign that that is how it would be. The Christian has every encouragement to enjoy what this world offers, whether it is the beauty of nature, good food, or the products of human creativity in the fields of art and material goods. Penny-pinching asceticism is not a Christian virtue. So we see Jesus in the gospel accounts going to parties, appreciating nature, savouring this world and human relationships as gifts of a generous God.

But we see another side, too. We see Jesus urging the rich young ruler to sell all that he has and to give the money to the poor, surprising his disciples by saying it will take a miracle for rich people to get into the kingdom of God (Mark 10:21–25). There is a painfully radical choice to be made between earthly wealth and heavenly wealth (Luke 12:13–21; 32–34), between God's kingdom and everything else (Luke, 12:22–31; 14:33), between God and money (Luke 16:13). It is all very demanding, and if Christians had put as much energy and imagination into the missionary task as we have put into inventing ways of side-stepping this demand, the world would be a very different place.

And yet it is too simplistic to suppose that Jesus told every follower of his to sell everything and have nothing more to do with wealth. For he himself was supported by the generosity of a group of wealthy women (Luke 8:2f.). He valued the use of people's homes (Luke 10:38f.; Mark

14:14f.). He did not shun the rich, nor did he propound theories about the evil of ownership of private property. Jesus was indifferent to theorising about wealth, because he looked for the coming of God's kingdom. 'He adopted the same scandalously free and untrammelled attitude to property as to the powers of the state. . . . The imminence of the kingdom of God robs all these things of their power *de facto*, for in it "many that are first will be last, and the last first" ' (Mark 10:31).[6]

Under the rule of God we discover that God supports our lives and there is no need to fret about our material needs. And because we are freed from such anxiety we can share freely with others. This is the point where Jesus left no room for compromise. He condemned not the creation of wealth, but the possession and protection of wealth for personal pleasure and security, while the poor man lies unheeded at the door (cf. Luke 16:19–31). He knows that in the coming kingdom there will be no rich and no poor. All will have their needs supplied by God. And those who belong to the kingdom must live out the implications of that kingdom, now. If we refuse to take seriously this call to be open-handed with our wealth, we are like those Pharisees who sneered at Jesus's declaration that 'you cannot serve both God and money' because they loved money too much. And Jesus's words to them are aimed afresh at us: 'You are the ones who make yourselves look right in other people's sight, but God knows your hearts. For the things that are considered of great value by man are worth nothing in God's sight' (Luke 16:14f.). To be attached to what is 'worth nothing in God's sight' is a perilous situation to be in. If the kingdom of God is real to us, we have no choice but to demonstrate by a joyful quality of life that 'a person's true life is not made up of the things he owns, no matter how rich he may be' (Luke 12:15). This demonstration must surely include a commitment to sharing our resources with those who have less, and limiting our own consumption of resources where failure to limit it deprives others of a share.

Jesus and the Bible do *not* teach that wealth is evil because it is always gained at the expense of the poor, though that is often the case (e.g., Amos 5:11; Mark 12:40; James 5:1–6). But they *do* say that to have wealth and not to be generous with it for the help of those in need is incompatible with membership in God's kingdom (Luke 16:19–31; 2 Corinthians 8:13f.; James 2:14–17; 1 John 3:16–18). We are called not to poverty, but to love. Listen to these Filipino peasants, commenting on the story of the good Samaritan:

> If you say that the test of love is how much you are willing to get hurt for the person you love, let us be clear that in ordinary day-to-day life, what really hurts most is to part with money or property. And it seems . . . that Christ really knows how to test human nature. For when someone asked him once, what is the test of love, he answered in the form of a story describing the test in terms of money . . . Christ's answer is dramatically clear: 'If there should be more expenses, I shall pay.' The answer is in financial terms—in terms of action against hunger, and sickness, and misery.[7]

Now of course all this raises big questions about how such attitudes and actions are to be worked out in the details of our lives. Jesus gave no rules. He left us to work it out, and he expected that there would be different implications for different people. If he did not have to be concerned with consumer goods and investment in arms dealers and church property, we do. The message which Jesus incarnated in his own time we are called to incarnate afresh in ways appropriate for our own day.[8] Lest we lose heart at the complexities of it all, let us remember that it is the *personal* relationship created by sharing which is characteristically Christian. Even the cup of cold water counts in the kingdom of God. I have myself been deeply moved to receive a portion of watermelon from the hands of Christian gypsies in southern

Greece, and a banana from a fellow-passenger on a train in India.

Our attitude to this world's goods, then, derives from the tension between these two key principles: we enjoy the things which God our creator has made, yet in view of the coming kingdom we do not cling to them but share them with open hand and heart. As Paul puts it, 'those who use the world's wealth must not count on using it to the full. For the whole frame of this world is passing away' (1 Corinthians 7:31, NEB). This basic stance is beautifully expressed by an unknown writer of the second century:

> The Christians are distingushed from other men neither by country, nor language, nor the customs which they observe. For they neither inhabit cities of their own, nor employ a peculiar form of speech, nor lead a life which is marked out by any singularity. . . . They dwell in their own countries, but simply as sojourners. As citizens, they share in all things with others, and yet endure all things as if foreigners. Every foreign land is to them as their native country, and every land of their birth as a land of strangers. . . . They are in the flesh, but they do not live after the flesh. They pass their days on earth, but they are citizens of heaven. They obey the prescribed laws, and at the same time surpass the laws by their lives. They love all men, and are persecuted by all. . . . They are poor, yet make many rich. . . . To sum up all in one word—what the soul is in the body, that are Christians in the world.
>
> (Letter to Diognetus, c. A.D. 150.)

Briefly, we mention three other examples of the tension created by hope. There is a tension between *suffering and glory*. Because the conflict between good and evil, between God and the forces ranged against him, goes on until Jesus's coming, Christians expect to suffer. We know that, like our Master, 'we must pass through many troubles to enter the Kingdom of God' (Acts 14:22). It may be the suffering of persecution by hostile neighbours or by an anti-Christian state, it may be the loss of a job because you are unwilling to adopt an unethical way of working. It may mean the suffering of bearing other people's burdens or the loneliness of being misunderstood and unsupported in a situation on the frontiers of the Christian mission.

Such suffering reminds us that the kingdom of God has not yet fully come. But it *is* on the way. Because suffering is the prelude to a glory which has already begun to be revealed, and because it is the way that Jesus himself went, the New Testament passages about suffering breathe an extraordinary sense of joy and purpose. Always in suffering there is hope—even Jesus on the cross said, '*My* God . . .' And the suffering is itself a sign that the sufferer is destined by God for the glory of his kingdom. 'My dear friends, do not be surprised at the painful test you are suffering, as though something unusual were happening to you. Rather be glad that you are sharing Christ's sufferings, so that you may be full of joy when his glory is revealed' (1 Peter 4:11f.; cf. 1:6–9; Romans 5:2–5). It follows from this that, whilst it is right to pray for God's sustaining power through suffering, and even for deliverance from it, we should not be bewildered if the suffering is not removed from us. If we pray and 'nothing happens', it is our 'triumphalist' theology rather than our attitude of prayer that is wrong.

Suffering can become the door to hope, because it pushes us into the arms of the God of resurrection. No day was ever more loaded with hope than Good Friday. As Pascal said, 'It is a happy time for the church when she is sustained by nothing other than God.'[9]

The thought of suffering leads us to the question of physical suffering and the possibility of *healing*. Here again, we must learn from the tension between the present and future comings of God's kingdom. Because the kingdom has come, healing of the body is a real and marvellous possibility. God heals both through medicine and through prayer and the work of the Spirit. Jesus pointed to his healings as signs that the rule of God had dawned (Matthew 11:2–6), and Paul spoke of the spiritual gift of healing continuing in the church during the present era (1 Corinthians 12:9, 28; 13:8–10). Yet Jesus did not heal all people. Paul himself had his 'thorn in the flesh', which was probably a 'painful physical ailment' (2 Corinthians 12:7, GNB). And he says he left Trophimus ill (2 Timothy 4:20)—apparently not expecting him to be instantly healed.

Jesus's healings were signs, advance notices of what God's kingdom would be like. They showed that God's destiny for his people is a life free from pain and imperfection. The people healed were living demonstrations that the blessings of the kingdom were already overflowing into history. But it is cruel deception to teach that any sick person may be healed 'if only he has enough faith'. We are to pray for healing in trust and without apologising as though there were something presumptuous about such prayer. But we are to wait in hope, understanding that, if healing is not given now, it most certainly will be given in the ultimate purposes of God.

Finally, there is a tension in the realm of *thought, faith and doubt*. The fact that Christ has already come as God's self-disclosure means that our faith and thinking have something solid to chew on. We are not left groping in the dark, wondering what God is like and whether he will ever reveal his character and purposes to mankind. But there is still a 'not yet' in this intellectual realm as in other aspects of our lives. Only when God's rule fully comes shall we 'know as fully as God knows us now' (cf. 1 Corinthians 13:12). To claim more knowledge about God than God has in fact revealed is the same kind of mistake as to pretend that we have already passed beyond the reach of temptation and sin.

There are two implications of this. In theology, we must recognise that our knowledge and understanding of God's truth is partial until Jesus comes again. Whilst God has given us real truth and enough of it for our salvation and our life in the world, we must acknowledge that many things remain mysterious to us. And we must admit that our particular way of expressing God's truth may not be the only true way to understand it. There is need for respect and humility before other people's ways of understanding, though all must submit to judgment and correction by what God has already made known in Christ.

The second implication is more personal. It is that doubt is not something which should necessarily surprise us or make us feel guilty. As long as our knowledge is partial, and is based on trust rather than sight (2 Corinthians 5:7), doubt may be part of our experience. Doubt is quite different from unbelief, which is a refusal to trust. Doubt trusts, whilst acknowledging the darkness. It hangs on, believing that in God's good time faith will give way to sight, and darkness to sight, in the light of God's presence. What we see now is 'like a dim image in a mirror', compared with our seeing then 'face to face' (1 Corinthians 13:12). Yet Paul is not saying that we can see nothing at all!

The whole theme of tension in the Christian's life is magnificently summed up in Romans 8. Here Paul describes the conflict between Spirit and flesh (verses 5–11), the need for moral effort and openness to the Holy Spirit's work (verses 12–17), the experience of suffering and incompleteness (verses 18–25), but also the resources provided by God's grace to meet this conflict (verses 1–4, 14–16, 26–30), and the assurance of final victory (verses 31–39): '. . . there is nothing in all creation that will ever be able to separate us from the love of God which is ours through Christ Jesus our Lord.'

Hope for the world?

So far in this chapter we have thought about hope mainly as it affects the life of the individual Christian. We must now ask what hope there is for the world and for the ongoing life of society. Is there *any* hope, or must we accept the predictions of the most pessimistic doomsters? Early in 1980 Jean-Paul Sartre said this:

With this third world war which might break out one day, with this wretched gathering which our planet now is, despair returns to tempt me. The idea that we'll never be done with it, that there's no purpose, only petty personal ends for which we fight. We make little revolutions but there's not a human end. Nothing concerning man, only disorders. One can't think such things. They tempt you incessantly, especially if you're old and can think, 'Oh, well, anyway, I shall die in five years at the most.' In fact I think ten, but it might well be five. In any case the world seems ugly, bad and without hope. There, that's the cry of despair of an old man who'll die in despair. But that's exactly what I resist, and I know I shall die in hope. But that hope needs a foundation.

Within a month he was dead, apparently without having found the foundation for which he searched. His words sum up that unresolved conflict of despair and hope which affects so many thoughtful people today. We watch the earth's population increase and its natural resources diminish. We are surrounded by the technical capability both to explode the planet and to improve greatly the standard of living of its poorer nations. We see nations lurch from one uneasy crisis to another. We Christians, like other people, wonder what God is doing.

Our general unease finds sharper form in the question: would God allow a nuclear war to happen? Would he not preserve us from such horror? If such an unthinkable thing were to happen, would it not multiply amongst the few survivors the disillusionment which led many to abandon God after the 1914–18 and 1939–45 wars? I am bound to say that in a world where God has allowed human beings to exercise free will there can be no absolute guarantee that a nuclear war would not happen. Many people in Jerusalem in the sixth century B.C. believed they had an absolute guarantee that Jerusalem and the Temple were safe for ever. They sang of this guarantee in psalms such as Psalms 46, 48, 132. Then came the destruction of the city by

227

Nebuchadnezzar in 587 B.C., and they were shattered by despair and puzzlement at the purposes of God, as the book of Lamentations shows. To us the destruction of the Temple may seem a trivial thing compared to a nuclear holocaust. But to the Jews it was everything. To them it felt like the end of the world. The utterly unthinkable had come to pass.

It is beyond our imagining what the effects of a nuclear war might be, and how its survivors might begin again. We dare to hope that God would restrain us from ever starting it. But if it were to happen, we could find resources for hope. We could draw courage from the fact that there was a new beginning after the destruction of Jerusalem and the exile, and again after Good Friday. And we could discover the reality of the God who 'brings the dead to life and whose command brings into being what did not exist' (Romans 4:17).

The Marxist vision

One approach to the future of the world with an overwhelming claim to be taken seriously is Marxism. I will not try to describe it fully, but will refer to some features of Marxism which particularly affect our topic, and then make some comments on them. I am aware that in these days Marxism takes many forms, but I will refer to some central tenets of classical Marxism.

Karl Marx's theory arose out of anger and concern: anger at what he saw happening to working people as a result of the industrial revolution, and concern that things should be changed so that such oppression might be replaced by a good life for all. French writer Merleau Ponty wrote, 'One does not become a revolutionary through science but through indignation.' And Che Guevara, 'Let me tell you, at the risk of looking ridiculous, that a true revolutionary is led by great feelings of love.'[10] Marx's collaborator Friedrich Engels was contemptuous about a contemporary Christianity which 'did not want to accomplish the social transformation in this world, but beyond it, in heaven, in eternal life after death, in the impending "millennium" '[11] And Marx wrote, 'The social principles of Christianity preach cowardice, self-contempt, abasement, submission, dejection.'[12]

Marx observed how the laws of economics are closely related to men's relationships in society. Indeed, he claimed that all aspects of human society could be explained in terms of economics. In particular, he saw how the new methods of production in the industrial revolution concentrated power in the hands of fewer and fewer people (the owners of the means of production). The vast majority of people are forced to sell their labour to the factory-owners, who pay them as little as they can get away with paying. Thus man is valued merely by how much economic 'punch' he can muster. He is 'alienated' because the social and economic situation prevents him from being truly himself. Marx envisaged that the growing class-struggle between the owners of capital and the working men would get worse and worse because, built into the capitalist system, was this process whereby the wealth gets concentrated in a few whilst poverty of the poor increases. And this provided him with his revolutionary theory.

For this process taking place in the outworkings of capitalism is part of an inevitable process taking place through the *epochs of history*. By a process of thesis and antithesis, or action and reaction, history is moving through seven inevitable stages or epochs—the primitive, the communal, the slave, the feudal, the capitalist, the socialist and the communist. In each case a conflict is set up in society between an established pattern (thesis) and a newly emerging factor (antithesis), which is resolved in the creation of a new situation (synthesis), which in its turn becomes the thesis initiating the next stage of history. And then the pattern is repeated. The important thing is that this development through the course of history is fixed and unalterable. You can no more stop it progressing than you can stop the tide rising up the beach.

And the Marxist revolution consists in recognising that this is the case, and working with it. The revolutionary can 'speed up' the arrival of the socialist era by intensifying the class struggle and thus hastening the collapse of the capitalist system. Socialism (the epoch in which the Eastern bloc countries are now) is the epoch when the state has control of the means of production. Communism (not yet attained anywhere) is the great goal, when there will be an abundance of production, and goods will be distributed to all according to their needs. Then the state's machinery of armies and police will wither away. Wars will be no more, men will no longer be alienated from their work and environment. Individuals will be able to express themselves in creative work and leisure. Through the change in his environment, the nature of man himself will have been changed for the better.

The kingdom of God without God?

How should a Christian react to Marxism? First, by an attitude of repentance. For the Marxist criticism of religion has too often been justified.

Secondly, there are some aspects of Marxist doctrine with which we must agree. We must share the Marxist's indignation at the cripplingly unequal distribution of wealth within nations and between nations, and at the alienating character of work—and unemployment—for so many people under capitalism. Marxists are right to declare the injustice of a system where those who control wealth (whether individuals or groups or nations) have power over those who do not have wealth, and control the system so as to keep things that way. They are right to insist that evil resides not only in individuals but also in systems and structures of society. They are right to want change, and to look for a programme for change which all people, especially the powerless, can strive after.

Yet, for all its attractiveness and power to capture the imagination, Marxism cannot provide a solid basis for the

230

future of human society. For, in the first place, it is full
of internal contradictions which arise from its being what
Emil Brunner called 'a Christian dogmatic with a minus
sign affixed. The whole system,' he suggested, 'can be
deduced from the thesis that God is an illusion.'[14] It claims
to offer a new 'revelation' about man and history, explain-
ing how human society has developed and will develop.
But where does the 'revelation' come from? It comes from
Marx's own analysis of history. But it is illegitimate to
turn an analysis of history (which must be subject to tests
of truth or falsehood as history continues to unfold) into
a 'revelation' about unalterable laws of history (which no
one is allowed to criticise). Moreover, since Marx's system
functions without God, and finds the origin of everything
in the material world, there is no logical *reason* why his
series of epochs should end with the communist epoch.
He cannot say *why* history should not be an endless
succession of epochs. And a materialistic system has no
basis for ethics. It can only describe what 'is', it cannot say
what 'ought' to be done. It is quite inconsistent with the
theoretical basis of Marxism to express moral indignation
at the injustices of capitalism. Unless you have a basis for
ethics from outside matter, you cannot say what is the
purpose of life and the goals towards which society should
move.

Secondly, Marxism's claim to be scientific is wrong,
because it ignores too many facts. It deals in stereotypes
which are often quite remote from the realities of a
situation. It is nonsense to divide people in complex western
societies into exploiters and exploited. Marxist analysis
does not allow for the 'affluent worker' who looks to partici-
pate in management. And in Latin America the situation
is complicated because there are two different kinds of
exploited people—the Europeanised urban poor and the
Indians, original inhabitants of the land.[15] And then there
is the oppression by the more advanced Marxist nations
over the poor countries of the developing world. It is not
only western countries who have a vested interest in keeping

poor nations poor and dependent.[16] And only by ruthless control of the media and of the movement of their people do the communist countries maintain the plausibility of their stereotypes.

Thirdly, Marxists fail to understand the origin of man's 'alienation'. They trace the reality of evil back to inadequacies in the economic process. But they are not radical enough. For they cannot tell us how such inadequacies got into the system in the first place. And they cannot explain why those things which are recognised as sins in a capitalist society remain to haunt a Marxist society. They cannot explain why people in iron-curtain countries feel alienated by the impersonal nature of state bureaucracy, or why financial incentives and privileges are necessary for the ruling people. The insistence that man is perfectible through the perfecting of the social system is a refusal to recognise that alienation begins from man's rejection of a true relationship with God, which in turn leads to alienation from their own true humanity, and alienation from each other through attempts to 'play God' over each other. There is not much wrong with the Marxists' vision of what the ultimate communist society would be like. The problem is that man has not within himself the power to get beyond the imperfections of the intervening socialist epoch on the way to that utopia.

Fourthly, Marx stressed (in his second thesis on Feuerbach) that truth can only be demonstrated by practice. If we apply this test to Marxist countries (and we have already noted how hostile to critical assessment they in fact are), we can observe that there have been significant strides forward in providing for the material needs of people. The massive industrialisation of Russia and the removal of hunger in China are obvious examples. But there is a human cost: extermination of dissidents, colonisation of independent nations, suppression of information from the outside world. The present is savagely sacrificed for the sake of the future. A specific example of the contradiction in Marxist practice is the way in which concern for the oppressed *before* the revolution turns into oppression by the revolutionaries *after* the revolution. The loving concern which motivates Marxists before the revolution is real, and puts many Christians to shame. But it leads to new forms of oppression because Marxism has no God, and therefore no means of self-criticism, no defence against the corruption of power. A system which is built on conflict, and seeks to remove oppression by removing the oppressor cannot exorcise the sources of conflict from society.

Finally, any quest for a perfect society which has no possibility of a life beyond death is illusory. It offers nothing to those who are sacrificed in the present time for the sake of those who are expected to enjoy the promised utopia. And even for those who experience the future perfect society, their enjoyment of it will be short-lived. Jürgen Moltmann writes:

> All utopias of the kingdom of God or of man, all hopeful pictures of the happy life, all revolutions of the future, remain hanging in the air and bear within them the germ of boredom and decay—and for that reason also adopt a militant and extortionate attitude to life—as long as there is no certainty in face of death and no hope which carries love beyond death. [17]

What hope is there within history?

Marxism falls victim to the same problems as other ideologies which look for a perfect society at a future point within history. Marxists try to realise the kingdom of God—without God. A God-given vision of what is desirable for human society is turned into a perfection which man thinks he can achieve without God. A hope for society on the way towards the perfect kingdom of God which lies beyond the present course of history is turned into an absolute hope for perfection within history—for there is nothing that lies beyond. Yet, in truth, only an awareness and worship of

233

the God who perfects his kingdom beyond history can deliver us from the worship of state and party which bedevils Marxism. Only the belief that the kingdom of God has come, and yet will not fully come until the end of history, can give us a true perspective for our hopes for society. As Miguez Bonino writes:

> Against every evolutionary idealism, faith looks at history as the arena of a permanent—although not undecisive—conflict. Christian eschatology prompts us to move in the direction of the Kingdom, but it also leads us to recognise the penultimate and partial character of all our achievements.[18]

But to criticise Marxism is not to endorse capitalism. There is no inbuilt morality in capitalism, any more than there is an ethical basis for Marxism. If Marxists sacrifice the present for the sake of the future, capitalists risk sacrificing the future for the sake of the present, since their working for profit today gives very low priority to the conservation of the earth's resources for tomorrow.

> The basic ethos of capitalism, [writes Miguez Bonino] is definitely anti-Christian: it is the maximising of economic gain, the raising of man's grasping impulse, the idolising of the strong, the subordination of man to the economic production. Humanisation is for capitalism an unintended by-product while it is for socialism an explicit goal. Solidarity is for capitalism accidental: for socialism, it is essential. In terms of their basic ethos, Christianity must criticise capitalism radically, in its fundamental intention, while it must criticise socialism functionally, in its failure to fulfil its purpose.[19]

David Edwards and Derek Farrow are more cautious than Miguez Bonino about socialism, less critical of capitalism.[20] But the point is that, whichever basis you start from, it needs modifying in the light of basic Christian insights about the nature of man and the purpose of God.

A better world

There were once some monks in Sicily who passed their days making, and then unmaking, wicker baskets. Since the world was passing away, they saw no point in doing anything to change the world. Today Christians have no choice but to be committed to striving to make the world a better place. Our understanding of Christian hope drives us not to escape from the world, but to work for its transformation. Only if we are able to argue this and to practise it have we a convincing response to the attraction of Marxism. So what grounds are there for believing that Christianity offers hope of a better world within history?

First, God's plan is a plan for the whole world. 'This plan, which God will complete when the time is right, is to bring all creation together, everything in heaven and on earth, with Christ as head' (Ephesians 1:10). In the previous chapter, I expressed my view that passages such as this are statements about God's all-embracing desire or purpose for his creation, and not necessarily a declaration that every individual will find salvation. But that does not alter the fact that God's plan embraces the whole world, and therefore his people should seek to share his broad horizons.

Secondly, Jesus has won the decisive victory over the demonic forces which work through the political and social structures of the world (Colossians 2:15; Revelation 12–13). Therefore there is hope for change.

Thirdly, the rule of God has already dawned. Even though God's rule has not yet come in its completeness, its power is at work in the world. And there is continuity between the present and future manifestations of that rule. Therefore there is power for change. The outworkings of God's rule are not totally reserved for the period after Christ's return.

Fourthly, the rule of God does not confine its self-disclosure to the church. Just as Jesus's healing ministry, for example, overflowed to the blessing of people who did not personally respond to his offer of forgiveness and call to discipleship, so the influence of God's rule overflows the boundaries of the church. God is pursuing his goals in the history of the world and outside the church. Therefore Christians are to live like their incarnate Lord, in the midst of the world and to promote God's will in it.

Fifthly, there is the demand of the kingdom, which involves recognising how God is exercising his rule, what he is doing, and getting involved with that. If the coming of God's rule in Jesus's ministry meant fighting disease and bondage to evil, working against divisions in society and commercial exploitation, his followers are not at liberty to abandon such demands in preference for something else. We are certainly not free to concentrate on 'spiritual' concerns to the neglect of what Jesus called 'the weightier matters of the law'—justice, mercy and honesty (Matthew 23:23). We have to remember that 'justice' in the Bible constantly means not an impartial and impersonal dispensing of verdicts in a court of law, but a vigorous action to set wrongs right and to restore the fortunes of the defenceless and the oppressed. Hence it is much closer to 'mercy' than is normal in our modern English usage.

In the Old Testament prophets, to practise steadfast love and justice is an indispensable part of 'knowing God'; since God practises these things, no one can claim to know him who does not reflect these qualities in his life (see Jeremiah 9:24). And Isaiah 58 confronts the problem of a nation which has apparently got all the spiritual things right. They worship, they pray, they fast. But God says:

The kind of fasting I want is this:
Remove the chains of oppression and the yoke of in-justice, and let the oppressed go free. Share your food

with the hungry and open your homes to the homeless poor. Give clothes to those who have nothing to wear, and do not refuse to help your own relatives (Isaiah 58:6f.).

And we see clear echoes of that passage in Jesus's parable of the sheep and the goats, with its message that our ultimate liberation depends on the reality of our commitment to the earthly liberation of men and women.

Another way of stating the demand of the kingdom is to say that we who are subjects of God's kingdom are called to live *now* by the values of the kingdom which is coming. Others may dismiss the commitment to universal love and justice as a counsel of perfection, to be put aside until some more convenient time. We cannot do that.

The guidelines of the kingdom

The hope of the kingdom of God gives guidelines for the kind of progress we should look for in human society. But before looking at the guidelines which this hope suggests, let us note the importance of having a vision of what we are striving for. We often recall the words of Martin Luther King: 'I have a dream that my four little children will one day live in a nation where they will not be judged according to the colour of their skin but by the content of their character . . . I have a dream today.' That Christian vision of a nation living as God meant it to live drove him to action. It kept him going when things got tough and dangerous. But where there is no such 'dream', nothing happens. Indeed, the worrying thing about the prophecies of doom which surround us today is that they may become self-fulfilling prophecies. If you are convinced that civilisation is going to collapse around your ears, it probably will, because you will do nothing to stop it happening. From our vision of the kingdom of God, then, we draw our guidelines. There are guidelines first about goals, and then about methods of working towards them.

First, the kingdom of God *reverses common assumptions and structures* in the present world. Rejoicing at the expected impact of the Messiah who is to be born of her, Mary sings:

> He has stretched out his mighty arm
> and scattered the proud with all their plans.
> He has brought down mighty kings from their thrones,
> and lifted up the lowly.
> He has filled the hungry with good things,
> and sent the rich away with empty hands
>   (Luke 1:51–53).

God is working to reverse the values by which most societies function, and he calls his people to work with him. Radical changes are required, and that is painful for those of us in comparatively rich situations in rich countries. The directions of change are determined by the nature of the kingdom.

The kingdom of God will be *universal*. Therefore our vision for a better world must embrace the whole world. A Christian is never free to advocate a solution to a social or political or economic problem which is a solution for 'me' or 'my group' or even 'my nation' at the expense of others. Human beings—unlike ants or bees—are not genetically coded to live together in harmonious co-operation. We use our free will to assert our independence over against others. So the Christian's commitment to the kingdom means he must fight against attitudes and social policies which drive people apart: for example, economic policies which worsen class divisions within a nation. And it means he must advocate policies of international trade and co-operation where the rules are not fixed in favour of the rich and powerful. He must ask himself what kind of lifestyle or living standard is appropriate for his brother in Sri Lanka or Brazil or Angola, and what the consequences of that goal would be for his own society. International development specialist Lester Brown says:

It has long been part of conventional wisdom within the international development community that the two billion people living in the poor countries could not aspire to the life style enjoyed by the average North American because there was not (enough) iron, ore, petroleum and protein to provide it.[21]

The kingdom of God will also be *peaceful*. Peace in the Bible does not mean only the absence of war, or a serene state of mind. It means well-being at every level, in relation to oneself, to others, and to God.[22] It is important to stress that peace in its full sense will not arrive until Jesus returns, and that according to the New Testament true peace is available only through relationship with him. Otherwise, peace (or the Hebrew 'shalom') becomes a misleading slogan emptied of its basic meaning. Nevertheless, the promise that the kingdom will be a kingdom of peace tells us that God desires people to experience well-being and good relationships in all areas of life. He does not separate the 'spiritual' from the 'physical', the 'eternal' from the 'worldly', as though only one side of this division mattered. Therefore we have to work for the removal of causes of conflict, and to pursue liberation from oppression and fear at the various points where they affect men's lives— liberation from economic and political domination and dependence, liberation from discrimination on grounds of race or sex, liberation from the ecological disasters which ensue from uncontrolled industrial growth, as well as liberation from the evil and unbelief which underlie so many of these major problems.

The kingdom will be a kingdom of *justice*. Therefore justice must be our goal for human societies. Justice in the Bible is not the impersonal and impartial dispensing of verdicts in accordance with the law. It involves acting to set things right, delivering the victims of injustice, recognising that it is possible to do things which are within the law and yet are unjust in God's eyes. Justice does not require that we make everyone earn the same, eat the same, think the same, enjoy the same. It does require that we work against exploitation, and against the economic systems which benefit the rich at the expense of the poor. Multinational companies, the new imperialists, have a lot to answer for when they drive out of business the small producers in developing countries, and transfer profits to investors in wealthier countries.[23] The wealth which *is* created by foreign investment within developing countries goes mostly to the wealthier sections of society, enhancing the gap between rich and poor. For there is vast injustice within developing nations, too.

The relationship between justice and world development is *the* great ethical issue for our day, an issue over which the credibility and integrity of nations and churches is at stake. The Brandt report, *North-South: a Programme for Survival* (Pan, London, 1980) proposes a possible way forward. It remains to be seen whether short-term vested interest will set us firmly on the road to moral suicide, or whether the proposals will be enacted or improved on. But justice is not only about world development. It is about nursery education for children who have had a bad start in life; it is about bus services for rural communities, homes for the homeless, and a host of other things. And seeking justice lies at the heart of seeking God's kingdom (cf. Matthew 6:33), for it is at the heart of the character and concern of God.

But the kingdom also will be a kingdom of *love*. There is a lot to be said for the view made famous by Reinhold Niebuhr that justice is the way in which love operates when dealing with societies *en masse*. You cannot love 'the poor' or 'the police force' in the same way as you can love the person next door. Yet the Christian insight into the meaning of love preserves us from the kind of justice which seeks right structures to the neglect of personal concern. Our striving for a better society must march under the banner of concern for people rather than things, for better relationships rather than better systems. Ask a teacher or a parent about the educational system in Britain. The chances are that he will lament that in the 1960s and 1970s the triple pressure of economics, ideology and confused aims has reduced well-being in our secondary schools for both pupils and staff. Whenever we look to improve a situation, we must think first about relationships, then about proposed new structures as they may affect relationships, then about relationships and persons again.

The way of the kingdom

Our thinking has already begun to spill over from the goals we should seek to the methods for achieving them. Perhaps it is here, rather than in the goals themselves, that a distinctively Christian approach may emerge. Here it is love, love, love all the time.

Love involves *solidarity* with the oppressed. Listen to this poem by Vinicio Aguilar from Central America:

> Where was god, daddy; where, where, where
> when the commissioners
>   broke the fence,
>   burnt the farm,
>   destroyed the harvest,
>   killed the pigs,
>   raped Imelda,
>   drank our rum?
> HE WAS UP THERE, boy.
> Where was god, daddy; where, where, where
> when because we complained
>   the state judge came and fined us
>   the bailiff came to arrest us
>   and even the priest come to insult us?
> HE WAS UP THERE, boy.
> Well, then, daddy; we must now tell him plainly
> that he must come down sometimes
>   to be with us.

You can see how we are, daddy,
with no fields sown, no farm, no pigs, nothing, and he
as if nothing had happened. It isn't right, you know,
    daddy.
If he's really up there
let him come down
Let him come down to taste this cruel hunger with us
let him come down and sweat
in the maize-fields, come down to be imprisoned,
let him come down and spew on the rich man
who throws the stone and hides his hand,
    on the venal judge,
    on the unworthy priest,
    and on the bailiffs and commissioners
    who rob and kill
    the peasants;
because I certainly don't want to tell my son when he
    asks me one day:
HE WAS UP THERE, boy.[24]

If God is to be known 'down here', his presence must be made real, 'incarnated' in the caring of his people. He who loves acts in solidarity with the needy. He works for development not merely by pouring in money from a distance, not by promoting development for people, but by engaging in development *with* people. He works for racial harmony not only by organising protests against apartheid in South Africa, but also by being alongside the black youngsters in the youth club and urging local employers to give them a fair deal when selecting employees.

Whilst acting in solidarity with the oppressed, love also is directed towards *oppressors*. For *their* humanity and their salvation are at risk through their oppression. They dehumanise themselves more than they dehumanise the oppressed. Love seeks to draw the sting of conflict by working for reconciliation. If it is retorted that it is impossible to side with the oppressed and at the same time to love the oppressor, we must reply that this is precisely

242

the attitude of God (Matthew 5:43–48). It is the attitude of Jesus who, whilst hanging on the cross, prayed for his crucifiers.

This means also that love *abhors the way of violence*. It is widely agreed nowadays that Jesus rejected violence as a strategy for his mission. But it is not widely agreed that this binds his followers also to reject violence. It is argued that in modern circumstances very different from those of Jesus's time, violent revolution may be a necessary evil. And if there can ever be a 'just war', there can in principle be a 'just revolution'. Yet even though we must grant that Jesus's circumstances were different from those of modern times, and that he had a unique mission which is not to be imitated in every respect by his followers, it seems to me difficult to defend the view that Christians should advocate precisely the opposite of what he practised in relation to his enemies and the oppressors of his people. The cross of Jesus surely has more significance than that as a pattern for his people.

The issues are very complex, and cannot be gone into here. But let not the discussion take place with cold detachment and without feeling towards the dilemmas of those who resort to violence. No condemnation of revolutionary violence has a right to be heard unless it has first learnt to see how often the violence of the oppressed is divine judgment on oppressors. And as the report *Violence, Nonviolence and the Struggle for Social Justice* stresses:

> Certainly the fact that some Christians are acting violently for justice and peace whilst others are acting nonviolently is a problem. But the greatest problem is that most of those who name Christ as Lord are not consciously acting on the matter at all.[25]

Love deals with all things, including economics, '*as if people mattered*'.[26] If our goals for society are to be achieved, wealth has to be created in order to make that possible. Economic activity and manufacturing industry are not dirty games. But no so-called 'laws of economics' can be allowed to operate without regard to the human cost. There must be safeguards against exploitation of cheap labour, dehumanising types of work, pollution, and the rape of the earth's resources. When the world has the technical know-how to abolish malnutrition and yet spends a million dollars a minute on its armed forces; when half the world's research is on the development of military equipment, there must be sustained efforts by governments and peoples towards a radical shift in the balance of expenditure.

Finally, love seeks to encourage a society where people are not dependent, nor purely self-reliant or independent but rather *interdependent*. For human beings find their true selves only in relationship with others. This again is a pattern which has implications for international co-operation (as the Brandt Report stresses) as well as for national and more local policies.

Such, then, are the basic insights into the nature of the society for which we seek. Turning them into detailed plans for action is the hard part, yet it is important to grasp the overall vision if the detailed plans are to have any direction.[27] As Christians we have confidence in progress towards the goal because we believe that God's rule already overflows into the world. And at the same time we can accept failures without giving up hope, because we know that the perfect society will not arrive until, at Jesus's coming, the kingdoms of this world become the kingdom of our Lord and of his Messiah.

Even though the Christian's vision of the kingdom of God is a theological basis for social change which will not necessarily be shared by others, he can co-operate with people of many different persuasions who are prepared to share the same objectives. It should not surprise us that such objectives can be embraced by people of differing religious viewpoints. For the kingdom of God is the goal of his creation, it is what human beings are made for, and so we would expect a broad range of people to recognise that such goals fit in with human nature and human ideals.

Yet Christians cannot stop at advocating, along with others, a particular route towards a better society. They have two distinctive tasks. First, there is the task of *evangelism*. I shall say little about this here since the subject is covered at length in other books.[28] Let it simply be said that the winning of people to Christian discipleship must never be made subservient to the search for a better society. For salvation—that is, 'eternal' relationship with God through faith in Christ—is not the same as liberation from political, economic or other oppression. Desirable though these goals are, they do not in themselves bring a person to God. Also, in the quest for a better society the need for better people, transformed by the grace of Christ, is paramount. Those who influence the direction of society must be called to repentance, called to 'seek the kingdom of God first'. Those who are dehumanised by the 'system' must hear the message of hope, just as 'the poor' of Jesus's time heard from him the announcement of God's rule. All must hear of his power to change people and transform situations. We dare not give people only 'the food that spoils', essential though that is. We must lead them also to 'the food that lasts for eternal life', the real and 'living bread which came down from heaven' (John 6:27, 51).

The church as a sign of hope

But evangelism is not enough, either. The church's other task is to be in its own life a sign of God's kingdom, a preliminary embodiment or 'pilot-plant' of what God's final kingdom will be like. The church, says Moltmann, 'is like an arrow sent out into the world to point to the future'.[29] However much some modern theologies may shunt the church into a siding when considering God's relation to the world and his purposes for it, the biblical writers keep pushing it back on to the main line. The letter to the Ephesians, for example, places the church at the heart of God's plan for the world, and even assigns it the task of proclaiming God's wisdom to 'the angelic rulers and powers in the heavenly world' (Ephesians 3:10). And James 1:18 calls the church the 'firstfruits of his creatures' (RSV)—an embodiment now of what is his purpose for all.

With all its imperfections, it is the community of those who have been 'brought safe into the kingdom of God's dear Son' (Colossians 1:13), it is the bride destined for the marriage-feast of the Lamb (Ephesians 5:22–33; Revelation 19:5–9). This understanding of the church is crucial for its life and mission. For, as Edward Schillebeeckx writes, 'Who could believe in a God who will make everything new later if it is in no way apparent from the activity of those who hope in the One who is to come that he is already beginning to make everything new now?'[30] And Leighton Ford: 'The world is not looking for perfection. It is looking for a substantial demonstration of the peace of God—a community where shalom is really to be found.'[31] Where the church truly, though not perfectly, embodies the kingdom's qualities of justice, peace and love, it is indeed a sign of hope. And because these qualities can only operate as people relate to each other, it is the church rather than the individual Christian which is the sign of the kingdom. How is the church the sign of the kingdom?

First, in its life as *community*. The inter-relationship of God's people in heaven is anticipated in the church. This was recognised as a quite astounding feature of the early church, as the Holy Spirit was seen to break down age-old barriers between Jew and Gentile, slave and free, rich and poor, men and women (cf. Galatians 3:28; Colossians 3:11). The church since then has a mixed record in its attitudes to the Jew, the slave, the poor, the woman, to whom it has often brought despair rather than hope. This is why issues such as the ordination of women and the church's commitment to the world's urban and rural poor cannot be treated as marginal issues, if we are to be a sign of the kingdom.

Second, it follows from this that the church points to the kingdom by its *unity*. For the same reason, this too cannot be a marginal issue. If it is God's purpose to break down hostility between men and nations, and if in his kingdom there will be no divisions, no second-class citizens, then the church is called to make unity visible and believable now. That may not mean that we are to come together under one ecclesiastical structure. It certainly does not mean that every local church must become exactly like every other church—as though the universal church were to consist of a chain of identical Wimpy Bars or Hilton Hotels. In the New Testament period, local churches exhibited great variety in their structures, and even in their ways of expressing doctrine, yet they recognised each other as proper churches of Christ and were related to each other through their common allegiance to the risen Jesus, and through the activity of apostles and other travellers. In the church today, history weighs heavily upon us, our denominational loyalties to the past erect barriers between us. We have gone soft on the gospel and hard as diamonds on the structures. How can we break free from this and recognise each other's standing in Christ, except perhaps by allowing the weight of the future to bear down upon us?

In God's kingdom there will be no bishops, no synods, no divisions over baptism. In the light of the kingdom, such issues (unlike the ones mentioned above) *are* marginal matters. If we are to be a church which looks and points to the future, we must find ways of respecting and accepting members, patterns of ministry and structures in the different denominations. We must work together. And since people will be in God's kingdom because of their trust in Jesus, and not because they have held to a particular detailed doctrinal basis, our search for unity must involve those with whom we may not agree on every aspect of the faith. Calvin wrote in his *Commentary on Hebrews*:

To what end did Christ come, except to collect us all into one body from that dispersion in which we are now wandering? Therefore the nearer his coming is, the more we ought to labour that the scattered may be assembled and united together, that there may be one fold and one shepherd (on Hebrews 10:25).[32]

Thirdly, the *church's growth*—in numbers, in the quality of its life, in the breadth of its service—points to the kingdom. For it is part of the ongoing movement of God, who will have in his kingdom 'people from every tribe, language, nation and race' (Revelation 5:9f.), and expects the church to be 'faultless on the day of our Lord Jesus Christ' (1 Corinthians 1:8).

Fourthly, the church is a sign of hope by expressing the quality of a *pilgrim*. To most people the church is an institution, and a slow and backward-looking one at that. We cannot help being an institution in some sense, and we have to maintain some continuity with the past— for that is where God revealed himself in Christ for our salvation. But to be a pilgrim, like Abraham and his fellow-travellers in Hebrews 11, means to be ready for change, responding to new situations, being willing to abandon what was right for yesterday in order to be ready for the challenge of tomorrow. Since it is not in the nature of institutions to change any more than the minimum that is necessary for survival, nothing but the fresh wind of God's Spirit can blow from us the accumulated baggage of the past and thrust us forward on the path to the future.

Finally, the church is a sign of hope in its *worship*. In worship we break through the barriers of time and space, and anticipate the worship of heaven. In a remarkable passage which makes this point, the writer to the Hebrews says:

You have come to Mount Zion and to the city of the living God, the heavenly Jerusalem, with its thousands of angels. You have come to the joyful gathering of God's first-born sons, whose names are written in heaven. You have come to God, who is the judge of all mankind, and to the spirits of good people made perfect. You have come to Jesus (Hebrews 12:22–24).

The central act of worship is the *Lord's Supper*, at which we 'proclaim the Lord's death until he comes' (1 Corinthians 11:26). This meal celebrates Jesus's death and resurrection to save all people, and is a foretaste of the 'messianic banquest' in God's final kingdom. Just as the Jew ends the passover service with the words, 'Next year in Jerusalem!', so for the Christian the Lord's Supper points forward to the coming of his kingdom.

Prayer, too, is at the heart of worship, and at the heart of prayer is the Lord's Prayer. Because this was intended by Jesus as the distinctive prayer of his followers (Luke 11:1f.), it summarises what Jesus wanted us to be concerned about. The first two petitions express our longing that God be known and honoured, and that his rule should come on the earth. The last three petitions deal with things which hinder his rule in us—anxiety about the basic needs of life, sin which needs forgiveness, the temptation to give up the struggle for the kingdom when the going get tough. But at the same time the prayer reveals the nature of the God for whose kingdom we pray; he is a father with a plan to fulfil, who meets the needs of his children, who forgives them and sustains them in the face of trial. When the church prays this prayer it is a sign of the kingdom, because it is focusing on God's true purpose, and is drawing strength for its witness to that God and that purpose.

For only in worship can the church's vision for the future be sustained in the face of difficulty, failure and frustration. If God is the one who brings his kingdom—both within history and beyond history—then to focus on him is the most hopeful, the most revolutionary act of all.

'*All this and heaven too!*'

Christian hope, then, is hope focused in Christ and his kingdom. It relates to every level of human life, both within history and beyond history. We do not have to choose between this world and the world to come, because the purpose of God embraces both. An earthly hope without the prospect of life beyond death is illusory and short-lived. But a real hope of eternal life with God sets us free from anxiety about death, and frees us to work for the transformation of this world. It gives us a true vision of God's purpose for this world, and assures us that 'nothing we do in the Lord's service is ever useless' (1 Corinthians 15:58).

Whether the coming of Jesus is near or distant, hope remains steady. For it lives in the knowledge that the coming kingdom has already dawned, that the Holy Spirit lives 'in our hearts as the guarantee of all that God has in store for us' (2 Corinthians 1:22), and that the God who will raise the dead has already raised Jesus our Lord. So Paul can say from a full heart, 'May God, the source of hope, fill you with all joy and peace by means of your faith in him, so that your hope will continue to grow by the power of the Holy Spirit' (Romans 15:13).

Notes to chapter 7

1. *Instead of the Trees* (Heinemann, London, 1977), pp. 29–31.
2. *Christian Holiness* (Lutterworth, London, 1960), pp. 26f.
3. Quoted in A. Outler, ed., *John Wesley* (OUP, New York, 1964), p. 378.
4. M. Ford, *Janani : the Making of a Martyr* (Lakeland, London, 1978), pp. 75f, 87.
5. *James Galway: an Autobiography* (Chappell/Elm Tree, London, 1978), p. 181.
6. M. Hengel, *Property and Riches in the Early Church* (Eng. tr., SCM, London, 1974), p. 30.
7. C. R. Avila, *Peasant Theology* (WSCF, Bangkok, 1976), pp. 28–30.
8. A helpful book on a wide range of practical matters concerning use of money is D. Farrow, *Through the Eye of a Needle* (Epworth, London, 1979).
9. *Pensées* 14.
10. Cited in J. Miguez Bonino, *Christians and Marxists* (Hodder, London, 1976), pp. 76f.

11. 'On the History of Early Christianity', in Marx and Engels, *On Religion* (Schocken, New York, 1964), p. 317.
12. 'The Communism of the Paper *Rheinischer Beobachter*' in *On Religion*, p. 84.
13. For an attractive modern presentation of 'The Marxist Hope', see J. Klugmann in G. B. Caird *et al.*, *The Christian Hope* (SPCK, London, 1970), pp. 49–68.
14. *Dogmatics*, vol. 3, p. 358. For some of the points which follow I rely on J. A. Kirk, 'The Meaning of Man in the Debate between Christianity and Marxism', *Themelios* 1.2, Spring, 1976, pp. 41–9, and 1.3, Summer, 1976, pp. 85–93.
15. See P. Hebblethwaite, *The Christian-Marxist Dialogue* (DLT, London, 1977), pp. 101f.
16. Miguez Bonino, *Christians and Marxists*, pp. 89–91.
17. 'Hope and Confidence: a Conversation with Ernst Bloch', *Dialog* 7 (Winter, 1968), p. 49.
18. *Christians and Marxists*, p. 129. On this whole theme see the discussion of utopianism in H. Thielicke, *The Evangelical Faith*, vol. 1 (Eng. tr., Eerdmans, Grand Rapids, 1974), pp. 386–403.
19. *Christians and Marxists*, p. 116.
20. Edwards, *A Reason to Hope* (Collins, London, 1978); Farrow, *Through the Eye of a Needle*, pp. 96–105.
21. Quoted in R. J. Sider, 'Rich Christians in an Age of Hunger', *Evangelical Review of Theology* 4.1, April, 1980, p. 72. Sider's book, *Rich Christians in an Age of Hunger* (Hodder, London, 1977) is a major study of the whole issue of world development and its implications for policies and lifestyles in wealthier countries.
22. See D. K. Gillett, 'Shalom: Content for a Slogan', *Themelios* 1.3, Summer 1976, pp. 80–4.
23. One example is Carnation Milk's operations in Peru—see the careful account of F. Sand, 'The Andean Marauders', *The Other Side*, July 1980, pp. 24–31.
24. *International Review of Mission* 66, 1977, pp. 249f.
25. (WCC, Geneva, 1973), p. 19. On this whole issue see M. Hengel, *Was Jesus a Revolutionist?* (Fortress, Philadelphia, 1971); R. Sider, *Christ and Violence* (Lion, Tring, 1980); J. A. Kirk, *Theology Encounters Revolution* (IVP, Leicester, 1980), appendix B.
26. E. F. Schumacher's book *Small is Beautiful* (Abacus, London, 1975), is subtitled 'A study of economics as if people mattered'.
27. For down-to-earth suggestions about what the local church can do about such issues, see G. Dow, *The Local Church's Political Responsibility* (Grove, Bramcote, Notts., 1980).
28. D. Watson, *I Believe in the Church* (1978); and *I Believe in Evangelism* (1976); M. Warren, *I Believe in the Great Commission* (1976); E. Gibbs, *I Believe in Church Growth* (1981).

29. *Theology of Hope*, p. 328. This understanding of the church is developed especially in his book *The Church in the Power of the Spirit* (Eng tr., SCM. London. 1977).
30. *God the Future of Man* (Eng. tr., Sheed & Ward. London, 1969), p. 183.
31. 'Evangelism in the Age of Apollo', *I Will Heal Their Land*, ed. M. Cassidy (Africa Enterprise, Pietermaritzburg, 1974), p. 18.
32. On the general theme of church unity and Christian hope, see C. E. Braaten, 'The Reunited Church of the Future', *Journal of Ecumenical Studies* 4, 1967, pp. 611–28.